AGENT GARBO

BOOKS BY STEPHAN TALTY

Mulatto America:
At the Crossroads of Black and White Culture

Empire of Blue Water:
Captain Morgan's Great Pirate Army, the Epic
Battle for the Americas, and the Catastrophe
That Ended the Outlaws' Bloody Reign

The Illustrious Dead:
The Terrifying Story of How Typhus Killed
Napoleon's Greatest Army

Escape from the Land of Snows:
The Young Dalai Lama's Harrowing Flight to
Freedom and the Making of a Spiritual Hero

Agent Garbo:
The Brilliant, Eccentric Secret Agent
Who Tricked Hitler and Saved D-Day

AGENT GARBO

The Brilliant, Eccentric
Secret Agent Who Tricked
Hitler and Saved D-Day

STEPHAN TALTY

HOUGHTON MIFFLIN HARCOURT | Boston | New York
2012

For information about permission to reproduce selections from this book,
write to Permissions, Houghton Mifflin Harcourt Publishing Company,
215 Park Avenue South, New York, New York 10003.

www.hmhbooks.com

Library of Congress Cataloging-in-Publication Data
Talty, Stephan.
Agent Garbo: the brilliant, eccentric secret agent who tricked Hitler and saved D-Day /
Stephan Talty.
pages cm
ISBN 978-0-547-61481-6
1. Pujol, Juan. 2. World War, 1939–1945 — Secret service — Great Britain.
3. Spies — Great Britain — Biography. I. Title.
D810.S8P883 2012
940.5'8641092 — dc23
2012005470

Printed in the United States of America
DOC 10 9 8 7 6 5 4 3 2 1

For Alfie Wright,
teacher and friend

CONTENTS

PART IV: BREAKOFF

CAST OF CHARACTERS

The Axis

Alfred Jodl: Chief of staff of the German High Command, tasked with implementing Hitler's strategic orders. Executed for war crimes after a trial at Nuremberg.

Friedrich Knappe-Ratey: Code-named Federico, the Abwehr agent who vetted Juan Pujol and was one of his two main contacts in the Madrid station.

Karl-Erich Kühlenthal: The second-in-command of the Abwehr's Madrid station and the man who effectively controlled Garbo.

Colonel Baron Alexis von Roenne: The chief intelligence officer for Foreign Armies West.

Erwin Rommel: Nicknamed the Desert Fox, field marshal in the German army who led the Afrika Korps in the Middle East and Army Group B in the defense of occupied France.

Gerd von Rundstedt: Prussian aristocrat and field marshal of the German army who commanded the forces in the West.

The Allies

Johnny Bevan: Former stockbroker and head of the London Controlling Section (LCS); known as the Controller of Deception.

Desmond Bristow: MI6 operative in the Iberian section and the first man to debrief Juan Pujol in London.

Brutus: Roman Garby-Czerniawski, Polish air force captain who became a double agent for the Allies. A key operative in establishing the false Order of Battle during Fortitude South.

Dudley Clarke: Brigadier in the British army, founder of the commando unit A Force and the man who developed many of the theories and practices used by the Allied deception forces.

Tommy Harris: MI5 officer who worked closely with Pujol on the Garbo operation.

Edward Kreisler: Politically connected American entrepreneur and art gallery owner who became Araceli Pujol's second husband.

Guy Liddell: MI5's head of counterespionage.

J. C. Masterman: Oxford don and head of the XX — or Double Cross — Committee.

Cyril Mills: MI5 officer who was first assigned to Pujol, before being replaced by Tommy Harris.

Kim Philby: MI6 officer who served as head of the Iberian section. Later revealed to have been an agent for the KGB.

Araceli Pujol: Juan Pujol's wife and his early co-conspirator.

Juan Pujol: Spanish double agent who worked for MI5 under the code name Garbo.

Gene Risso-Gill: MI6 officer in Lisbon who first interrogated Pujol in 1941.

T. A. "Tar" Robertson: Intelligence officer who headed up MI5's B1A unit, which managed all double agents in England.

Lieutenant Colonel Robin "Tin-Eye" Stephens: Head of Camp 020, the interrogation center for suspected Axis spies in south London.

David Strangeways: British army colonel and head of R Force during World War II. Rewrote the Operation Fortitude cover plan and implemented many of its components.

Tate: Wulf Schmidt, the original MI5 double agent, who parachuted into England before being sent to Camp 020 and agreeing to spy for the Allies.

Nigel West: British author and espionage expert, real name Rupert Allason, who rediscovered Juan Pujol in 1984.

INTRODUCTION

I
N THE MIDDLE of the snowless English winter of 1944, General Dwight D. Eisenhower, the Allied commander overseeing the forthcoming invasion of Europe, was anxious to get the hell out of London. It was January, less than six months before D-Day, and it seemed to him that every Allied officer and VIP in the capital felt personally entitled to barge into his bustling office and bend his ear. The visitors never stopped, interrupting him and his staff, whose typewriters and footsteps and male voices created a constant, purposeful buzz in the rooms at 20 Grosvenor Square. The American ambassador, John Winant, was forever knocking on his door. Churchill was incorrigible. Today — he glanced down at his appointment book — Noel Wild of Ops (b) was due in, the head of an obscure sector in Eisenhower's sprawling command: deception.

The general had been an early skeptic of deception, the shadow bureau of spies running around the Continent claiming they could fool Hitler and turn the tide of war. General George S. Patton, who much to his own disgust had been drafted into the effort as head of an imaginary one-million-man army called FUSAG, summed up the initial feelings of Eisenhower — and the current attitude of many other military and political leaders: "This damned secrecy thing is rather annoying," he wrote, "particularly as I doubt if it fools anyone."

Eisenhower had changed his mind about deception after witnessing its effectiveness firsthand in the Mediterranean. But in January 1944 he had many *actual* objects to worry about: destroyers and French railroads and the landing vessels called LSTs, which were maddeningly scarce and threatened to sink the invasion before it began. These very real and important things, not espionage, were what consumed his days.

As he strode through his headquarters, bald, handsome and electric with physical vigor, Eisenhower appeared confident, "a living dynamo of energy, good humor, amazing memory for details, and amazing courage for the future." His staff loved his relentless optimism, but inwardly and in his private letters to Mamie, the general agonized about what was about to happen. He was smoking four packs of Camels a day, and a journalist would later describe him as "bowed down with worry . . . as though each of the stars on either shoulder weighed four tons."

If and when the Allies took the beaches of Normandy, Eisenhower hoped to join them. Going to France would return him to an old haunt. He'd spent a year there that few of his visitors knew about, the idyllic seasons of 1928–29 when Eisenhower — somewhat slimmer and with more hair — traveled the roads of Bordeaux and Aquitaine with an army driver, eating picnic lunches on the grass borders of country lanes and grating the ears of the farmers with his rudimentary French before winning them over with a flashing smile. That year at the end of the Roaring Twenties had been one of the best of his life. The career officer had been in France to write a guidebook for World War I battlefields and the graveyards of American troops, austere places where the soldiers' families came to honor their dead.

It had seemed a pleasant assignment then, but Eisenhower's memories of France had lately attained a darker shading: if D-Day wasn't successful, American cemeteries would sprout around the hills and hedgerows of Normandy like the native wood hyacinths. The French would need acres and acres of rich farmland for the graves of the 101st Airborne alone, more for the young men of the Big Red One; the white crosses would blanket the Norman countryside. Western France would become the graveyard for an entire generation of American GIs, the men that Eisenhower made a point of dashing out to visit every chance he got.

The invasion numbers were daunting. Eisenhower hoped to land five divisions on the first day of the operation. Waiting for him in France and the Low Countries would be fifty-six German divisions. The Fifteenth Army was perhaps the most crucial: it was strung out from Turhout in Belgium (the 1st Panzer Division) to Amiens (the 2nd Panzer Division) and Pontoise in France (the 116th Panzer), place names that Eisenhower knew well. There were ten German armored divisions that were "thought to be held as a centrally controlled mobile reserve, whose function would be to drive any invading force back into the sea before it had time to establish a lodgment." The Allies would calculate that most of those reserves would be sent to the Normandy bridgehead within one week of the invasion. That one week, however, was critical.

If Noel Wild and his deception outfit failed to deceive the enemy about the true target of the invasion, those German divisions would begin to flow south and attempt to destroy the Allied invasion force on the roads and in the small towns of Normandy. If the deception succeeded, the panzers would stay right where they were, waiting for the "real" landing. But how could that be achieved? Who could disguise the largest invasion force in history from Berlin's watchful eyes?

Finally, Lieutenant Colonel Wild knocked on the door. He was a "slim, elegant little man" and — though this didn't impress Eisenhower much — an Old Etonian. The two men chatted for a few moments, then Eisenhower made a very modest request. "Just keep the Fifteenth Army out of my hair for the first two days," he said. "That's all I ask."

Wild saluted and walked out.

His chat with Noel Wild was one meeting among the many that Eisenhower held that day and he probably forgot about it almost immediately. If he thought about it at all, the commander most likely believed his request — forty-eight precious hours free of the Fifteenth Army — was asking too much.

On the same day, approximately two miles from Eisenhower's frenetic headquarters, a rather ordinary-looking man named Juan Pujol was taking the Underground to work at a nondescript office on Jermyn Street. Though short and thin, Pujol carried himself like a member of the unseated European royalty that had found themselves at loose ends in London during the war. His shoulders were thrown back and a winning smile arced across his lips. The young Spaniard had an almost boyish face, a wide forehead, a prominent nose and a strong chin. The dominant feature of his face were the warm hazel eyes, flecked with green, that occasionally flashed with amusement and hidden depths. Pujol commuted to work every day from his house in Hendon, where he lived with his glamorous but unhappy wife and his two young children.

Dwight Eisenhower was the all-powerful commander of the Allied forces in Europe; every ship's quartermaster, every tank gunner, every medic was technically under his command. Pujol, on the other hand, was the emperor of an imaginary world. He was the linchpin in the plan to fool Hitler into believing the attack was coming not at Normandy but up the French coast at Calais. His mission was to keep the Fifteenth Army that was causing Eisenhower such deep worry out of the action. Only a handful of men, such as Lieutenant Colonel Wild, even knew who Juan Pujol was; he walked the London streets unrecognized and unprotected. But this brilliant spy, who three years before had been a failed chicken farmer and hotel manager at a one-star dump in Madrid, was the jewel of the Allies' counterintelligence forces. Churchill avidly followed his adventures; J. Edgar Hoover would one day clamor to meet him. His code name was Garbo; a British officer had given him the name because he considered Pujol "the best actor in the world."

In his quest to fool Hitler, Garbo was surrounded by a rather bizarre supporting cast that included a handful of other double agents, a mysterious half-Jewish case officer nicknamed Jesus, a vast supply of props and specially trained commandos, his own invented army of some twenty-seven nonexistent subagents, even an advance man who scoured the country looking for places Garbo's specters could stay while on their espionage missions to Dover and Edinburgh. But mostly, he had the Germans' confidence. The Führer's intelligence agency, the Abwehr, believed in Garbo above all others. They were convinced he was their secret weapon inside England, a spymaster who had sent them so many invaluable reports (carefully crafted with MI5's help), who had recruited so many valuable sources (all pure inventions), and who believed in fascism so fervently that he could hand them the time and place of the invasion. And if Hitler knew when and where Eisenhower would land his troops, the Führer believed that the Nazi victory was assured.

For Eisenhower, Hitler was a cipher, quite possibly mad: "a power-drunk egocentric . . . one of the criminally insane." Pujol had less experience with military leaders than the American general but more with fascists: he had actually met and fought with them. And he'd spent months trying to get inside Hitler's mind, to imagine what the German leader was thinking and then, from six hundred miles away, to obscure entire divisions and armadas from the Führer's eyes. Pujol's view of Hitler reflected the spy's Catholic boyhood and the scenes of executions he'd witnessed as a young soldier in the Spanish Civil War. "I had the idea that this man was a demon, a man who could completely destroy humanity."

That cool January day, Pujol emerged from the Underground station and walked down Jermyn Street. He arrived at his building, ascended the stairs to his office, greeted the young British secretary, Sarah Bishop, who kept the records of his spectral army, and said hello to his MI5 case officer, Tommy Harris, the man they called Jesus, already filling the small room with the smoke of his black Spanish cigarettes. Pujol knew that D-Day, his final test as a spy, was coming, and he was increasingly nervous, even as he looked — like Eisenhower — cheerful and confident.

Pujol had failed in almost everything he'd tried in his thirty-two years: student, businessman, cinema magnate, soldier. His marriage was falling apart. But in one specialized area of war, the espionage underworld known as the double-cross game, the young man was a kind of savant, and he knew it. After years of suffering and doubt, Pujol hoped he was ready to match wits with the best minds of the Third Reich.

"I wanted to start a personal war with Hitler," he said. "And I wanted to fight with my imagination."

Pujol sat down at his desk. Perhaps he asked Sarah Bishop about her evening. Or he exchanged a few words with Tommy Harris about lunch at the nearby Martinez Restaurant, one of their favorite haunts. But despite the close bond between the two, forged over two years of creating intrigues and counterplots spread across Europe and round the world, the enigmatic Harris was keeping not one but two secrets from his star agent: the deception plan that would hide D-Day from Hitler — code-named Operation Fortitude — was in deep trouble. And, even more worryingly, an Abwehr spy in Lisbon had recently revealed that he knew all about Garbo and could soon expose him to the Gestapo, ending his quest once and for all.

Unaware, Pujol began to write a message to the Germans in a beautiful, sloping hand. He was acquainted with secrets. He had a few of his own.

I

THE MAKING OF A SPY

1

Tom Mix in Barcelona

J UAN PUJOL WAS BORN into turmoil, even though no one realized it at the time. The baby boy was entered into the Barcelona Civil Registry as Juan Miguel Valentín García Guijarro
and the date of birth given as February 28, 1912, although the baby
had actually been delivered two weeks earlier, February 14, the "Day
of the Lovers." What was more troubling was the missing name of his
father. In the appropriate box, the registrar listed the baby boy as il-
legitimate.

It was a not uncommon story. Pujol's mother, Mercedes García
Guijarro, had grown up near Granada, in the southern region of
Andalusia, the beautiful and high-spirited daughter of a family that
was so devout they were known to locals as *Los Beatos* (The Blessed).
The family moved to Barcelona when Mercedes was eight, and when
she was in her early twenties, the trim-waisted and effervescent
woman went to work in the factory of Juan Pujol Pena, who lived at
70 Muntaner Street, a respectable and historic address in the heart
of the Catalan bourgeois district. Pujol Pena was a highly successful
dye merchant, completely self-made, whose factory was "famous for
its dark shades," especially the deepest jet black, which was an important color in Catholic Barcelona.

The merchant's first wife was alive when Mercedes began working
in the factory, but passed away soon after the young woman started
there. Pujol Pena and Mercedes began a relationship — whether
before or after the first wife was dead is unknown. At the age of
twenty-two, Mercedes gave birth to her first son, Joaquín, and then
a daughter named Bonaventura. Juan followed, and inherited from

his mother a "complicit expression in his ironic gaze" that the British operative Desmond Bristow would catch years later. A younger sister, Elena, followed two years later, after Juan Sr. and Mercedes had married.

The ironic gaze and his small stature were about all Pujol took from his mother. He looked strikingly like his thin, elegant father and he would inherit Pujol Pena's liberal outlook on the world, as opposed to Mercedes's stark Catholicism. When Juan was four, his father finally accepted the young boy and his two older siblings as his legitimate children. It was a fortunate moment for Juan: to be a bastard in status-conscious Barcelona in 1912 was a serious matter.

Yet most of the turmoil that churned Pujol's early years had an inner origin. As Pujol grew up in a house full of nannies, chefs, seamstresses and chauffeurs, with vacations to the shore in his father's gleaming Hispano-Suiza, his parents quickly saw qualities in their second boy that they couldn't trace to either of their personalities. Pujol was wild, very wild, or as his mother saw it, bad, very bad. "In my house, the name 'Juan' was constantly ringing," he remembered, "followed by *'What have you done this time?'*" Pujol banged into walls, scraped his limbs raw, crashed into banisters and, in one memorable incident, plowed straight through a floor-to-ceiling window on his tricycle, sending glass crashing into a thousand pieces all around him.

Miraculously, he emerged unscathed. "I really believed that Don Quixote in his adventure with the windmills was not so destroyed as I was," he later wrote. But that day was the exception. "I was constantly covered in bandages through my whole boyhood." Though they loved him, Pujol's brothers and sisters would hide their toys from Juan, convinced that anything he touched would soon be shattered.

His family despaired. Mercedes, especially, couldn't understand her son. He was incorrigible: threats, punishments, near-mortal injuries seemed to have no effect on a trail of destruction that stretched wider and longer the older he grew. But what looked like sheer mayhem to his parents and the rest of his family were, for the boy, marvelous and exuberant adventures that he saw in his mind in blazing, sharply defined color, always with him as the hero of the tale. As

Pujol tore around the mansion, he became a knight, a desperado, a daredevil, an explorer or, his favorite role model, Tom Mix of the Hollywood westerns that he attended as faithfully as Mercedes did Catholic Mass. "That cowboy was doing these wonderful things, and I decided that I should imitate him."

Pujol would later describe his boyhood imagination as something that he had no real control over. Like some alien host, it compelled him to do things. "The contents of my fevered fantasies," he wrote, "ran my imagination." Whatever bloomed in his brain, Pujol would set out to do. Most boys have adventures spinning through their heads at all hours of the day, but Pujol actually seemed to live solely in his dreams, lost to the real world. "I wanted to be the beloved hero of a Hollywood silent movie." But no one else saw the sets and the props, only Pujol with the crazy look in his eye, approaching at top speed. On the soccer field, he was even more terrifying; his nickname was Bullet.

He wasn't malicious, and in fact he had a good heart, always rushing in to help when the neighborhood runt was losing a fight. "I didn't hurt anybody, I was just very, very naughty." Pujol's mother tried to snatch him out of his fantasies and mold him into a nice Catalan upper-class boy, a boy she could fully love. "Punishments and retribution" rained down on Pujol's head one after the other, but they rarely had any effect. Pujol's genial father could only sigh.

When he was seven, Pujol was sent away to a strict boarding school, run by the Marist Fathers. Pujol's older brother, the "sturdy and straightforward" Joaquín, was forced to go along to watch over Bullet. In the Spanish expression, it was Pujol who broke the dishes but Joaquín who paid for them.

The priests did their best, but Pujol would always be a mediocre student. He hated the boarding school, and waited impatiently for his wonderful father to arrive on the train, as he did faithfully every Sunday, to take Juan and Joaquín for walks by the sea. There Juan Sr. would tell his boys entrancing stories about the world and dispense advice about life. "He taught me to respect the individuality of human beings, their sorrows and their sufferings. He despised war and bloody revolutions, scorning the despot, the authoritarian . . ."

The Marist discipline wouldn't stick, but the seaside lessons would. In Pujol's four "interminable" years with the Marists, however, he did manage to become fascinated by history and especially languages. Eventually he would be able to speak five: Spanish, Catalan, French, English and Portuguese.

The elder Juan had more to worry about than a high-spirited boy. Barcelona in the 1920s was a prosperous city known as "the Unrivaled," with nearly one million citizens and heavy industries that led the world. The city's cotton industry was second only to mighty Liverpool's, and the first railway engine in the world had been built in its thriving factories. The young Pujol loved going to the train station, where he would watch the steam engines blowing and hissing as they pulled out of the grand terminal. "My imagination would travel with them as they sped away to remote destinations to the echoing sound of a whistle."

But there were good reasons for a young boy to want to escape Barcelona: it was a combustible, highly dangerous place to grow up in, a place where the leftists' idea of a joke was to soap the stone steps of churches so that the hated Catholic bourgeoisie would slip and break their necks when leaving Mass. The Catalan capital often seemed on the verge of tearing itself apart: waves of riots, strikes and violence left dozens of mutilated bodies on the streets; radicals burned down churches and convents, fascist gangs responded with kidnappings and mass murders. Political coups seemed to be the city's leading industry. "One day a right-wing faction sitting outside a coffeebar would be machine-gunned," Pujol remembered, "the next day it was the turn of the left." Anarcho-syndicalists battled Catholic workers, proto-fascists shot communists, military supporters bombed antimonarchists. Assassination became so common that when a politician or union leader was found dead on the street, it was said almost casually that he'd "been take for a *paseo*," a stroll.

As a leading industrialist and a progressive, the elder Juan was a potential target of several factions. "Every morning my father went to work, he said goodbye to us as if for the last time; each parting was heart-rending." The paterfamilias despised the violence and poison-tipped rhetoric that had become so common in Barcelona. He was a committed humanist who believed in science, progress and, above all, tolerance. (Mercedes's sympathies no doubt lay with the Catholic traditionalists who backed Franco.) Finally, the tension became so thick that Juan Sr. moved his family away from the city center to the northern suburb of Putxet, where after living in a succession of apartments they settled into a magnificent home on Homero Street.

Pujol grew up strong, athletic, "a hefty fellow of fifteen, with an incipient beard," as he boasted later. He was charming, loved to dance and quote Catalan poetry, to hike in the mountains and sweet-talk the local girls. But he found his lessons to be "endless and dull," and after one particularly loud fight with a teacher, he marched home and announced that he was dropping out. Cannily, Juan Sr. agreed, with one proviso: the impulsive teenager had to go out and get a job. Pujol agreed, promptly marched off and talked his way into an apprenticeship at an enormous hardware shop just off the world-famous Rambla.

His duties were to sweep the floor, run errands, deliver packages and replace the tools that the shop assistants had left out after demonstrating them for customers. It was his first real job, and the long hours and menial tasks quickly wore him down. As his father had no doubt foreseen, Pujol lasted only a few weeks before quitting the shop. Then he zoomed to the opposite extreme, locking himself in the family library and delving deep into the arcane philosophical and literary texts that lined the walls. Pujol was searching for a vocation, and like everything else, he pursued it at top speed. The teenager was all velocity and no direction.

The young man's intense, headlong nature also propelled him into a series of mad love affairs. "I've always adored romanticism, and I've always been a slave of what is usually called the weaker sex." When he met Luisita, a vivacious dance-crazed girl from Andalusia, he pursued her all the way to Granada, begging his father to drive him there in the family's Hispano-Suiza. In Granada Pujol discovered that his beloved had a violently jealous boyfriend. Pujol sent Luisita poem after poem and declared his everlasting love, but the girl chose the brute, and Pujol's father had to drive back to Barcelona with his heartbroken son weeping in the passenger seat. "I was destroyed; the chef of the house couldn't find anything to make me happy. A few months after I left, Luisita married that abominable cretin."

One day when he was nineteen, Pujol began to feel knife-like pains in his abdomen that doubled him over. His appendix had burst. He was rushed to the hospital and into the operating room. The surgeon successfully removed the appendix, but three days later, as Pujol recovered in bed, the incision became infected. The young man raved with fever, wavering between life and death. In between hallucinations, he would awaken to find his father by his side, day and night, holding his hand and saying nothing, only crying. It was the first time young Pujol had seen his father's tears.

The fever seemed to burn something out of Pujol. After he recovered, he made another hairpin turn in his life: he would stop dreaming of romance and foreign travel. He gave up studying Aristotle. Instead, he began taking classes in — of all things — poultry management. After a six-month course at the Royal Academy of Poultry Farming at Arenys de Mar, Juan Pujol became a fully certified chicken farmer.

This about-face was clearly a major capitulation to his family, and to reality. "I felt my stubbornness, my not studying and continuously disappointing my father were going to bring me to a bad end," he later explained. He even took up with Margarita, a sensible and tender Barcelona girl who was very like his mother: "prudent, very religious" — and afraid of sex. The mad charms of girls like Luisita, as well as the adventures of Tom Mix and Don Quixote, were quietly put on a shelf.

In 1933, Pujol reported for compulsory military service. Soon he was sporting around town in the tailored officer's uniform of the 7th Light Artillery Regiment, sworn to serve the leftist Republican government against all enemies. After a few months, Pujol had learned to ride a horse and salute correctly. It was of his last successes before death and war darkened his life.

After a series of small strokes, his sixty-seven-year-old father soon took to his bed. The 1934 flu epidemic had struck Barcelona, and Juan Sr. was sick with the virus. In another room, Pujol was also laid out with the flu, and the two of them spent their days only yards apart, their faces burning with fever. On January 24, a doctor was called. Half delirious, Pujol listened from his room as the physician examined his father, the only sound the murmuring of his mother and sisters. Though sleepy and dazed, Pujol heard the doctor say that an injection was needed. He heard the thump of the front door closing and the rapid footsteps of a servant running off to the nearby pharmacy. A few minutes later, the sound of the door again: the servant had returned with the medicine. There was silence and Pujol imagined the doctor poking his syringe into the vial, then rolling up his father's sleeve, holding his pale arm as the needle slipped into the vein. And then Pujol heard a scream that he would never forget. "Everybody was crying and shouting. I heard someone cry out, 'What happened? What happened?' My mother and my sisters were crying, crying. I could hear the doctor saying he couldn't understand what had happened, why the injection had that effect." Finally, someone rushed in and told Pujol the news. His father had died the instant the doctor pushed the syringe's plunger.

Pujol, too ill to attend the funeral, was devastated. His father had been his closest friend, the ideal of what a man should be. "The flight of his soul from the world left me oppressed and overwhelmed," he said. "I had lost the one I loved the most, forever." To make matters worse, his father had died knowing that his son was struggling. As he listened to his family tell how the workers at the dye factory had taken his father's coffin on their shoulders, tears streaming down their faces, and how children from the San Juan de Dios Hospital had joined in the procession, paying tribute to the man who'd quietly paid for their medicines and their beds because it was the decent thing to do, the wayward son cried and contemplated a hard truth: he'd fallen short in his father's eyes.

With his father gone, Pujol struggled to find a place for himself in increasingly chaotic and violent Barcelona. Perhaps sparked by boyhood memories of Tom Mix, he bought a movie theater, then sold it and bought a smaller one. Both failed miserably. A trucking company bought and run with the long-suffering Joaquín bled red ink and had to be closed. Then a chicken farm. Everything collapsed in frustrated hopes, costing the family untold sums. "He was a *terrible* businessman," says Pujol's eldest son, who would go on to be a successful entrepreneur and art gallery owner. Pujol simply wasn't a practical thinker; he threw himself into things with passion but little planning or strategic vision.

Finally, at twenty-four, Pujol took up a sales position with a poultry farm in Llinás del Vallés, just under twenty miles north of Barcelona, and got engaged to the quiet Margarita. Was he in love with her? "I don't know. She was very nice to me but I was bored," he would say years later. Pujol had seemingly reconciled himself to a life of anonymous work and family life in a small town in Spain. He owed his family that much. And he needed to eat.

Then, on July 17, 1936, Spanish soldiers in their Moroccan barracks staged a revolt. The Spanish Civil War had begun.

2

The Training Ground

J ULY 18 WAS A blisteringly hot Sunday. Pujol had planned a day trip with friends to Montseny, a mountainous region thirty miles northeast of Barcelona. But then fragmented reports of the barracks rebellion came in over the radio: General Franco and his troops in the Canary Islands were joining the fray; officers and men across the nation were swelling the ranks of the coup against the Republican government. As Barcelona tensed, Pujol made his way through empty streets to his fiancée's house in Calle Girona. There he heard the news of escalations and fresh outbreaks of violence: cathedrals and political headquarters were burning; priests were being hunted down and murdered by leftist radicals; a general strike had been called by antifascist unions; food was already growing scarce and people were killing each other in the streets. Rebel fascist units had stormed the Telefónica building and the Hotel Colon, and marched toward the intersection of Paseo de Grácia and Diagonal, where a workers' militia waited to oppose them, rifle stocks growing slick in their hands.

Soon it became clear that Barcelona was firmly in the grip of the Republican forces. As a cavalry officer, Pujol was required to report for duty, but he refused to take up arms "in such a fratricidal fight." Even if he had to die, he wouldn't kill a fellow Spaniard.

Politically, Pujol was his father's son. "I loved liberty, tolerance and religious liberty," he said. He hated the wild rhetoric of the communists and the anarcho-syndicalists, who declared that "nothing great has ever been achieved without violence . . . the possession of revolv-

ers and machine guns distinguished the free man from the slave."
Franco and his Nationalists were just as extreme in their hatreds,
but Barcelona was a leftist city, its buildings draped with communist flags and the red-and-black banners of the anarchists. "Every
shop and café had an inscription saying that it had been collectiv-
ized," wrote George Orwell. "Even the bootblacks had been collectiv-
ized and their boxes painted red and black."

Pujol shared none of the left's infatuation with the Republicans.
He'd seen the massacres, seen the bodies being pulled from the church
ruins. His younger sister Elena and his mother were arrested by the
Republicans on charges of supporting Franco, but the family managed to contact an anarchist friend, and the pair were "snatched from
certain death" and returned home unharmed. Pujol's older brother,
Joaquín, was sent to the Republican front; like his brother, Joaquín
didn't believe in the cause and soon deserted, slipping through the
hills of Girona province, starving and near naked. The family's dye
factory, on whose profits the Pujols depended, was taken over by the
workers who just a few years earlier had carried his father's coffin
on their shoulders. Pujol despised the vicious war that tore families
apart, the massacres in bullrings, the shadowy groups of men known
as "uncontrollables" who hunted fascists and their peers on the right.
He saw firsthand what one thoughtful anarchist called the release of
"a brutish appetite, a thirst for extermination, a lust for blood incon-
ceivable in honest men before."

Barcelona was Pujol's first experience of war — and of espionage. In
Spain, the spy game shared little with the remote gentlemen's pastime
popularized in pulp novels. It was all-pervasive, blind and savage. "A
horrible atmosphere of suspicion had grown up," wrote Orwell, who
arrived in the city in late 1936. "Various people were infected with
spy mania and were creeping round whispering that everyone else
was a spy of the Communists, or the Trotskyists, or the Anarchists,
or what-not." Men and women were executed on the mere charge
of "Trotskyist treachery." Even those who weren't spying, as Orwell
wrote, somehow *felt* that they were. Pujol would emerge from the
Spanish Civil War naïve about the techniques of espionage, but not

about its costs. People were put up against a wall and shot in Barcelona on the strength of a rumor.

Not wanting to fight for the Republicans, Pujol took his chances as a fugitive and holed up at his fiancée's family home, one of many young Spaniards who fled the ranks of both sides. For months he lived there, unable to leave the premises, glued to the radio as gunshots echoed outside and the airwaves filled with reports of massacres. It was too risky for him to speak above a whisper or glance out the window, and every time the doorbell rang he had to hide. Capture could mean being shot as a deserter.

Just before Christmas 1936, Pujol was in the kitchen cracking hazelnuts and walnuts with a hammer, the shells flying everywhere. Enjoying himself, he forgot about the need for silence; in fact, he was making such a racket that at first he didn't hear the knock at the front door. An informer had turned Margarita's family in for storing valuables for pro-Franco families who'd fled Barcelona. When the police poured through the front door, they marched straight to the spot where the jewelry was hidden, a lintel between two rooms. Then they began to search the rest of the house. When the police reached the kitchen, they found Pujol, hammer still raised to smash a walnut. He was arrested at gunpoint and marched out of the house, along with his fiancée's father and brother, into a waiting car.

Had Pujol and the others been found by an irregular posse of full-blooded radicals, they would most likely have been "taken for a stroll" and executed. But luck was with them: the somber group was brought instead to the local police station, which meant they were in the hands of more moderate Republicans. Pujol breathed a sigh of relief — which quickly evaporated when he was accused of being a deserter. "I was petrified, fearing that I might have to pay with my life," he recalled. The young lieutenant was taken to the dungeon below the station and locked in a dark, cold cell.

Day after day, as his warders brought his meals, Pujol could only sit in the gloom and listen to the voices of his jailers and fellow inmates. Every day the door to his cell would be opened and a police officer would sit down and interrogate him. "I kept assuring [them] I had only been in the house because I was engaged to the eldest daughter, but they continued to question me remorselessly." The war was growing even more savage, with atrocities and mass killings on both sides. The execution of a suspected Nationalist sympathizer would barely be noticed.

After a week in the jail, in the middle of a freezing night, Pujol awoke with a start. The cell door had swung open and a man he'd never seen before was standing in the dim light. The man whispered for him to get up and come with him. Pujol, half asleep, stumbled after the stranger as he led the prisoner through a bewildering series of hallways and offices in the predawn darkness. Pujol now realized that the man was no policeman; Pujol had unwittingly become part of a jailbreak. At every turn he feared running into a Republican militiaman in one of their mismatched uniforms. A deserter might catch a break, but a deserter-cum-escapee was certain to be shot. Finally, the stranger reached ahead and pushed open a small door, and Pujol felt a rush of cold air against his face. The man handed him a piece of paper and pointed toward the starlit road.

His fiancée, the pious and prudish Margarita, whom he wasn't even sure he loved, had saved his skin. She'd contacted a secret Catholic organization called the Socorro Blanco (White Aid), which ran a kind of Francoist underground railroad for fugitives. But now Pujol was on the streets of Barcelona, a hunted man without the identification needed to pass the Republican checkpoints. He looked at the address on the paper and began walking quickly, keeping a sharp eye out for the barricades behind which soldiers stood guard around the clock. The dizzying fall from the dreamy existence of his childhood was nearly complete. "I had . . . become a criminal."

The address led him to the Gothic Quarter, one of Barcelona's tough and dirty working-class neighborhoods. Pujol climbed the stairs of the apartment building listed on the paper, not daring to turn on the hallway light. Feeling his way forward in the dark, he touched the smooth surface of a wooden door and knocked gently. He heard footsteps. A woman slowly opened the door. Without a word, she gestured him inside. The flat was a Socorro Blanco safe house occupied by a taxi driver, his wife and their bright-eyed nine-year-old son. Pujol was safe for the time being.

Unable to get word to his family, Pujol spent his days in the cramped apartment, often hungry, as food in Barcelona was becoming increasingly scarce. When Pujol had to speak to his protectors, they would turn up the radio to muffle the conversation. Otherwise, he lived in silence. He helped the boy with his math and history lessons — the schools in Barcelona had closed during the war — by whispering his corrections in the nine-year-old's ear. Outside, he could glimpse fathers and mothers lining up for food and could feel the impact as bombs thudded into nearby houses. At night, Pujol had difficulty sleeping, his vivid imagination serving up nightmares in which a sudden knock on the door was followed by arrest and a firing squad.

The only relief from the boredom were moments of unexpected terror. One day, when he was whiling away the time with the taxi driver's son, with the parents away, the knock on the door finally came. "*Policía*," a voice shouted. Pujol silently pointed to the boy's bedroom, and the boy nodded. As he hid himself, Pujol heard the child open the front door and inform the policemen that his mother was shopping and his father was out fighting the fascists. The boy invited the men in and casually showed them the apartment as they asked detailed questions. When he came to the room where Pujol lay hiding under the bed, the boy flung the door open, hit the light switch and in a bored voice announced that this was where he slept. The police nodded and passed by.

After months of this precarious existence, in the summer of 1937 the taxi driver took his family to live in a small village in Lleida, in western Catalonia. Pujol was left alone. He had to strain to be completely quiet, as the neighbors believed the apartment had been left empty — no radio, no clattering of dishes, no singing to pass the time. When he walked across the floor, he shuffled to keep the noise down. The apartment windows were kept shut even during the blazingly hot Barcelona summer, so Pujol roasted; when winter came, his teeth chattered with cold. He couldn't turn on a lamp, afraid the glow from behind the drawn curtains would be seen from the street. Pujol's eyes, like those of a nocturnal animal, became sensitive to bright light. Only the surreptitious visits of a girl from the Socorro Blanco with packages of food under her arm broke the monotony and kept him from starvation. She came every three days, but as the weeks passed the time between visits stretched longer and longer.

Pujol was a naturally buoyant person, a lover of life, but in time he fell into a deep depression. He lost nearly fifty pounds, and his skin grew pale from lack of sunlight. "I began to look like a decrepit old man of forty, even though I was only twenty-five. I became desperate and knew I could not hold out much longer." Pujol asked the volunteer to get him fake papers so that he could walk the streets again, and after a long delay she came back with a forged ID showing he was too old for the army. It wasn't a difficult thing to pull off: Pujol had aged so much that his appearance matched the fake details.

The fugitive walked out into the streets of Barcelona and at first failed to recognize his native city, with its burned-out husks of buildings and its citizens in rags. Distraught over the reports of fresh bloodshed coming over the radio daily, he decided it was time to leave Spain. "The years of enclosure and persecution shaped my personality and most of my dreams were dashed and destroyed. The bitterness of so many hours of dejection and woe, deprivations, deceptions . . . made my spirit into a rebel one, more disobedient and obstinate." In order to plan an escape over the border, he first found work managing a chicken farm in Girona in the northeast, not far from France. He nodded as his neighbors repeated the latest Republican slogans; he was an undercover pacifist, unattached to either side, already learning how to be a kind of double agent in his own country. In his free time, Pujol went for long walks in the hills to build up his strength for the ordeals ahead, carefully noting the distances in a small notebook. He was walking thirteen miles a day, then twenty, until one day he arrived back in Girona and realized he'd hiked forty miles, all the way to the top of Mount Puigmal, from which he could see the French border. His health slowly returned.

There was one problem with his escape plan: border guards had recently shot and killed a number of fugitives. Pujol contemplated fleeing but soon changed his mind. Instead, he decided to go over to the Nationalist side, where he hoped he'd "be left alone to live my own life." To do that, he first had to rejoin the Republicans, go through training, get his commission and be sent to the front. Only then could he make a run for the enemy lines. Even to begin the ruse, Pujol had to deceive. Using a false name and forged papers, he went to the barracks in Las Atarazanas and signed up for the army. The Republican officers cheered his selflessness; Pujol's fake ID showed that he was past the age for compulsory service, but here he was, a diehard volunteering for the cause.

After two weeks of bare-bones training, Pujol was sent to Montblanc, near the Ebro River. The war, and the Nationalist army, was only a few miles away. Pujol volunteered as a signals officer and was sent to the front as part of one of the International Brigades made famous by Hemingway and Orwell. The appeal of the war had faded for the Europeans and Americans, however, and Pujol found himself among fellow Catalans, often shooting at their cousins and uncles a few hundred yards away across a hilly landscape cut into zigzag trenches and pitted with bomb craters. The casualty rate was over 50 percent.

Though he'd claimed to be experienced in signals, the new recruit didn't know Morse code or semaphore. Instead of sending messages, he was ordered to lay telephone cables from the rear command areas to the front lines. On the northern bank of the Ebro, he ducked as a rebel bomber screamed overhead and dropped explosives on a Republican pontoon, which was being used to ferry combatants across the river. "The bombs hissed as they descended, thunderous explosions followed and the air was filled with millions of splinters as huge columns of water gushed upward."

Pujol took up his position in a trench cut into a slope of the Sierra de la Fatarella and listened to the voices of the Nationalist troops as they called through their megaphones, mocking the half-starved enemy, asking them if they were eating lentils again. That was the only Republican meal: lentils, perhaps with a trace of lard or a bit of pork. Desertion was rife. The punishment, if you were caught, was death. One day, Pujol watched as the company barber, who'd been caught trying to sneak over to Franco's lines, was stood up in front of the battalion and shot. His corpse was left to rot in the sun as a warning to the other men. Pujol decided to risk an escape anyway.

Walking the front line, checking the telephone cables for breaks or cuts, Pujol kept an eye on the no man's land between the trenches.

He could see the helmets of the Francoists outlined against the setting sun. He listened to the chatter from the other side, trying to zero in on the trench closest to the Republican lines. Finally, one evening early in the new year of 1938, he picked up two hand grenades and steeled himself for "the craziest act I ever did in my long and adventurous existence." Two other ragged and starving Republicans had agreed to go across with him. They waited for the right moment.

The sky was clear and a full moon lit up the battlefield. At around 7 p.m., the three men crouching in their trench turned to each other and nodded. As Pujol adjusted his gear one final time, the other two, their nerves frayed to the breaking point, startled him by jumping out of the trench and dashing wildly down the hillside, sending a small avalanche of rocks and pebbles ahead of them. A sentry called out. Pujol wasn't yet out of the trench and already his cover was blown. Prepared to die to escape an army he'd grown to hate, he climbed the trench wall and pitched himself into no man's land.

Stumbling down the hill in the half darkness, Pujol heard a patrol take up the chase behind him. He made it down the slope and crossed the river at the foot of the mountain, then angled toward a stand of pine trees that offered cover from the bright moonlight. Once he reached the trees, however, he became disoriented and began running uphill, before realizing he was ascending the same small mountain he'd just scrambled down. He was panicking, heading straight back to the Republican lines and certain death.

Bullets cut through the night air around him. Pujol reversed course as tiny geysers of dirt spattered against his wool pants. He sped up, taking giant steps, half running and half falling down the hill toward a patch of reeds that lay at the bottom. When he reached the stand, he rolled into the reeds and out of the moonlight as the patrol nipped at his heels. Panting, he tried to control his breathing as the soldiers beat the grass with their guns, hoping to flush him out. Their voices, angry and frustrated, grew closer. "There were six of them. I lay there shaking in fear and covered with sweat," he later wrote. He began to pray to the Virgin Mary to keep him hidden.

Pujol felt the cool metal of the grenades in his sweating palms. If he pulled the pins and lobbed the grenades at the voices, he'd be free. But he was lying in this dirt because he despised bloodshed. He

couldn't do it. After a tense fifteen minutes, he dashed up the opposite hill — the correct one this time — to a nearby stand of trees. He
found a narrow ditch just wide enough to hide a man. He lay down
in it, covering himself with leaves and twigs. The voices of the patrol,
close by, soon stopped; the men were taking a cigarette break. Pujol peered through the leaves and saw the silhouettes of their faces
against the sky.

The Francoists began their nightly banter, their mocking voices
floating over the reed bed. "Hey, Reds, what've they given you to eat
today?" A rain cloud passed in front of the moon, sending a shadow
over the battlefield. Pujol placed his two grenades on dry ground and
slowly reached down to untie his boots, listening for any change in
the soldier's voices, any hint they'd heard him stirring. Now his boots
were off and he could tiptoe silently. He crouched down, making his
way through the reed bed and out the other side.

His bare feet gripped the loose gravel of the hillside as he raced
uphill and threw himself over two stone walls, using the shouts of
the Nationalists as his beacon. His heart racing, he suddenly heard
a voice that seemed impossibly close to him. "We're coming to you,"
the man said. Pujol nearly fainted, thinking the patrol had caught
him — but it was one of his fellow escapees. He had made it across.

Once they were safely behind Nationalist lines, Pujol and the
other two fugitives were presented with plates piled with food. They
ate until their stomachs hurt. Stone-faced interrogators put them
through "endless hours" of questioning: Where were the Republican
positions? What was morale like? Next, the men were sent on a supply train back to Zaragoza, where they were herded into the concentration camp at the University of Deusto, in the Basque province.

Pujol had risked his life for freedom. Now he found himself
dressed in filthy rags like all his fellow prisoners, watching lice races
in the camp barracks, complete with betting and cheering sections
for each contestant. He slept on the hard wooden floor, his days ruled
over by abusive guards. He fell ill and was brought, vomiting, to the
camp's infirmary. His dream of liberty, like all the others, had gone up
in bitter smoke.

Pujol had only one thing of value left, a beautiful and expensive
fountain pen, a reminder of his past as a child of Barcelona's upper

class. He sold the pen to a soldier and, with the proceeds, bought a much cheaper pen, some writing paper and stamps. Pujol wrote to everyone he knew, relatives and distant acquaintances that he remembered from his boyhood. Finally, a kindhearted family friend, a brother superior of the order of San Juan de Dios, the Catholic mission his father had supported, showed up at the camp to berate the Nationalists and secure his release. Again his long-suffering family had come to the rescue of their luckless son.

Pujol was taken to Palencia and then on to a hospital in the city of Burgos, where he was diagnosed with acute bronchitis and sent to the wards. At last he could enjoy small pleasures, such as sleeping in a clean bed and playing cards with his fellow patients as the daughters of the best families of Burgos cared for them. One especially caught his eye, a dark beauty named Araceli, who worked as a nurse and whom he later ran into at the Hotel Condestable. The hotel had one other guest that would have an impact on Pujol's life: Kim Philby, war correspondent for the London *Times*, Russian spy and future head of the Spanish section of MI6.

The Civil War ended on April 1, 1939, with General Francisco Franco taking control of a broken, hate-addled nation.

Pujol was in as bad shape as his country. "Years of hiding and persecution had made me bitter; my dreams had been shattered; my life seemed to have been nothing but disappointments and privations; I hated being a soldier and longed to escape to a new life." He received his discharge from the army but refused to join the Spanish Phalanx of the Assemblies of the Nationalist Syndicalist Offensive, also known as the Falange, the party headed by General Franco. Doing so would have greased the wheels for Pujol in business and social life, but by now he despised the fascists as much as he had the communists.

The war had remade Juan Pujol. It had eaten up his youth, left him physically wasted, mocked his ideals, disillusioned and humiliated him, reduced him to a pale ghost. His family fortune was gone and his beloved country was in ruins. He'd lost most of his hair. He looked far older than he was. He had no medals or war service with which to kick off a brilliant career.

But the conflict had given as well as taken. He found himself walking the streets of a blasted, mourning Madrid no longer willing to settle for an anonymous life as a chicken farmer in the back reaches of the capital. Instead of grandiose dreams, he now had something more world-ready: a survivor's wit sharpened to a razor's edge. He'd learned how to talk his way past firing squads and to convince people of whatever he wanted to convince them. He wasn't the hero he'd wanted to be; he was far from being his noble father. "I am only his shadow," he would later write. But he was a far tougher man than he'd been a few years before. It was as if the stuff of his fantasies had been brutally reprocessed into a working knowledge of how human beings functioned under pressure.

Even more importantly, Pujol realized that playing it safe had gotten him nowhere. Why remain a chicken farmer when the world was being turned upside down? He was willing to risk things again — everything, if necessary. And he'd found someone who was just as eager to take the plunge with him.

3

Araceli

ARACELI GONZÁLEZ CARBALLO, the dark stunner of a nurse that Pujol had met in the Hotel Condestable, was a dreamer like Pujol. Growing up, her mother nicknamed her Antoñita la Fantástica, after the fictional character in a series of popular children's books starring a Madrid girl who traveled the world chasing adventure and who, as one reader put it, "symbolized extravagance and almost a hint of madness."

But unlike Pujol's ambitions, Araceli's were tuned to beautiful things, fine clothes and social glamour. "There is a part of the family that believes they descend from Alfonso XI," she would later write, while confirming that one grandmother "belonged to the house of the marquis of Carballo." All very important considerations in status-conscious Spain.

Pujol had always alternated unhappily between two romantic poles: devout Catholic girls like Margarita, humble and a little boring, who must have pleased his mother, and women with fire in their eyes: wild, music-mad, flamboyant like Luisita, the girl who'd married the "abominable cretin." Perhaps, like his career choices—chicken farming vs. philosophy—they represented the two forces that repelled and attracted him: a desire to please his family and be the good son, and the compulsion to seek out all-or-nothing encounters with destiny. Araceli was very much from the flamboyant camp, and in pursuing her ardently, Pujol made declaration: I will take a chance on life. Poor Margarita, who'd saved his life more than once, wasn't heard from again.

Pujol's fires burned deep inside, but on the surface he was often quiet and reserved. It was Araceli who had the show-stopping personality. When she entered a room, it was as if the lights had been turned up. With lustrous black hair, flashing eyes, a pale, creamy complexion, she was impossible to miss. Decades later, her granddaughter would smile ruefully and say, "She was the most seductive woman I ever met. My boyfriends always ended up falling in love with her."

Araceli had grown up in the province of Galicia, in the small northwestern town of Lugo, the only extant town in the world still surrounded by intact Roman walls. It was as ancient and insular as it sounded. When Araceli claimed that "Lugo was the kind of place where people died in the bed they'd been born in," she meant it literally. Instead of receiving a first-class education that would allow them to make their way in the world, Araceli and other girls of her station were sent to "ladies' school" and then to be trained in a minor profession where they could meet a respectable husband. Araceli was steered into nursing. "It was the best way to leave us without culture," she wrote bitterly. "I always wanted to talk, to reason, to discuss." Everything modern and exciting was far away: "We lived in a fantasy world of the good girls of Lugo."

Araceli rebelled. After her nurse's training, she raced off to the regional center, Burgos, and volunteered to treat the wounded. She took with her an enormous wooden chest, custom made by one of the finest carpenters in her hometown, which held all her dresses, shoes and warm coats. The closet became a kind of movable Lugo, lugged by moving men to each new residence she found herself in, filled with memories of the happy but smothering town she'd left behind.

Araceli was fiercely intelligent, adventurous, dramatic and a bit vain. "All my friends would say, you have to fly away and see the world, you're too special for here." They were right, actually: Lugo was too drab and backward to hold her. But Araceli also had the grit to back up her ambitions. A friend and fellow nursing student, Cachita, remembered their first day of working at the hospital in Lugo, where the Nationalist wounded were brought in from the front. Araceli and Cachita were told to clean up one of the treatment rooms. Cachita, who'd grown up with maids at home just like Araceli, was appalled at the blood-soaked wrappings and pus-smeared bandages. She stormed out; cleaning was beneath her. Araceli, to Cachita's amazement, not only stayed but proceeded to pick up the dressings, sweep the floor and make the room fit to receive more wounded. It wasn't work for a society girl: wrapping amputated legs, smelling the gangrene and the blood, watching young men die. But Araceli didn't turn away.

Pujol and Araceli met in the spring of 1939. "I went to Burgos and that's where my destiny was waiting for me," Araceli said. Meeting Pujol "was where my life began." She called him Juanito and he called her Aracelita. They were both young, in their mid-twenties, and bursting with ambition. "Where he was weak, she was strong, and vice versa," their daughter Maria said. And they were both dreamers: Antoñita la Fantástica and the boy who wanted to be Tom Mix.

As the two fell in love, Franco's super-Catholic, hysterically nationalist regime clamped down on the country. In Navarre, men in short-sleeve shirts were banned from cafés, and women had to adhere to strict rules of dress — which makeup was suitable and which too provocative. Books by Jews and Freemasons were publicly burned in Pamplona. Movie censors snipped parts of the Gettysburg Address from D. W. Griffith's 1930 film on Abraham Lincoln, which must have cut at Pujol's Hollywood-loving heart. The regime's suppression reached all the way down to the menus of neighborhood *cervecerías:* "Russian salad" became "National salad," as Moscow was still affiliated with the defeated Reds. Newspaper editors received official edicts telling them articles were to be written in "the language of Don Quixote" as opposed to the more modern vernacular. Identity cards had to be carried at all times. On them, each citizen was given one of three possible ratings: "Addicted" to Franco's cause, "Indifferent" or "Disaffected." The disaffected were fired from their jobs.

Pujol hated extremism and intolerance above everything else, and here they were, running roughshod over the Spanish. He hated the suffocating atmosphere of Francoist Spain, the near outlawing of free thought. Not only that, Franco made his sympathies clear when it came to the increasingly tense "phony war" between Hitler and the future Allies. Spain's police and Seguridad — the intelligence service — worked closely with the Nazis: passports for Spanish citizens were granted or denied based on German lists of who was trust-worthy. Those suspected of speaking against the Führer were often kidnapped and brought to Berlin for trial. The rabidly anti-British press was under the thumb of the sinister and all-powerful Hans La-zar, a Turkish Jew turned Catholic and a rabid Nazi who'd married a Transylvanian baroness and come to Madrid as the press attaché for the German embassy. Lazar reportedly had a bedroom done up as a chapel, complete with plaster saints and candles. He slept under the altar. With his jet-black eyes glinting behind a monocle, this mor-phine addict threw extravagant dinner parties featuring goose liver flown in from Paris, parties attended by everyone who was anyone in Madrid. He was considered the best-informed man in Spain, and the two hundred newspapers under his control fed Nazi propaganda to a receptive nation. Under Lazar, Spain practically became a Ger-man colony.

Madrid and its suburbs in the winter of 1939 gave a preview of what London could reasonably expect from war. "The countryside . . . was pockmarked by shell holes," said the MI6 officer Desmond Bristow, who passed through Madrid just after the ceasefire was de-clared. "The empty trenches wound their snakelike courses, twisted tanks and trucks lay around, all presenting a scene which not only saddened me, but gave me nervous twinges . . . As we slowly rat-tled northwards, the dangling power-lines, broken telegraph poles, bomb-shattered and machine-gun-bullet-marked walls, really wak-ened me to the destructive elements of war."

Desperate to survive in the city, Pujol answered an ad in a Madrid newspaper and took a job as the manager of the three-star Hotel Ma-jestic near the city's famous Calle Velázquez. The thirty-room hotel had once been an elegant destination for the middle classes, but dur-ing the war its suites had been commandeered by the International Brigade. It was now a half-wrecked shell, its central heating system constantly on the blink and its hallways grimy. "It didn't even deserve one star," Pujol sighed, but the Majestic gave him a place to stay and a meager income.

Pujol hoped, like his entrepreneurial father, to build the hotel back into a thriving gem, but soon it became clear that there would be neither funds nor paying guests to bankroll a functioning furnace, let alone fresh wallpaper. He walked the shabby halls growing more and more depressed. He'd found a tenuous foothold in the dark city, but he refused to settle in. "Francoist Madrid was too small for him and Araceli," said a Spanish journalist. "They were looking beyond the horizon." It was easier said than done, however: getting a passport in 1939 Madrid was a nearly impossible task, requiring luck and connections in high places.

On September 1, 1939, German panzers rolled over the Polish border. World War II had begun. For Pujol, Hitler was "a maniac, an inhuman brute." He was shocked by the suffering of the Polish people as the Nazi SS swept through town after town, executing resisters. "My humanist convictions would not allow me to turn a blind eye to the enormous suffering that was being unleashed by this psychopath."

Pujol had stayed on the sidelines in the Spanish Civil War, with its multiple factions and brutal extremes, but this was different: one side was evil and one was good. Everything he held dear — humanism, tolerance, freedom — lay with the Allies. He threw his allegiance to them and never wavered in his loyalty.

But what could Pujol do? He was a hotel manager, an ex–chicken farmer and a committed pacifist. He had very little money. There were no openings for men like him in the Allied ranks, and besides, he was trapped in Madrid. Pujol stewed in the wrecked Hotel Majestic, listening obsessively to the radio, whispering to friends about the Nazis and suffering what sounds like mild symptoms of post-traumatic stress: "I would be tormented by odd pieces of information and graphic details which merged in my imagination into a confused and horrible nightmare." By 1940, the news on the wireless got darker and darker. In April, Denmark and Norway fell. The next month it was the turn of Belgium, Holland and France. On May 26, the tragedy at Dunkirk unfolded. On June 10, Italy entered the war on the German side. Two weeks later, Pétain surrendered in the name of France. Hitler seemed unstoppable.

The only relief was his marriage to his beloved Araceli in April 1940, in Madrid. Otherwise, Pujol listened, brooded and plotted, both his despair and his convictions growing stronger as the days passed.

After months of talking with Araceli, Pujol decided he had to find a way to volunteer for the Allies. Perhaps he could go to London and work for the BBC, write and produce shows in Castilian on freedom and politics. Or *something*. The details were vague. But he desperately wanted to be part of the fight.

There was more to it. Perhaps Pujol wanted to prove himself worthy of this vibrant woman on his arm. Perhaps he realized that life as a hotel manager wouldn't hold Araceli for long, that she deserved — no, required — something altogether more rare and dramatic. Certainly she'd given him a shot of confidence.

The lure of espionage spoke to some of the deepest and earliest desires within Pujol: it promised to give his imagination a chance to run riot in the world, and at long last answer the echoes of his father's entreaties — *do good, believe in your fellow human being*. He'd tried to be a dutiful son, but he had no talent for business and he'd been a farce as a soldier. Spying would allow him to honor his father and at the same time declare his own rather eccentric personality, which happened to find great joy in the thought of tricking fascists.

How exactly he came upon the scheme that would turn him into one of the war's great double agents is somewhat mysterious. There was no master plan. "If a Pythian oracle had foretold the checkered existence that lay before me," he said later, "I would have sneered sarcastically at the soothsayer, so little intention did I have of behaving the way I actually did." But the germ of the idea came with news reports from Hitler's Germany. Pujol was always listening to the BBC or paging slowly through a Spanish newspaper, then rushing off to the local café to argue about what he'd just read. And he kept hearing phrases that chilled him: "Aryan race," "superior being." Gradually Pujol came to believe that the "diabolical dogmas" that had come to rule Spain were going to be implemented in Germany. Spanish censors attempted to withhold all news of concentration camps and "extermination through work," but word leaked out. And Pujol decided he had to act. "I must do something, something practical," he said. "I must make my contribution toward the good of humanity."

Step one: leave Spain. A little caper over the Portuguese border gave Pujol a shot at the passport he'd need to get to Allied territory. A guest at the Majestic who called himself the Duke of Torre knew of two elderly pro-Franco princesses who craved a supply of whisky, then unobtainable in Madrid. "They considered such a drink essential, given their social position and entertaining commitments." Pujol looked the capable type. Could he get them a case of good Scotch? Pujol told the Duke and the spinsters to find him a passport and a visa, and the deal was as good as done. The trio of Francoists soon acquired the documents, so Pujol drove his two elderly coconspirators and the Duke over the Portuguese border, bought six bottles of Scotch on the black market and wheeled home in high spirits, the contraband tucked safely in the trunk. The passport was Pujol's reward for the jaunt. There were hundreds, if not thousands, of Madrileños trying to become informers or spies who would have looked at the document with barely disguised envy.

But what to do with it? In his room at the hotel, Pujol felt twenty-odd years of frustration well up within him. He wanted to take a stand for a world he'd witnessed only in the novels he'd read and in the stories told by his father so many years ago, walking by the seashore: "We were just fighting for the right to survive. And we had to feed our optimism in order to live. I yearned for justice. From the medley of tangled ideas and fantasies going around and around in my head, a plan slowly began to take shape."

Pujol was ready to take the next step. He possessed a talent that hadn't fit anywhere before — not in the peacetime economy of northern Spain, not in the ranks of two very different armies. But perhaps in espionage he would finally find his purpose.

He'd decided he would use his riotous and unrivaled imagination to help defeat the Third Reich.

On a cold day in January 1941, Juan Pujol walked into the British embassy in Madrid and volunteered his services.

"Your services of *what?*" was the response.

Pujol couldn't or wouldn't explain. (In fact, even he didn't know what he was offering. "I must confess that my plans were fairly confused.") His original idea had been to offer to produce radio programs for the BBC. But his ambition had outrun his brain. He only repeated his request and stood there, shoulders thrown back, his warm hazel eyes burning with intensity. It became a game for the embassy staff, as the Spaniard was handed on from receptionist to secretary to clerk to minor official. Finally, having got no further than the embassy's lowest rungs, Pujol was told to write down exactly what he proposed to do for England, and was shown the door.

Pujol was green, but he wasn't that green. Madrid was practically a suburb of Berlin in 1941, the papers full of pro-German slogans and the cafés crowded with German agents and their local informants. Even to write down some nonsense about the BBC would mean risking his life. He was beginning to believe that espionage, not a radio show, was the best way he could serve the cause. There was only one problem: he didn't know anything about espionage. Yet he did not give up, and he was not alone. Araceli tried next. She went to the embassy with an enigmatic offer of getting information for the Allies. She was turned down flat.

These refusals didn't reflect on the Pujols' skills as potential spies. Instead, they reflected a complex political reality the couple knew nothing about. The British ambassador to Spain in 1940 was Sir Samuel Hoare, an Oxonian and longtime Conservative politician who had once — as an officer in MI6 — recruited the young Benito Mussolini during World War I. The future Il Duce was then the thirty-four-year-old editor of an influential and virulently right-wing newspaper. England was eager to keep Italy on the side of the Allies, so it paid Mussolini the princely sum of 100 pounds a week ($9,300 in today's dollars) to publish fiery editorials against the Germans. Mussolini's controller, Sir Samuel, later became an establishment politician who saw plenty of skullduggery as he waded through various international skirmishes between the wars. He knew espionage, and he wasn't necessarily opposed to it. But his mandate in 1941 was to keep neutral Spain out of the war. So Sir Samuel passed the word to the Madrid head of MI6, a man named Hamilton-Stokes: he would tolerate no incidents or spy capers under his watch. Pujol and Araceli had been turned down as a matter of policy, not because of the merits of their offer.

Unaware of the backstory, Pujol was downcast. But the stubbornness that had always been part of his nature took over. He'd decided by now that he would present himself to the British as a potential double agent. This was even crazier than his previous offer to spy. He didn't know anything about espionage, and he knew even less about Germany's spy service, the Abwehr. But he knew he needed material to offer the British, something concrete he could carry in his pocket and produce with a flourish at the right moment. So he decided to offer his services to the Germans first, gather what nuggets of intelligence he could, then present them to the British embassy.

As a gambit, doublecrossing the Germans was exponentially more dangerous than Pujol's first idea. But a man whose first nickname was Bullet didn't give up easily.

In their room at the crumbling hotel, Pujol and Araceli worked up a plan, going over and over the details and reworking the approach. They quickly realized they needed to learn more about the Germans, to do what would later be called "oppo research": find out what the enemy was thinking. "Out of *amour-propre,* I decided to prepare the ground more carefully," he said. Here Pujol did something that was to be vital to his remarkable rise: he tried to think like a German. "In order to offer myself to the Nazis, I first studied their doctrines." What did they want, how did they carry themselves, how did they speak, what would intrigue them? Pujol was doing more than studying some dog-eared Nazi tracts about land in the East and Aryan strongmen; he was doing what a good actor does. Learning his character, becoming the role.

From the Hotel Majestic, he phoned the German embassy. Pujol would tell two versions of what happened next, differing in mostly minor details but focused on the same Abwehr agent. In the first version, a man with a guttural voice, speaking bad Spanish, answered. Pujol, not messing around, asked to be connected to the military attaché. He gave the man some high-flown rhetoric about serving the masters of the "New Europe." The man asked him to call back the next day. Pujol hung up, pleased, and the next day the man told him to meet a member of the embassy staff the following afternoon at 4:30 at the Café Lyon in Calle Alcalá. This man was described as fair-haired with blue eyes, and he'd be dressed in a light suit and carrying a raincoat over his arm, sitting at one of the tables at the far end of the café. His name was Federico. The voice asked what Pujol looked like and what he'd be wearing the next day. Pujol happily gave him the details and hung up. "My contact with the Germans had started." (In the second version, the Federico meeting did not happen quite so fast.)

Pujol was excited but nervous. Going to the British embassy and playing mysterious was dangerous enough, but the Abwehr in Madrid represented an entirely new level of the game. The German embassy in Madrid was a hive of Nazi intelligence; it employed 391 people, 220 of whom were full-time Abwehr officers, split into sections for espionage, counterespionage and sabotage. These officers directed 1,500 agents spread all over Spain, who in turn had their own informers and subagents. The communications of this gargantuan network kept a staff of 34 radio operators busy around the clock sending coded messages to Abwehr headquarters in Berlin, by way of Paris. The Abwehr apparatus in Spain was directed with the knowledge and approval of Franco, who was well aware that Spain was honeycombed with Nazi spies. "All classes were represented, from Cabinet Ministers to unnamed stewards of cargo ships," reported a wartime memo. The embassy had its own wireless station, complete with a state-of-the-art radio tower. In walking into the embassy, Pujol was twitching the tail of a large and quite lethal animal.

Federico, the man Pujol was going to meet that day, was a twenty-seven-year-old Abwehr officer named Friedrich Knappe-Ratey (the Germans often practiced the standard spy protocol of assigning a cover name that was close to one's original name, so that the agent would instinctively respond to it). He was the son of a German father, an importer of electronics, including the first x-ray machine to be used in Spain. Knappe-Ratey had grown up in luxury, attended the best Spanish schools and even visited the country homes of the Spanish king Alfonso XIII. His MI5 file described him as "slight but rather athletic . . . hair fair, curly and brushed-back . . . well-dressed, appears to be a sportsman . . . rather Jewish in appearance . . . usually wears light gloves . . . placid, not communicative, wears a ring that he fingers continuously." Inside the Abwehr, he was an agent-runner who recruited and trained spies for a living. He himself was trained to spot fakes and ferret out lies, the first task of any Abwehr agent who dealt with "walk-ins" such as Juan Pujol.

Pujol arrived on time, spotted Federico at a table and walked over slowly, not wanting to appear overeager, all the while regarding the German with a casual smile. (In the second version Pujol later told, he met a different officer at his rendezvous and wasn't introduced to Federico until several weeks later.) When he sat down, he introduced himself as Mr. Lopez (the equivalent of an American calling himself Mr. Smith) and was met with a cold nod. Federico was giving nothing away; he immediately asked what the young Spaniard wanted. He regarded Pujol with his piercing blue eyes and a chilly expression. The walk-in had to convince the spy-runner, not vice versa.

Pujol became animated and gestured wildly, proclaiming his hatred of the Allies. He spoke extravagantly of the Third Reich and his adulation of Hitler. Pujol was carried away with the character he was playing, what MI5 would later call a "hot Nazi." Yet after another prediction of an "extraordinarily magnificent" victory, Pujol happened to glance at Federico and his heart nearly stopped. "It dawned on me that I wasn't making such a good impression on him as I'd first imagined." Federico drily asked him what exactly he proposed to do for the Nazis. Pujol fired off a list of fictitious diplomats and government officials he was supposedly friends with, "a thousand foolish things" spilling out of his brain. It was the start of a long parade of fabrications. Federico may have rolled his eyes, but he was intrigued enough to give the voluble Spaniard a second rendezvous two days later, at the Cervecería de Correos, opposite the Ministry of Communications.

Pujol said goodbye and strolled back to the hotel along the busy Madrid streets. He'd been making things up as he went along, but he'd clearly achieved something: he'd slipped into the character of an excitable maniac, a kind of cliché of the passionate Spaniard. And Federico had bought his new self. "It's something you have to know," Pujol told himself. "How to catch their confidence."

What's remarkable about Pujol's performance is that this was not the man that his friends and family described before or after. In real life, he was witty and genial. This "Mr. Lopez" was completely different, a veritable tornado. The most convincing explanation of how Pujol transformed himself lies with his new wife of under a year. It was Araceli who possessed the category-5 personality, the outsized gestures and the exuberance. It was as if Pujol had borrowed her persona for an afternoon and walked it around Madrid.

For the next two days, Pujol pottered around the hotel, "dreaming up new rigamaroles about Nazism." He knew he'd won only a partial victory: he'd convinced Federico that he was a virulent Hitlerite, but he hadn't told him how he could help the Germans win the war. That was the hard part: he had nothing concrete to offer the Abwehr man. He'd have to bluff his way forward, counting on his extraordinary ability to improvise.

When Pujol showed up at the *cervecería* for the next meeting, he picked out Federico sitting at a table. Instantly, he knew things had gone well back at the embassy: Federico was friendlier this time, greeting him with a warm smile. But when Pujol sat down, Federico told him that the Germans weren't interested in his proposal. Madrid was crawling with German agents; they didn't need another Spaniard informing on the informers. What they were really looking for was people who could go abroad and dig up military information on the Allies. Pujol mentioned the fact that he had a passport, which immediately placed him ahead of most other conspirators in the capital. If the Germans could get him a visa to travel to, say, England, he could pose as a newspaper correspondent and become an Abwehr mole in London.

Federico sat back and considered this, but didn't bite. Pujol desperately tried to come up with another idea, and one that he'd been turning over since the previous meeting popped into his mind — currency smuggling. Out came the next major fabrication. He began to spin out the details of a potential caper that could get him not just to Lisbon but beyond, into the heart of the enemy. He called it the Dalamal Operation.

Pujol claimed to know a Spanish secret agent who was tracking a man named Dalamal — no such person existed, of course — a Brit desperately trying to convert 5 million pesetas into pounds sterling. The Franco government was then desperate for foreign currency and had offered to cut through any red tape for Spaniards who were able to negotiate deals that would bring British pounds or French francs back into the country. This had opened up one of the few legal ways of leaving Spain. If the Germans could get the Seguridad to issue Pujol a visa, he would fly to London under the cover of being a currency smuggler, track down Dalamal and commence spying for the Abwehr. But Federico shot him down, calling the idea "complicated and absurd."

Pujol was stuck. He tried the British embassy again, asking for a visa, and was turned down. When he phoned the Germans to tell them the news, his contact said simply, "We know about your visit to the Consulate. We had you followed." He hung up the phone, chilled that he was now under surveillance.

Finally, a few days later, Pujol met with Federico and the German handed him 1,000 pesetas (about $1,500 today) and told him his first mission was to go to Lisbon, where he should obtain an exit visa. The cash was the first tangible evidence Pujol had received that he'd fooled the Germans. Pujol took the money and left for Lisbon alone on April 26, 1941.

4

The White City

L ISBON WAS THEN KNOWN as "the capital of espionage," a vast open market for illicit information, casual betrayal, currency smuggling, drugs, murder and deception. Portugal was neutral in the conflict, and Lisbon's airport was the only one in Europe that still maintained flights to both Berlin and London, making it the last stop before freedom for the one million refugees — including Peggy Guggenheim, Marc Chagall and Arthur Koestler — who passed through it during the war. Men, women and children from all over occupied Europe — Polish counts, Belgian millionaires, Bulgarian adventurers and Jews from every quarter of the new Reich — had washed up in Lisbon, where they mixed uneasily with a floating population of black marketeers, prostitutes, informants and double agents. Many of the refugees had no visas to travel onward, and they'd spent fortunes just getting to Portugal, trading in the family silver and selling their wives' engagement rings and diamond brooches to last another week or two. The only valuable left to them, the real currency of the capital, was information. "Everybody is a spy in Lisbon," says a character in Robert Wilson's World War II novel, *A Small Death in Lisbon*. "Anybody with ears to overhear can make a living."

On the shadowy boulevards of the White City, famous for its bone-colored buildings, intelligence was bought and sold and the corpses of unlucky double agents were discovered when the deals went sour. Ten miles north of the city, in the resort town of Estoril, the jewel of the "Coast of Kings," secret agents from both sides drank and dueled. Each side had its own watering hole in the glamorous town: MI6 and American OSS officers frequented the five-star Hotel Palacio, whose bartender reportedly made the best Manhattan in all of

Europe and whose maids were said to be part-time employees of one spy agency or another (one American visitor compared the place to the Mayo Clinic, because the face of every guest reflected some deep inner worry); the Abwehr favored the nearby Hotel Atlântico.

The place where they all met in the evenings, the nerve center for generalized espionage, was the Estoril Casino. Graham Greene, then working the Lisbon desk for MI6, gathered material here for his spy novels, including *Our Man in Havana*, which was inspired by Pujol's life. Ian Fleming, the creator of James Bond, gambled away his escudos while helping to plan Operation Golden Eye for British naval intelligence. Fleming believed that the man who'd cleaned him out at chemin de fer was the "chief German agent" in Lisbon. His drinking buddies disagreed, remembering only stolid Portuguese businessmen at the table that night. Nevertheless, Fleming would use the incident as the inspiration for *Casino Royale,* the first 007 novel.

Even the gaming tables were part of the spy game. The playboy and Allied double agent Dusko Popov, code-named Tricycle, used the Estoril to arrange meet-ups. Believing he was being watched, and unwilling to book appointments in plain English, Popov would follow his gorgeous blond secretary into the casino and head straight to the roulette table. "She . . . would play three times, the numbers indicating consecutively the date, hour and minute of our rendezvous." The spy moll would place her chips on one of two numbers, zero or 36. Zero meant the pickup would occur in Lisbon, 36 meant their usual spot in Estoril. "It was an expensive code," Popov remarked drily.

Juan Pujol arrived in Lisbon, found a room at the less-than-glamorous Hotel Suíço Atlântico, chosen for its proximity to the Spanish embassy and consulate, and immediately went to apply for a British visa. Still an amateur, he thought things would be just that easy. But the consulate told him to go back to Madrid and apply there. Pujol pleaded and stormed, but to no avail; he was just one of thousands of people trying to get out of Lisbon. Disappointed, he left and joined the hollow-eyed scrum of refugees aimlessly wandering the streets, hoping to meet the right connection to get them to the free world.

Days went by. Pujol drank in the hotel bars, hoping to buttonhole a Spanish diplomat, looking for an edge, an opening, while his Portuguese escudos ebbed away. His hopes rose when he met an agent for the Spanish security agency, the Seguridad, who was attached to the Lisbon embassy, a man named Varela, but nothing resulted from the brief encounter. Araceli, now pregnant, was waiting back in Madrid, trusting her husband would find a way for them to flee to England. "I was getting desperate," he remembered.

Hope arrived in the form of a fellow Spaniard. The hotel manager introduced Pujol to a friend, Señor Souza, a pudgy Galician who gave off the self-confident glow of a comfortable, well-connected man. On one of their excursions to Estoril, Señor Souza produced with a flourish a document that proved more than interesting to Pujol. It was a diplomatic visa from the Ministry of Foreign Affairs, embossed with Spain's coat of arms, stamped and signed in the indecipherable scrawl of a high official. Even better, in Pujol's eyes, the foreign minister had typed a personal note on the visa asking that every courtesy and assistance be granted to the bearer. Souza was planning to use the visa to take the Pan Am hydroplane whose whine could be heard every day in Lisbon harbor as it set off for South America, where he would undertake a special mission to Argentina on behalf of the Spanish government. Every other person in Lisbon wanted on that plane, but Souza had the document to claim a seat.

Pujol's eyes grew large. "I resolved to become better acquainted with the owner of such a magnificent document." He began to charm Señor Souza as they ducked into amusement parks and the nightclubs and cabarets of Rua Augusta, stopping at cafés to refresh themselves with coffee and to hear Portuguese *fado*, the national music. By the time they rolled back to the hotel, the sun was beginning to light the horizon beyond the sea. Pujol was an excellent companion, half genuine and half mercenary, and to repay Señor Souza for the meals they'd enjoyed, he invited the older man along for a week of gambling and sea breezes at the Casino Estoril. A makeshift plan was already taking shape in his mind.

Pujol was down to his last chance. Either he would pull in this big fish or his espionage career would likely be over before it had really begun. As he got ready for the trip, Pujol borrowed a camera and packed it in his luggage. Then he and Souza took the train to the resort town and, to save money, took a single room at the Monte Estoril

Hotel, three blocks from the casino. Pujol chipped in the rest of his bankroll, Souza did the same, and they hit the roulette tables. Their luck was running high when one afternoon Pujol began to complain of stomach cramps. He patted Souza on the shoulder and told him to keep playing, as the Galician had a hot hand. Souza nodded, thinking nothing of it. Pujol made his way back to the hotel, slipped into the room, pulled out the camera and found Souza's visa secreted in a compartment of the man's luggage. A few minutes later, he strolled out of the hotel, close-up shots of the document now stored on the film tucked in his suitcase.

A few days later, Señor Souza was preparing for his trip to South America and Pujol was back in Lisbon, standing in an engraver's shop. He held a crisp photograph of the visa with the Spanish seal carefully trimmed off. He asked the engraver to make a steel photographic plate of the image, and several hours later he was on his way, plate in hand, to 7 Rua Condessa do Rio, which housed an old printing firm. Pujol announced that he was an employee of the Spanish chancery, the Office of Public Records. He handed over the plate and the photograph and said he required two hundred copies of the visa as soon as possible. Pujol's confidence, and his natural instinct for the con — who would order *two hundred* copies if he only wanted one for himself? — allowed for no questions. The visas were printed, Pujol disposed of all but a dozen of them, and he was soon on his way to an office supply store. He told the workers there that the rubber stamp shown in the photo had been used so often that the imprint was beginning to blur. Could they make him an exact replacement? They could.

Next, Pujol stopped into a photography shop, posed for a head shot, cut copies of the picture to size, pasted them on the documents and signed his name. He now held in his hands something only a few of the tens of thousands of refugees in Lisbon could boast: a Spanish visa. It could take him anywhere in the world. Men would kill for that document. In a few short months, he'd gone from a bumbling amateur to an operative of the first rank. And he was completely self-taught.

He returned to Madrid, to Araceli and their new baby boy, Juan. The young family moved out of the crumbling Hotel Majestic into a small bed-and-breakfast on the bustling commercial street called

Gran Via. Pujol knew that he was exposing his family more with each step along the dark path of espionage. "I was fully aware of the risks I was running and always had a lurking fear that my operation would collapse." But he pushed on. Pujol called Federico at the German embassy and arranged a rendezvous.

The meet was at the Café Negresco, not far from the Puerta del Sol, one of the ancient gateways of the old walled city where centuries before couriers from distant countries would arrive on secret missions. Pujol sat down opposite Federico and began to weave a rich fabrication concerning the "Dalamal Operation," complete with currency smugglers named the Zulueta brothers (two very real, "picaresque" Basque-Cuban adventurers and police snitches he'd met at the Hotel Majestic), a surprise offer from the Bank of Spain's Foreign Exchange Police section, thousands of pesetas and pounds changed one for the other . . . It went on and on. Federico's mind must have whirled as Pujol regaled him with a highly detailed account of his adventures. Here the fledgling spy used a technique that would become one of his hallmarks: basing his fabulous tales in grains of truth, sprinkled like a bright trail through the lies. From now on, Pujol would always prefer to have his fantasies rooted in reality.

The nugget here was Varela, the real-life Seguridad agent whom Pujol had met briefly during his first days in Lisbon. Now Varela, instead of being a passing acquaintance, became the brains behind the Dalamal Operation. It was *he* who was secretly trying to exchange huge amounts of pesetas for British pounds, most likely on behalf of the Spanish government, which was starved for foreign currency. And it was Varela who was trying to get Pujol a diplomatic visa so he could go to London. Pujol had stashed the fake diplomatic visa back at the bed-and-breakfast, his hole card kept hidden for the right moment.

Federico bit. "He was becoming increasingly interested and spent hours advising and training me." In the next days and weeks, the spy and his runner met all over Madrid: the aquarium, the Café Calatrava, the Maison Doré. In the meantime, the Abwehr had its agents confirm that Señor Varela was a real person and worked as the head of security at the embassy. Pujol's contact, who'd actually never heard of him, checked out.

This went on for a month. Pujol must have been aching to dazzle Federico with the visa, but his patience was sublime. At one meeting, Federico told him his bosses at the embassy were very interested in his work, so long as what he'd been telling them was true. But he confided he'd recently been burned by an "agent" who'd absconded with the money Federico had given him. For the first time, Pujol realized that men like Federico had skin in the game, too: one more failure and the Abwehr agent could be sent to the front lines. "He did not wish . . . to be caught a second time." Pujol sensed an opening.

With Federico pressing for more, Pujol called up a man he'd met in Lisbon, a Spaniard named Dionisio Fernández. He told Dionisio that he wanted to return to Lisbon to meet a lover he'd met there (another lie), but his wife, as wives tended to be, was suspicious. Could Dionisio impersonate a business contact and send him a telegram requesting his presence in Lisbon?

Pujol was a very likable man, and his friends, even instant ones like Dionisio, always seemed ready to do him favors. The telegram soon arrived in Madrid: "You must return urgently. The matter is closed."

It was signed with the fake businessman's name that Pujol had given his friend: "Varela."

Pujol met Federico and handed over the telegram. Federico scanned the contents — surely noticing that it had been sent from Lisbon — and stuffed the piece of paper in his pocket. He asked for a meeting the next day. The process was accelerating. The next afternoon, Federico slipped Pujol 500 pesetas and told him to go to Lisbon and finalize the Varela affair. He also gave him a contact name in case he should need more money when in Portugal.

Pujol headed back to Lisbon, booked a hotel room and stayed as far away from the real Varela as he could. He called up Federico's contact to ask for more money, confirming to the Abwehr that he'd actually been in Lisbon. Then he headed back to Spain, met with the German spy-runner, confirmed that everything had gone well and told him the Spanish Seguridad was making all the necessary arrangements for him to work under Varela on the fake Dalamal Operation. He should have the documents soon.

It was time for Pujol to spring the trap.

. . .

Early the next morning, Pujol made a few calls, then phoned Federico, his voice charged with excitement. He demanded a meeting at a café across from the Seguridad building, not in a few days but *now*. "Alarmed and furious," Federico probably assumed that the crazy Spaniard had blown the Varela affair and was on the run. He agreed to meet Pujol in five minutes at the café. When Pujol walked in, he found Federico waiting impatiently. The diminutive spy sat down, nodded and said he had only a second to spare. In a low voice, Pujol calmly told the German agent what was going to happen next. *In two minutes,* he told Federico, *I'm going to get up and walk forty feet over to the Seguridad ministry, where a government messenger and car are waiting. They will take me to the Foreign Office, where the special diplomatic visa I'm carrying in my pocket will be stamped and sent on to Lisbon by diplomatic courier. I will travel to Lisbon and pick up the visa in person. From Lisbon, I will travel on to England, and there I will begin my career as a German spy.*

Federico gaped. Pujol now said that he wanted to show Federico the document, to dispel once and for all any doubts the Abwehr had about him. Looking around with exaggerated caution, he slid something out of his pocket and passed it under the table. Federico glanced down at the heavily embossed piece of paper and, after a second, nodded. Pujol slid the document back and put it in his lapel pocket. "Greatly impressed," Federico slapped Pujol on the back and congratulated him on his coup.

Pujol smiled and, as if he were the teacher and Federico the beginner, whispered that it wasn't safe for them to exit the café together. He would leave first. He said goodbye, got up and walked across toward the doors of the Seguridad ministry. There was indeed a young man waiting there, just as Pujol had said, scanning the crowd and intently looking for someone. The man wasn't a special messenger of the Franco government, of course; he was the son of the owner of the bed-and-breakfast where Pujol and Araceli were staying. One of the phone calls Pujol had made that morning was to this young man, who agreed to meet his guest in front of the building. For what purpose, he had no idea. Pujol's next call had been to a car service, which at his request had sent one of its vehicles to the ministry. It was now idling in front of the Seguridad's doors. Pujol greeted the hotelkeeper's son, they got into the car, and Pujol, in a loud voice that carried all the way to the interior of the café, called out, "Foreign Office." The driver nodded and they drove off.

Through the café window Federico watched the car motor away. In his mind, Pujol was now officially a secret agent of the Third Reich. "[He'd] swallowed the story hook, line and sinker," Pujol gloated. The spy even got Federico to send a telegram to the real Varela: "In a few days I'll depart for Lisbon. Signed, Juan."

Pujol was a modest man; he never bragged about what he was about to do. But returning home that night, he must have been brimming with pride. He'd done it. His life to that point had been one misadventure after another, some of them nearly fatal. His family had long regarded him as a lost cause, beloved but a little mad. The Marist Fathers at his school had thought him a dunce with anger issues. But now he'd bamboozled the Abwehr and was about to take Araceli to London, the center of Western civilization, to help save the world from "that psychopath" Hitler.

He was not yet a double agent, but he was fully a spy, and he had gotten himself out of Spain, ready to audition for the British.

"No conquest conquered me," he said. "And no defeat defeated me."

It was late spring, 1941. By this point in the war, Hitler had taken Poland, Czechoslovakia, Luxembourg, France, Norway, Belgium, Holland, Denmark and Austria. Greece and Yugoslavia were tottering and about to fall. A triumphant Hitler had promenaded through Paris the summer before. German U-boats were attacking merchant ships in the Atlantic, massive Luftwaffe raids were targeting Coventry and central London, and Rommel and his Afrika Korps were sweeping across North Africa. FDR had signed the Lend-Lease Act but America was still neutral, while Italy and Japan had allied themselves with the Third Reich and Stalin had signed a nonaggression pact with Hitler. In Germany, the program of euthanasia of the sick and disabled was more than a year old. *Kristallnacht* had occurred over two years before, and the first experimental use of poisonous gas at Auschwitz was now four months away.

5

The Game

WITH A FLURRY OF THEATRICS — more meetings, another fake telegram — Pujol prepared to start his career as an Abwehr spy. Now that the Germans were convinced of the Spaniard's bona fides, they rushed to bring him up to speed. Federico trained Pujol in secret writing and handed over four questionnaires detailing what the Nazis needed to know about England's war plans and preparations. Pujol memorized parts of the document and was then given a miniaturized copy he could carry to England. The questions ranged from the highly technical to the broadly strategic: "In what stage of construction is the aircraft carrier *Indefatigable*? What is thought of the possibilities of success of a German invasion? What measures are being taken against such an eventuality?" Pujol was given the code name Alaric, and his network was termed Arabel. Federico devoted all his working hours to training his new recruit, even taking him home to his apartment, at 73 Viriato Street, to teach him the art of ciphers.

"Why he had such blind faith in me I do not know," Pujol would write later. He was being too modest. His performance had been precise and convincing. He'd taken control of the game away from the much more experienced Federico. He'd intuited what the Germans wanted and how they would best be seduced. He hadn't ham-handedly presented them his scheme on a platter all at once; he'd made them work for it. He had charmed Federico, enticed him with his daring, then frightened him half to death with the phone call out of the blue demanding a meeting. As a finale, he'd stage-managed the ultimate reveal in the café with the eye of a Hollywood director.

"With the British he was British, with the Germans he was German," a journalist who met him much later on would say. Actually the opposite was true. Pujol created a completely original character, stuck to it until death and pulled less confident operatives toward his creation. But he *understood* the Germans like a German and the British like a Brit.

Federico was so taken with his new agent that he passed along the name of a German spy already working in London: Luis Calvo, a well-known newspaper correspondent. Perhaps the spy-runner was courting Pujol, trying to impress him with the Abwehr's extensive network in England. Or perhaps he was just talking shop. But instead of being impressed, Pujol erupted: he didn't want to know the names of any of their operatives, he roared, and how dare Federico offer him one? If they unmasked Calvo so easily, he snapped, did that mean they'd "out" Pujol to the next agent who came along? How dare he risk his spies' lives like that!

Federico, his future now partially invested in this fiery Spaniard, had to sit there and take the tongue-lashing. After all, Pujol was right. It was bad form in the spy world to give away an agent's real name to another agent unless absolutely necessary; it endangered both spies. Pujol didn't learn this from an espionage manual, he intuited it on the spot. He wasn't just thinking like a German, he was thinking like the spy-runner Federico wished he was.

For the last meeting, Federico had a surprise. His boss, Karl-Erich Kühlenthal, showed up to see Pujol off. Kühlenthal's MI5 file described him in detail: "Oval face . . . fleshy. Boneless cheeks. Fresh complexion, high color on cheekbones. Curved, hawklike nose. Searching grey eyes." He was a regular in Madrid cafés and *cervecerías,* where he was known as Don Pablo.

Kühlenthal handed Pujol several bottles of secret ink, ciphering codes to encrypt his first messages, a list of cover addresses to send them to and $3,000 in cash, the equivalent of about $44,000 today. The Abwehr was rich and not afraid to spend on good prospects. Kühlenthal shook Pujol's hand and gave him his marching orders: don't underestimate the British, be patient, don't expect a quick Nazi victory. Above all, try to develop a set of subagents who can be left behind like sleepers if you're forced to leave England.

With that, Pujol gathered up his young family and, in July 1941, headed to Lisbon to practice "my own bizarre form of espionage."

To get by the border controls, Pujol rolled up most of the $3,000 into a rubber sheath and inserted it into a half-empty tube of toothpaste. The rest went into a can of shaving cream. As he made his way to Portugal, he imagined he was carrying the keys to the kingdom, that the bottles of secret ink stashed in his luggage, the money and the secret codes would be enough to get him hired by the British as a double agent and whisked off to London. "[He] had no idea of the adventures and experiences which were to envelop him," recalled MI5's Tommy Harris.

After arriving in the Portuguese capital, Pujol rented a room from a poor fisherman in the Cascais district, outside Lisbon, and headed straight to the British embassy, making sure that he wasn't being tailed. "What follows may seem unbelievable but it is true," Pujol would write years later. "After all that I had done, all that I had gone through, all the subterfuges I'd invented, the deceptions and the chicanery, the tension and the strain . . . I was no further forward than I had been when I made my first attempt." The British turned him down flat. Again. For the third time. And the rejection forced Pujol deeper and deeper into a game he didn't fully understand. He couldn't just impersonate a spy anymore. He'd have to become one.

But he would have to do it from offstage, faking all the way. Pujol bought a map of England, a Baedeker tourist guide to the country and a copy of Bradshaw's railway timetables. He had never been in England in his entire life; now he had to convince his handlers that he lived there. He also got back in touch with the Spanish friend, Dionisio Fernández, who'd sent the fake telegram from Varela that said he was in Lisbon to carry on the affair with his mistress. Could he use Fernández's name to rent a post office box to receive letters from the woman without his wife finding out? Fernández agreed.

On July 19, Pujol sent his first message to the Germans in Madrid, pretending that he'd arrived in England. The "cover" letter in black ink was filled with the first impressions of a "passionate Catalan democrat" who'd fled to Britain to escape Franco. Between the lines, in invisible ink, Pujol carefully wrote out the real message: he'd made it safely to the British Isles and on the way had met a pilot with the Dutch airline KLM who'd agreed, after much persuading, to carry letters from London to Lisbon, to avoid the British censors. (This would later amaze Pujol's handlers in London, because the chief pilot on that route was a real English spy. Pujol didn't know this; it was a lucky fabrication.) There the pilot would mail the letters, which would have a Portuguese postmark, on to Madrid. The Abwehr could respond to the same poste restante address, and the messages would be ferried back to London by the pilot. The imaginary pilot thus became the first of the subagents that would soon pour forth from Pujol's brain.

Pujol waited anxiously for the response. Ten days later, a letter from Federico arrived at the poste restante box: "The method of communication is good and the letter developed well. We await with interest further news . . . Kindest regards and good luck."

The Germans had bought his KLM story. "I had become a real German spy." Now he could pretend to be in London while in reality living in Estoril, where he'd just moved from the fisherman's shack to a proper house, along with Araceli and his baby son.

There was, of course, one overriding problem with the plan: Pujol knew next to nothing about the country he was supposed to be living in. He didn't speak a word of English and was unfamiliar with its currency, its culture, its terminology, not to mention its regiments, army groups and the types of ships its merchant navy favored. How could he compose convincing reports about a place that was as distant and strange to him as the North Pole?

As he struggled to figure this out, the farce with the English continued. Pujol went to the British embassy in Lisbon and told the assistant to the military attaché everything: the secret ink, the Abwehr questionnaires, the names and descriptions of Federico and Kühlenthal. He wanted to make a deal, and fast. With Lisbon swarming with German spies, and with the Abwehr expecting precise reports about the Allied war effort, time was against him. If the Brits would get him to America — his new escape hatch — he'd happily turn over everything. It was his fourth approach to the British.

The assistant told Pujol an official would meet with him the next day at the English bar inside the Estoril Casino at 7 p.m. to discuss the proposal in detail. The following evening Pujol arrived at the bar and waited, nervously sipping a drink as the minutes passed. The promised official never showed. Pujol went back to the embassy the next day, found the assistant and demanded an explanation. The man palmed Pujol off by claiming he'd been unable to contact the official. The farce was now complete: the Nazis he despised were enamored of him, and the Allies for whom he was willing to risk his life regarded him as a nuisance. "Why, I kept on asking myself, was the enemy proving to be so helpful while those whom I wanted to be my friends were being so implacable?" Pujol stormed out of the embassy.

The spy needed more ammunition to get on that flight to London. He called on the real Varela, head of security at the Spanish embassy. Varela immediately demanded to know the meaning of a telegram that Federico had sent him days earlier, announcing Pujol's arrival in Portugal. Who the hell was Pujol to telegram him? The spy quickly charmed Varela out of his anger and patiently explained that he was a currency smuggler working on something called the Dalamal Operation. Varela calmed down and listened, but told Pujol nothing could be done about the scheme unless the real Dalamal (who didn't exist) came to Spain. Pujol was crushed — teaming up with Varela on a real operation would have boosted his credibility with the Germans — but at least, should an Abwehr agent phone the security official and ask about a Spanish spy named Pujol, Varela would confirm they were in touch.

With very few tools at hand, Pujol fell back on the one thing that had never failed him: his imagination. He began to dream up the team of subagents that Kühlenthal, the Abwehr chief in Madrid, had demanded. Not only would these imaginary people be able to feed him information from sources he didn't have access to himself, they could also take the fall if the information proved incorrect. First up was "Carvalho," a Portuguese with Nazi sympathies who lived near the Bristol Channel, an important shipping lane in southwest England. He could report on convoys and tankers steaming through the local waters and the shoreline defenses. (The fake spy's name was a silent tribute to Araceli, whose last name was Carbollo.) Pujol also recruited "William Gerbers," an imaginary Swiss national who could keep an eye on Liverpool. The spy's second letter to the Germans detailed these minor coups, as well as the news that the BBC in London had offered him a job as a freelance translator.

Pujol wrote the letters in a bombastic, florid style that the historian Thaddeus Holt once called the "verbal equivalent of the extravagant confections of Antonio Gaudí." It's an apt description. "I do not wish to end this letter," Pujol wrote at one point, "without sending a Viva Victorioso for our brave troops who fight in Russia, annihilating the Bolshevic [sic] beast." Not only did the style match the personality he'd created, but it had the advantage of taking up a lot of pages without conveying too much information. Any mistake could have cost him dearly, so as he sat in his house in Lisbon he concentrated on "recruiting" agents and wrote only one letter each month, sticking close to the theories of espionage that he'd developed over the past few weeks. "I tried hard to introduce new information gradually and to be cautious when I mentioned the new contacts I had recruited to help me." He made the information hard to come by, describing "in detail how I had grappled with a whole string of obstacles." His methods would have been well known to any mystery writer or con man — ground every revelation in lived experience, let the mark come to the con, not vice versa — but Pujol had to work them out on his own.

That couldn't last forever, though. Sooner or later he'd have to come up with some actual information. So in his third letter, postmarked in October 1941, he began to add some red meat to his reports: His subagent William Gerbers had spotted a convoy of five Allied ships leaving Liverpool, headed for Malta. That Mediterranean island, rich in Christian history, was a vital link in the British defenses, key to the Allied campaign in North Africa. Over a two-year period beginning in 1940, the Luftwaffe carpet-bombed the small island with 3,000 raids; in February 1942 alone, more than 1,000 tons of bombs would be dropped on the rocky outpost. German destroyers and cruisers regularly laid siege to the Allied tankers and freighters hoping to resupply the station. The news that a major convoy was on its way to the battered island would be of great interest to the Third Reich's war planners.

Despite this phony coup, Pujol was increasingly like a rat in a maze, looking for the exit. He traveled back to Madrid to try the British embassy again for a fifth attempt, showing one of the staffers the miniaturized questionnaires that Kühlenthal had handed to him, but the official sent him away. After this latest rebuff, Pujol was convinced his luck was going to run out, and soon.

Meanwhile, Federico was peppering him with fresh demands: "Try to find out the details of the formation of a new expeditionary force of several divisions: Where are they destined for, the Middle East or Far East?" "Try to get an agent into northern Ireland at the arrival port of American shipments. Ireland is very interesting and important." The Abwehr also asked him to obtain a series of pamphlets from the Institute of Statistics in Oxford, a way not only to get much-needed information but also to confirm that Pujol was indeed living in England. The last request was easier than it sounded. The spy simply went to the British Propaganda Office in Lisbon, claimed to be a "student of statistics" and asked a clerk to send for the publications. But the dozens of other inquiries were harder to answer from Lisbon. Pujol would have to improvise.

The spy began to scour the city for usable information. An advertisement in a Portuguese paper gave him a few facts about a British naval firm. A French newspaper had a small article on infantile paralysis and food rationing. A telephone directory yielded the name of a British company. Pujol rifled through the Blue Book, published by the Office of National Statistics, for the text of Churchill's speeches, and sent Federico the best bits. When he went to a Lisbon cinema to relax for a couple of hours (the movie itch was still with him), he watched a newsreel before the main feature that included a few seconds' footage of a Canadian warship called *Esquimalt*. Pujol sat up in his chair, instantly alert. His next report included a detailed description of the ship, including his completely made-up descriptions of its capabilities. A sketch of a "very secret apparatus which had been copied from plans" by his "sub-agent No. 3" had in fact been copied down by Pujol, standing in front of a Lisbon shop window that featured a picture of an Allied commando barge. Pujol scribbled out a quick drawing, which he refined later, then added an avalanche of false data on how long and wide the barge was and what armaments it carried, and for good measure he sent along a fake eyewitness report on how the thing maneuvered on water. Even a British propaganda leaflet — whether dropped from the sky or handed out by pro-Allied sympathizers — was turned into a lengthy report: "R.A.F. Pilot School situated near Sandwich, the camp is camouflaged and also used as a landing ground for coastal defense plans. It is on the right bank of the river Stour . . . just by the cross roads of the main roads leading to Ramsgate and Sandwich." Other things he just made up out of whole cloth, including enormous "amphibious tanks" he'd seen maneuvering on Lake Windermere.

Pujol was like a rag-and-bone man wandering the streets of Lisbon. Nothing was wasted.

But how to get the letters to the Germans? He didn't want to overplay the fake KLM pilot who was supposedly acting as his courier. Instead, Pujol went to a local detective agency, hired a man to impersonate the phony subagent named Gerbers, booked him a hotel room in Lisbon and had the Germans come knock on the door and collect the materials.

Despite their sketchy origins, many of his reports were quite convincing. When Tommy Harris later revealed to British intelligence that Pujol had made up most of his messages, the analysts there refused to believe Pujol had never set foot in England. His letters were so detailed and persuasive, so accurately rendered, that it seemed impossible that he was relying only on his wits. He'd convinced the *British* he was lurking in their cities when he was really a thousand miles away.

Federico's letters made it clear that the Germans were studying his reports closely. When he made the inevitable mistake, the Abwehr agent pounced: "You refer by number to the infantry regiment which you saw in Guilford but infantry regiments don't have numbers, they are known by names. Your report is therefore useless . . . I await your clarification!"

Pujol instinctively knew that he couldn't let the Germans speak to him that way. He shot back: "I am surprised at your announcement regarding the numbering of Regiments . . . Have you never heard of the organizations which are known as the War Office and the General Staff? Nearly a year ago these organizations, in order to avoid espionage, have referred to fighting units by numbers . . . I am in possession of proof of what I am now stating and of the orders which have been issued, one of which I came by during my travels." Would the Germans like to see the actual orders?

It was a bluff, of course. Pujol didn't have the orders and in fact the Germans were right: the English used names, not numbers, to identify their regiments. If the Abwehr demanded to see the documents, Pujol was finished. But the spy instinctively seemed to know how to play his German handlers. A few weeks later, after Pujol sent more folderol backing up his statements (but not the imaginary "orders"), Federico wrote back: "It is unnecessary for you to send us proof in evidence since we have absolute trust in you . . . I repeat that we here are most satisfied with your collaboration."

The secret to playing his handlers was calculating how badly they needed him. The counterattack had worked perfectly. Like a mistress furious that she'd been accused of cheating, Pujol had struck back at exactly the right moment, binding the Germans closer to him. He wouldn't be questioned; if they didn't trust him, he'd leave. MI5's Tommy Harris later shook his head at his agent's brass: "It can be said that from this point onwards it became evident that the Germans did not want to lose [Pujol] at any cost."

A few groaners passed without comment. "There are men here," Pujol wrote in a report "from" Glasgow, "that will do anything for a liter of wine." Anyone who'd really been to Scotland would have known that ale or whisky was the only thing longshoremen drank. He made glaring mistakes with English currency; he was copying amounts in pence and shillings from a railway guide, but he didn't know how to convert one into the other.

To further bamboozle the Germans, Pujol sent Araceli to meet with Federico, with a personal letter he'd written her. Araceli told the German officer that she suspected her husband was having an affair. "She became highly excited and said that she was convinced that her husband had run off with a woman and that Federico was an accomplice in his escapade." Federico revealed that her husband was in fact in England on a special mission for the Third Reich. Araceli screamed that Juanito was sure to be picked up by the British and shot. (Of course, she knew full well that Pujol was in Lisbon and in no danger.) Desperate to get this woman out of his office, Federico offered her a job in the German embassy. When that failed, he tried money — enough pesetas to stay in a five-star Madrid hotel. Araceli wouldn't be bought off, however, and to make her point about the danger her husband was in, she gave Federico a picture of the baby Juan to forward to Pujol, who would, she said melodramatically, probably never see his child again.

It had been a bravura performance. In his next letter, Federico gave Pujol a full report on the encounter, then added a line asking Pujol to please not send any more letters via his wife.

Back in Lisbon, the strain was getting to Pujol. His letters to Federico were now full of complaints of lack of money and correspondence. To Araceli, then in Madrid, he wrote: "Talk to me about the baby, for God knows how I long to see him, and hug him. I shall perhaps find him grown up into a man smoking a large Havana cigar." Even a minimally venal spy would probably have thrown in the towel and gone to work for the Germans by this point. But the thought apparently never crossed Pujol's mind; he wasn't some chancer looking to make a mint and take the hydroplane to Argentina. He really wanted to save the world.

But the spy also had a young family, and every visit to the British embassy increased the chance they would all end up in a concentration camp. In the opinion of one MI5 officer, at this point "[Pujol's] existence was precarious in the extreme. He remained permanently poised on the edge of a precipice over which some blunder or other must, as it seemed, soon impel him." The Abwehr's replies to his messages were not as enthusiastic as he'd hoped for, and they'd refused to supply him with more cash for living expenses after the original $3,000 had run out. Instead, they'd send him a grudging $50 here or $100 there. His star was clearly fading. "The farce was coming to an end." Pujol began looking into emigrating to Brazil.

The mission that had begun in his Tom Mix daydreams appeared to have run its course. But Pujol hadn't factored in one thing: the determination of Araceli González Carballo Pujol.

It was Araceli who sensed her husband's deepening pessimism and decided to do something about it. Having joined Pujol in Lisbon, she now put on her best outfit and made her way to the American embassy. We can imagine her dressed in her finest coat, aglitter with whatever jewels she'd brought from Lugo, marching into the rather grand embassy building and demanding to speak to someone of real influence. Araceli was not a woman to be denied. She was ushered into the naval attaché's office — far better than Pujol had done in his many tries at the British embassy — and almost immediately began to get results in a series of meetings with an attaché named Rousseau. "[She] mystified the American and . . . whetted his appetite." She also demanded $200,000 for the secrets she was about to reveal. It was an outrageous figure, but it was meant to be: Rousseau sat up in his chair and took notice of this commanding woman.

To convince the American that she and Pujol were real spies, Araceli felt she had to give Rousseau some proof of what they could do for his country. At their next meeting, she brought a letter written in French. Araceli didn't speak French, something Rousseau knew. In order to get the letter, she'd asked a friend to write out an innocuous telegram that she said her husband, a writer, wanted to send to his agent. The original letter read: "LeClerc Fils of Paris reports that both he and his Madrid agents are awaiting your orders as they now have everything ready to commence publication in all the agreed journals at a moment's notice."

The friend wrote out the text. Araceli took it and substituted some key words. The harmless "LeClerc Fils" became "Agent 172 of Chicago," "publication" became "sabotage," "Madrid" morphed into "Detroit," and "journals" was changed to "factories." When she was done, the letter read: "Agent 172 of Chicago reports that both he and his Detroit agents are awaiting your orders as they now have everything ready to commence sabotage in all the agreed factories at a moment's notice."

At the meeting with Rousseau, Araceli produced the letter with the message written in invisible ink, saying it was a secret communication from a man staying at her boarding house who she believed to be a German spy. She then whipped out a bottle of secret ink developer — Rousseau's eyes must have gone wide at that — and spread it across the page. The sinister message appeared. The American bent over to read it and immediately agreed to put her in touch with the British.

But there was a footnote that Pujol never learned about. He probably went to his grave unaware of what had really happened in that embassy in Lisbon. Araceli had been far more creative — and self-sacrificing — than he knew.

Rousseau set up a meeting with a British MI6 officer in Lisbon so that Araceli could tell her story. She brought along the miniaturized questionnaires and the secret ink bottles, but before she could take them out of her handbag the MI6 man — who took her for another adventuress hoping to get out of Lisbon by hook or by crook — made it clear that he doubted her integrity. Offended, she stood up to leave, and the Brit took 20 escudos from his pocket and threw it on the table. "Here you are. Take this for your trouble and your fare." He was calling this well-bred society girl from Lugo a hustler.

In her family, Araceli was famous for her ferocity. "She *never* stepped back — even when she was getting ready to sprint ahead" is how her daughter put it. Now a foreigner she'd never previously met had just paid her, a possible descendant of King Alfonso XI, one of the gravest insults imaginable. God knows what would happen if she told her husband. Harris wrote: "There is no doubt that had he learnt about this incident at the time the case would have been irrevocably lost." Pujol would probably have given the officer a beating. In the accounts of the meeting in the MI5 files, one can almost feel the blood rise to Araceli's face as she absorbed the insult.

Somehow she kept her cool. Rousseau quickly apologized for the officer's rudeness, and Araceli revealed that the "German spy" was actually her husband.

The improvisation of the "Agent 172" letter was a brilliant stroke, but then Araceli was a highly intelligent woman. Yet it's the self-restraint — not something that came easily to Araceli — that impresses the most. It's hard not to see it as an act of love for her husband, an offering to their shared mission.

6

The Snakepit

S T. ALBANS, TWENTY MILES outside London, was a typically English market town, solid and prosperous, a place of meadows and old manor houses of red brick. It was filled with quaint inns, as St. Albans had been the first coach stop on the road out of London since the Tudor era. At night, one could hardly hear the incendiary bombs falling on the capital to the south, only crickets and tree frogs.

But the sleepy suburb had once been the site of defiance and ancient gore, home to the Catuvellauni, a warlike British tribe that emerged before the birth of Christ. The Catuvellauni are believed to have led the first resistance against the armies of Julius Caesar, as they swept up from Rome, in 54 B.C. The town was renamed for Britain's first Christian martyr, St. Alban, who was beheaded by the Romans in an anti-Christian purge that swept England in A.D. 308.

Now, centuries later, St. Albans was again playing an important wartime role, one rooted not in violence but in cerebral conflict. In the fall of 1941, along with evacuated children arriving daily from London in airless buffet cars, holding hands as the train exhaled a final gust of steam and they stepped to the platform to meet their new foster parents, other passengers, young men in suits and dark hats, were met as soon as they disembarked and were whisked off in civilian cars. The men were offered a cigarette and taken to a brick estate that lay at the end of a private gravel driveway hidden behind tall hedgerows. It was an old Edwardian mansion called Glenalmond, now converted into a warren of small offices. Early in the war it had been quietly taken over by Section V of MI6. And it was here, in subsection (d), responsible for Iberia and the Spanish-speaking countries, that the intelligence officer Desmond Bristow, who would soon lead the debriefing of Juan Pujol, found himself on a crisp October day.

Desmond Bristow was a tough-minded young man who knew Spain and Spaniards intimately. Though born in Manchester, the son of a mining engineer, he'd been raised in Sotiel Coronada, in the southern Iberian countryside, before going up to Cambridge to study French and Spanish. Or to feign study — he'd been a terrible student. Instead of excelling academically, Bristow captained the famous Cambridge rowing team, and game for anything, once set fire to himself with gas before leaping into the river Cam to raise money for war veterans on Poppy Day. At twenty-two, the adventurous Bristow had found himself "bored" and "broke" in the winter of 1940 and so walked to the sandbagged War Office in Westminster and volunteered to fight the Nazis.

Bristow had come to the intelligence services after seeing something he would never forget. He'd originally been inducted into the British army as a private. One day after a series of grueling infantry drills, he'd found himself at Oxford Station on his way to see his girlfriend, Betty. As he waited, a special carriage heaved in on another track, and the eyes of those in the crowded station turned to watch as the car wheezed to a stop. In its windows were men with no arms or half their faces gone. "I watched in horror as hundreds of young men like myself limped, hobbled on crutches, or were carried on stretchers, with arms or legs missing and bloody bandages around their faces and eyes." The train had come from Dunkirk, where the British Expeditionary Force had just escaped after a chaotic retreat from France.

The sight made it clear that England was losing the war, and convinced Bristow with equal force that he wanted out of the infantry. He quickly transferred to the intelligence services. Nearly two years later he found himself in MI6, using his fluency in Spanish. Instead of killing German soldiers, he devoted himself to catching spies.

In late October 1941, the Iberian section's pleasant offices were located in a glass conservatory in the rear of Glenalmond, overlooking a grove of chestnut trees. The boys in the unit called this "the snakepit," presumably because they spent their time in it plotting against the venomous creatures of the Abwehr. Sitting in the room that autumn day, Bristow was so bored he almost regretted his decision to join MI6. He'd been assigned to leaf through an old Lisbon telephone directory, attempting to match the intercepted phone number of a possible spy with a name and a street address. As one of the most junior men in Section V, he often got the scutwork: poring over registers of hotel guests or studying long lists of airline passengers. It wasn't what he'd imagined espionage to be. There were occasional sessions of lively gossip and serious drinking in the snakepit — pink gins were the poison of choice — but the work was often sheer drudgery.

The room was ice cold and quiet. Bristow had managed to light a fire, but the rays of warmth hadn't yet cut through the chill. The other members of the section sat nearby: Trevor Wilson, the local Morocco expert and a former Abyssinian skunk-excrement exporter, and Tim Milne, a former copywriter who'd written ads for Guinness. By the bay window overlooking the chestnut trees was the most ambitious officer of them all: Kim Philby, the head of the subsection, sitting in a battered leather jacket he'd worn while working as a correspondent for the *Times* in the Spanish Civil War.

There was a knock at the door. It was the motorcycle courier who brought the daily pile of deciphered messages known as ISOS (Intelligence Service Oliver Strachey), the product of codebreakers who were assigned to Abwehr messages. The intercepts were picked out of the ether by towering radio masts erected at a place called Hanslope Park, where a crack assortment of intellectuals, mathematicians and Oxford scholars, led by a genius named Oliver Strachey, scanned the Abwehr's traffic between Madrid, Lisbon and Berlin. The man on the motorcycle handed the dour Tim Milne that morning's crop and hopped back on his machine.

Milne took the bulletins with a nod. It was his job to go through the intercepts and decide which would stay with the subsection and which would be routed to the German, French and Dutch branches.

"This sounds very odd," he said almost immediately.

The eyes in the room shifted from their work to the unexcitable Milne.

"What does it say?" Philby asked.

"Madrid's telling Berlin that their V-man, Arabel, has reported the formation of a convoy in the bay of Caernarvon."

The tension in the room spiked. There weren't supposed to be any German spies in England, not one. The intelligence services had managed to catch every agent parachuted into the countryside or paid off by the Abwehr. But here was a previously unidentified agent who was apparently watching a convoy gather in the upper reaches of northwest Wales. If true, England had a problem on its hands.

Philby grabbed the green phone sitting on his desk, a secure line to MI5. Snapping his fingers to battle the effects of his painful stammer, he called the Abwehr-research department. As the others listened to Philby's stuttering words, it became clear the rival agency had received the same message and was equally concerned about it.

Soon, as Pujol would later discover, "the British were going crazy looking for me." MI5 hurriedly checked the schedule of ships leaving Liverpool; none matched Arabel's description. Scotland Yard sent agents to remote Llyn Peninsula and scoured the boggy heath and the inns for suspicious characters, but found none. Commander Ewen Montagu, MI5's link with the Admiralty, sent a telegram saying that the Caernarvon convoy didn't exist. The men of Section V blew out relieved breaths — Arabel was clearly a phony.

More deciphered messages came in from ISOS, handed over by the motorcycle courier. It was Arabel again, reporting that the convoy had left Caernarvon, heading south, in strength. "We know there is no bloody convoy," Philby hissed. "Why and who is this Arabel and why is he so obviously lying?" They began watching for messages from Arabel every day. Yet the agent frustrated the men of the Iberian section by going silent for weeks before chirping up again, often with some ridiculous new bulletin: the staff of foreign embassies in London, he reported, had moved to the seaside in Brighton to get away from the intolerable heat. It was preposterous; only an idiot would even suggest such a thing. But a few of Arabel's messages hit close to the bone, giving half-accurate reports on British armaments or naval movements that indicated some access to English ports. The Germans responded avidly to every word. "The Abwehr's trust in this creative liar grew with every fishy message," wrote Bristow. The

Abwehr even agreed to pay Arabel's expenses, which strangely were always given in shillings, not pounds, as if the spy didn't understand British currency.

The proof of Arabel's high standing came when ISOS began intercepting messages showing that the Germans were scrambling their forces to ambush the convoy from Caernarvon — a convoy that didn't exist. The German navy diverted U-boats from their regular patrols to hunt the Allied ships; Italian fighter planes loaded with torpedo bombs were moved to Sardinia in case they were needed for an attack. Thousands of crucial man-hours, tons of fuel and important naval assets were being sent to fight a phantom. The Germans planned to ambush the five-vessel convoy at a point east of Gibraltar.

It was incomprehensible. Even Philby, generally acknowledged to be the section's best mind, couldn't understand what was happening. Either the Abwehr had fallen for a con man with hazy motives, or it was a complex ruse to get Arabel to London and inside the lair of the British High Command. Philby knew his spy history: in 1939, the Abwehr had attempted a similar stratagem, drawing out the British secret service with a fake triple agent, leading to the kidnapping of two SIS agents in the Netherlands. Were the Germans using the same scheme again? Philby couldn't be sure; he hadn't so much as identified Arabel yet.

MI5 chimed in with a theory: perhaps Arabel was working at the Spanish embassy in London, a well-known rat's nest of pro-Nazi Francoists; it was even believed that one Spanish diplomat sat every day in the bay window of Boodle's, the gentlemen's club in St. James's Street, across from the entrance to MI5 headquarters, and noted down the comings and goings of all the visitors for the Abwehr. Other analysts suspected that Arabel had to be working out of the anti-British stronghold of Ireland.

Philby and MI6 sent out the equivalent of an all-points bulletin on Arabel. During the war, thousands of foreigners entering the country were questioned at the Royal Victorian Patriotic School in Wandsworth, and now MI5 began questioning the refugees about Arabel. But even though the interrogators were exceedingly thorough, no likely suspects emerged.

The supposed date of the Gibraltar ambush came and went. New

ISOS intercepts revealed, of course, that no convoy had been spotted. The German submarines and Italian fighter planes were sent home. Astonishingly, however, the Germans blamed the fiasco not on Arabel but the notoriously erratic Italians. The agent's stock was still sky high.

Arabel disappeared from Section V's screens as the winter of 1941 passed. Then on February 5, at 10:30 in the morning, the ISOS courier again appeared at Glenalmond, the tires of his motorcycle slipping on the ice as he pulled to a stop. Kim Philby was in London for the day, meeting with MI5. It was left to Bristow to sort through the telegrams, and he quickly spotted one postmarked Lisbon. He tore it open, saw that it was from MI6, and read that a Spanish national named Juan Pujol had approached a Lieutenant Demarest, the American naval attaché in Madrid, with a curious offer: he wanted to spy for the Allies in London. Pujol also mentioned that he'd been sending the Germans messages from Lisbon.

A thrill ran through Bristow. He was convinced they'd finally found Arabel and that the spy was trying to switch sides. He ran upstairs to the office of Colonel Felix Cowgill, head of MI6's Section V. Cowgill thought the telegram intriguing, but he didn't want to alert the Nazis that their codes had been broken and that Section V was reading their communications, nor did he want to hand Pujol over to his rivals in MI5. He told Bristow to wait until Philby returned. When the lanky spy walked through the door of Glenalmond, knocking the snow off his shoes, Bristow buttonholed him and showed him the telegram. "I think it might be Arabel," Bristow said excitedly.

"By God, Desmond," Philby exclaimed, "I think you're right." He agreed to send an agent to meet with this Spaniard and entice his story out of him. After months of trying, Pujol had gotten the Brits' full attention.

The German reaction to Pujol's fake convoy had impressed everyone. "If it was within Pujol's power to cause such mischief unwittingly," wrote the espionage historian Nigel West, "what might be the results if his efforts were directed in concert with other weapons of deception?" Back in St. Albans, Philby contacted MI6's head of station in Lisbon, asking him to set up a "discreet interview" with this Juan Pujol. MI6 chose its most effective Lisbon officer, Gene Risso-Gill, a well-bred Portuguese with a thick, short-cut beard, to conduct the first interview.

On an unseasonably hot February evening, Risso-Gill waited for Pujol at a horseshoe-shaped café overlooking the white sands of Estoril beach. "Never before or since have I been so nervous," he remembered. "I thought every German agent was watching me, [that] everybody around the area and in the café was a German agent." As the seagulls swooped and cried overhead and the sardine fishermen dressed in their brightly patterned homemade sweaters pulled in the day's catch on the broad beach in front of him, Risso-Gill waited, watching the crowd. Eventually a small, well-dressed man emerged from the welter of refugees, walked up to the bar and spoke to the server in good Portuguese, tinged with a Spanish accent: "Tea with lemon, no sugar, please." Risso-Gill studied the man, then sidled up to him. "The view is much better at the table by the steps leading down to the beach," he said casually. The man looked over. The code words were the ones agreed to for the rendezvous. Juan Pujol smiled and the two men walked to the table, and there Pujol handed over the bottles of secret ink and began to tell his story. He was in the Allies' hands at last.

Just over two months later, after wrapping up his affairs, Pujol was smuggled out of Lisbon on a British merchant ship headed for Gibraltar, without any luggage, leaving Araceli and little Juan behind, to be brought over later. Risso-Gill personally walked him up the gangway, escorted him past the Portuguese national police guarding the ship and showed him to his room. "My legs were shaking," Pujol recalled, as Risso-Gill whispered in his ear that there was no need to worry, it was a short journey. The captain had been alerted to their unusual passenger, and given instructions on whom to hand him over to once they arrived. Two men met Pujol at the Gibraltar dock, passed him "a wad of sterling notes" and told him to buy some clothes; prices on the Rock were one-third of those in England. After two days on the island, he flew to Plymouth on a powerful Sunderland seaplane.

As the Sunderland descended toward the black strip of runway, Pujol had a flash of foreboding: "I was suddenly acutely aware that I was away from home and about to enter an alien land. Would the English be friendly toward me? Would they believe my story . . . ? Would they understand my motives for all that I had done and honestly believe that I wished to work for the good of mankind?" As he walked down the plane's gangway, Pujol felt the first bite of English frost. "Terrible cold," he remembered. "Cold outside and icy fear inside."

Only days after that, he was upstairs in a room at 35 Crespigny Road being debriefed and meeting his future case officer, Tommy Harris, for the first time. It had required a long and often tortured apprenticeship, but the career of the most important Allied spy of World War II was about to begin in earnest. "It seemed a miracle that he'd survived so long," Harris would later write. "It was crazy," Pujol agreed. "I had no idea what I was doing."

II

GARBO'S RISE

7

A Fresh Riot of Ideas

PUJOL HAD FOOLED the Germans, but an even more rigorous test awaited him: getting past MI5.

On the morning of May 1, 1942, Desmond Bristow stood outside the front door of the small Victorian house at 35 Crespigny Road and blew a breath into the crisp London air. The place was an ordinary-looking two-story detached home, rented from a Jewish officer in the British Armed Forces. Upstairs, Pujol was sitting in a room furnished with four simple chairs and a table, a guard outside the door. For the past three days he'd been telling Bristow the story of his life. Soon the M16 officer would have to tell his superiors whether he believed it or not.

For Bristow, there were two possibilities: either this charming man was telling the truth, or he was a German triple agent trying to infiltrate the Allied war machine and destroy it from the inside.

The British agent glanced up and down the street, looking for Tommy Harris, the brilliant half-Jewish MI5 operative who would help Bristow conduct the next round of interrogation. Nothing.

Bristow had been sent in soon after Pujol's arrival, and for hour after hour he'd been asking the Spaniard to repeat key parts of his story; he'd backtracked, intentionally mixed up names and dates and tried to confuse the almost handsome and very personable young man. Analysts in London had studied Pujol's intercepted messages line by line and sent Bristow intricately plotted questions designed to trip up the alleged spy. But Bristow hadn't been able to lay a finger on him. The Spaniard would simply nod and go back to the contested point and unspool one unbelievable episode after another in a thoroughly believable way.

As they spoke, something in Pujol's hazel eyes made Bristow uneasy. Every now and then the MI6 agent would catch a certain "mischievous glint" there, a glint suggesting that Pujol's answers were the product of something other than complete and utter honesty.

Where was Tommy Harris? Crespigny Road was full of commuters on their way to London offices, but not the tall, soulful-eyed Harris, impossible to miss. If anyone could tell whether Pujol was the real thing, it was Harris, whose nickname inside the agency was Jesus.

Finally, Harris arrived and the two agents went upstairs, nodded at the man standing guard and walked inside. Pujol stood and greeted the agents and the three got down to work. On the desk were copies of every message Pujol had sent to the Abwehr. There were thirty-eight in all, written between July 1941 and March 1942. They went over the handwritten reports in detail, studying how Pujol constructed his sentences, how he used periods and commas, even how he crossed his *t*'s and dotted his *i*'s. They worked steadily through the day, the housekeeper — a woman named Miss Titoff — bringing coffee in to relieve the stress. All the while Tommy Harris watched Pujol, watched him speak, watched his eyes, watched how he read the messages, watched how he told his stories. "Tommy seemed to have the size of Pujol very quickly," Bristow remembered. "[He] manipulated his new agent in any direction he cared to."

As the sun warmed the interior of the small room, the three men came to the crux of the matter, the question Bristow had asked over and over again. Why was Pujol here? Why had he risked his life and that of his Spanish wife to spy for the Allies? Pujol nodded and said that his older brother, Joaquín, had been traveling in France when one day he stumbled on a terrible scene: the Gestapo conducting a wholesale slaughter of innocent people. Hearing Pujol tell it, the agents could almost hear the screams of the terrified men and women and the bark of the Walther PPKs, the Gestapo's gun of choice. When Joaquín had returned home and told Juan the awful story, his younger brother had decided he had to fight Hitler, no matter the cost.

It was a grisly and moving story. It was also a complete fabrication.

Harris listened, nodding occasionally, rolling and smoking the Spanish black cigarettes he preferred. "[Pujol's] motives for working against the Germans were obvious," Bristow said. "He had all the right answers."

As dusk approached, Bristow grew exhausted and suggested to Harris that they get a beer at the local pub. The two men said their goodbyes and walked down the path to Crespigny Road, Tommy Harris's eyes twinkling.

What do you think? Bristow asked.

Harris raised his eyebrows, shook his head and smiled.

"Desmond, he is obviously Arabel, but I do find it hard to believe such an outwardly simple man still has the Germans fooled and had us worried for so long."

Bristow nodded. He'd wondered the same thing. How could this naïve young man, not quite a rube but no master spy, be conning the best minds in the Abwehr?

As they walked toward the local hotel — Harris, the sophisticate, had suggested to Bristow that they have a glass of wine instead of a lager — the MI5 man gave his verdict. He told Bristow, "He is such a dreamer . . . but he is going to be a marvelous double agent."

Upstairs, Juan Pujol took another drag of one of Tommy Harris's Spanish cigarettes and watched dusk fall across north London. It's hard to believe, from what we know of him, that he wasn't smiling.

As Pujol settled into his new role those first few weeks, gorging himself on enormous English breakfasts — he hadn't tasted bacon in six long years — his hosts were just beginning to find a foothold in the shifting game of espionage.

One of the first requirements of intelligence is to acquire a picture of who the enemy is and what he intends to do. Early in the war, top Allied officers often had little insight into either of those things. One officer recalled a story about Major General Mason-Macfarlane, director of military intelligence for the aging field marshal Lord Gort, commander of the British Expeditionary Force, one of the most important Allied leaders. One day Gort stuck his head around Mason-Macfarlane's door.

"Bulgarians?" he asked. "Good chaps, aren't they?"

"No, sir, not very good," Mason-Macfarlane said.

"Oh! Bad chaps, eh? Pity, pity!" said Gort before disappearing.

When the old-school officer left, Mason-Macfarlane could only spread his hands wide "in a gesture of resignation."

This ignorance extended to espionage, at least in the beginning. When the war started, the War Office had only a hazy idea of German strategy or capabilities. This was illustrated when an air raid signal sounded in London on September 3, 1939, the day after the outbreak of hostilities. The War Office's entire staff descended to their bomb shelter, where a former military attaché who'd been through the Spanish Civil War listened to a series of blasts and told everyone that they were German bombs. The sounds had actually been doors slamming in the offices above; there'd been no air raid, because the Luftwaffe didn't yet have the resources to mount one and Hitler's strategy at the time was to lure England into a peace treaty, not attack it.

Double agents worked in an area of intelligence that fell under the broad name "deception," which was carried out by a host of outfits with a blizzard of acronyms: BiA, LCS, MI5, A Force, JPS, R Force. Despite the array of outfits, deception wasn't a popular tactic in the British military at the beginning of the war. "We are bred up to feel it is a disgrace ever to succeed by falsehood," stated a plaque on the wall of Churchill's bunker-like headquarters underneath Westminster. They were the words of Sir Garnet Wolseley, former commander in chief of the British army, from 1869. Wolseley's point was that anyone who believed those words was doomed to fail, and that deception was essential in all wars. But if falsehood was a necessary part of beating the Germans, few British officers felt that way, at least early on.

It didn't help matters that, because of the wartime squeeze on office space, the headquarters of MI5 were moved to the moldy cells of Wormwood Scrubs in west London. Common criminals could be seen milling around the prison's exercise yard as intelligence analysts tried to get inside the minds of the German High Command. "Don't go near them," a warder told female staff about the prisoners. "Some of them ain't seen no women for years." The cell — now office — doors had no handles on the inside, and some MI5 agents spent terrifying hours locked in the malodorous, soundproof rooms.

Britain's early deception efforts were often comically inept. Dennis Wheatley was one of the first recruits to the effort, a stout, bibulous former wine merchant and successful novelist who wrote tales of intrigue and occult magic with such titles as *To the Devil — a Daughter* and *They Used Dark Forces*. In 1941, he joined something called the Joint Planning Staff, an arm of the War Office, after writing a series of colorful papers on military strategy, some of which were read by King George VI. Wheatley found the response to this "newfangled business" of deception to be tepid at best. Generals didn't want to lend their tanks and regiments to fool the Germans. Admirals blanched when it was suggested they redirect a destroyer or two to support an elaborate "crack-brained" plot that had emerged from Wheatley's fertile imagination. British officers called the deception schemes "a racket," "a lot of nonsense," "a shocking waste of time and material." Some generals even refused to believe the Allies were engaged in such a thing, since information was given to the fewest possible decision makers. "The very fact that the Allies were engaged in deception *at all*," writes the historian Thaddeus Holt, "was a secret almost as closely held as Ultra or the Manhattan Project." In fact, Pujol's secret would be held far longer than J. Robert Oppenheimer's.

And the original leaders of the deception effort were far from first rate. Wheatley's first boss was a crusty old one-legged lieutenant colonel named Fritz Lumby, who every morning would limp into the office beneath Whitehall on his wooden leg and spend the first hour doing the *Times* crossword puzzle. Down the hall, Churchill met with his cabinet in the war room, under huge red-painted steel girders, and in gas-proof, flood-proof offices that featured four-foot-thick concrete ceilings. Close to Wheatley's office was the transatlantic phone to the White House and FDR, the world's first hot line, housed in room 63 with a sign that read "Keep Locked" and connected by cables to the enormous Sigsaly scrambler in the subbasement of Selfridges department store. Everyone believed room 63 was a working toilet for the exclusive use of the prime minister. Down the hall, a sign posted in a hallway noted the "Schedule of Alarms." If the klaxon sounded for two minutes, a German ground attack was expected. A royal marine in a dark blue uniform and white gun holster and shoulder strap stood guard around the clock. He was there to protect Churchill and the War Cabinet. As for Wheatley and Lumby, they could have expired from sheer boredom in their office and their deaths would barely have been noticed.

The two deceivers spent hour after sleepy hour waiting for orders in what the novelist called "the lost section." To pass the time, Lumby developed an unusual filing method: he gleefully confided to his subordinate that once, when a folder detailing some operation had become too big for his liking, he simply took it out and burned it. One steel filing cabinet was filled not with secret documents but with bottles of gin and Scotch, for the regular afternoon snort. Wheatley, who was a social animal with friends all over London, went out for three-hour lunches with "cloak and dagger men" and plowed through courses of "smoked salmon or potted shrimps . . . a Dover sole, jugged hare, salmon or game, and a Welsh rarebit to wind up with," then went back to the office and collapsed for a long nap. On March 28, 1942, Lumby left a despairing memo in Wheatley's tray: "The day has brought forth nothing — not even a lemon."

When the pair did concoct a scheme to fool the Germans, it was often badly misguided. One of Wheatley's proposals especially seemed to come straight out of one of his garish potboilers. On April 10, 1942, the same day that Pujol was boarding the British merchant ship on his way to Gibraltar, Wheatley submitted a memo called "Deception on the Highest Plane." In it, he stated that the Germans had probably lost their faith in Hitler, as he'd failed to conquer England and had added the United States and Russia as opponents. (In reality, Hitler enjoyed wide support in Germany in the spring of 1942.) So the ex-novelist proposed that the deception planners give the enemy a new leader to deliver them out of the darkness. He suggested that British intelligence create a figure who would, like Christ, be the son of poor parents, emerge after a period of seclusion, appear magically in various places all over the German countryside and conduct a "demonstration of supernatural powers" that would rally even hard-core Nazis to his message of "peace, universal brotherhood and passive resistance to all further war activities." Lumby adored the idea, suggested the name Bote ("messenger" in German) for the imaginary leader and added that, to really whet the Teutonic imagination, Bote should be rumored to be a descendant of the emperor Barbarossa.

MI6 and its informers and spies would then spread stories about Bote, which would force the Nazis to issue denials that such a man existed. The controversy would somehow suck legitimacy away from Hitler and eventually, somehow, lead the Germans to the negotiating table. (In another memo, Wheatley had fixed the date for the Nazi collapse, rather optimistically, at November 8, 1942.) A ridiculous scheme if ever there were one, the plan showed Allied intelligence at its most out of touch.

Deception and "psywar," which included the spreading of rumors, were separate disciplines. Psywar aimed to sap enemy morale; deception aimed to induce the enemy to do or not do something concrete and specific. But innuendo was used effectively in both crafts. When they were desperately trying to stave off a German invasion of the island in 1940, the Brits had put out the story that they'd discovered a way to set the English Channel on fire. The idea had come to Major John Baker White, an officer in the Directorate of Military Intelligence, while witnessing a demonstration of a new weapon of war: a kind of sprinkler system where a flammable mix of gas, fuel oil and creosote was fed by underground pipes to sprinkler heads that created a fine mist. Once lit, the mist could turn any beach in England into a searing wall of flames. The device was never used, but the image of a burning beach got inside White's head. How smashing it would be, he thought, if we could convince the Germans that we could set the entire *ocean* aflame.

Unlike Dennis Wheatley, White began with an insidious, primordial instinct — the fear of being burned alive — and carefully built on it. He went to British scientists and asked if it was possible to set the English Channel on fire. They told him it was, provided that you had almost unlimited amounts of money to spend on equipment and fuel. White didn't care about that; he only wanted something that was within the realm of possibility. He carefully began feeding the macabre rumor through his network of informants and touts: in the Café Bavaria in Geneva and the Ritz in Madrid, places where spies and diplomats and Germans gathered by night, his agents whispered about this horrible new invention. Next, he spread the story in Cairo, New York, Ankara and Istanbul.

A few weeks later, a German pilot was captured after ejecting from his plane over Kent, and brought to an interrogation center at Trent Park in Cockfosters, north London. He admitted that the pilots and commanders of the Luftwaffe were already familiar with the "burning sea defenses" that British scientists had invented. Three days later, another captured German airman gave up the same details. When some RAF planes dropped incendiary bombs on German soldiers practicing for the invasion of England, the most critically injured victims were sent to occupied Paris for treatment. Suddenly the rumor had undeniable evidence to back it up: French partisans — who'd heard about the burning sea scheme through their own sources — believed the men were part of a secret invasion force that had tried to cross the English Channel and had been broiled alive.

The rumor now spread like crazy. French citizens stood behind German soldiers in the cafés along the Champs-Élysées, rubbing their hands together as if they were warming them over a campfire. A Belgian shopkeeper was brave enough to advertise men's swimming trunks in his front window "for Channel swimming." Faced with this fast-moving virus, the Germans panicked. They began to test ways of making their invasion vessels fire-resistant. A barge in Fécamp, Normandy, was lined with asbestos, loaded with German soldiers and pushed into a pool of burning gas. The vessel came through the test; the men didn't — the entire crew was consumed by the flames and died. Some of the blackened corpses tumbled into the water and drifted to shore, where they gave further evidence of the horrors awaiting any German attackers. Sefton Delmer, a broadcaster who would one day write a thinly disguised account of the Pujol case, even went on the air and gave the German invasion forces some language tips: *Ich brenne* (I burn), *Du brennst* (You burn), *Er brennt* (He burns).

The "flammable sea" idea showed the power of what the Germans called "nerve warfare." It was, in a way, the perfect rumor, the one every deception officer dreamt of. It was terrifying, scientifically possible, and it spread exponentially.

Dennis Wheatley's Jesus-in-Berlin idea was nothing of the sort.

But, astonishingly, an even more bizarre variation of Wheatley's plot was adopted by British intelligence. In April 1942, the British secret service began putting out rumors of a "mysterious personality," now called simply Z, who instead of resembling Jesus Christ looked "a little like Bismarck when he was young" and had formed a secret underground organization to take back Germany. Prominent Germans, including the airplane designer Willy Messerschmitt, were said to be supporting him and had been "buying up corner houses to be used as machine-gun posts that would dominate the main square of cities when the time came to rise against Hitler." For some inscrutable reason, only people who spoke perfect English could join the clandestine group.

The Z craze failed to catch on in Berlin and Düsseldorf. When he heard about the operation, Wheatley was appalled. "Obviously, [they] missed the whole point of my paper," he lamented. "I have rarely heard anything more crazy."

Though Juan Pujol had an image of suave MI5 officers effortlessly bamboozling their opponents, in reality British deception often struggled to find a way into the German military mind.

MI5 managed the agents. It assigned a case officer to each double agent and saw to his day-to-day needs. It screened the candidates for the double life, including real German spies who'd entered England, weeded out the venal and the stupid ones, of which there were many in the four hundred or so candidates, chose the best and provided them with everything they needed to become conduits to the German High Command. If the incoming spies couldn't be turned, they were often imprisoned and used as "reference books," living encyclopedias on German spy techniques. MI5 kept secret offices throughout London, disguised as legitimate businesses, where agents could interview recruits; it arranged for apartments for the double agents to live in and provided housekeepers, guards, clothing coupons, ration books, identity cards, a wireless operator to transmit messages and even female companionship (case officers sometimes hired prostitutes for their lonely operatives). Then there was the matter of the "appointed scribes," active British soldiers who were asked to write the letters of any imaginary subagents; if a subagent's handwriting looked the same as the spy's, Berlin would grow suspicious. When a scribe died — taking with him his inimitable longhand — the fake sub-agent often had to be killed off, unless a man with the exact same cursive style could be found quickly. (This would later happen to Pujol's "Agent No. 6," whose real-life letter writer perished in a plane crash.)

Obtaining all these things — from real soldiers to whores — in wartime London required great imagination and secrecy. "The running of double-cross agents entailed not only the deception of the Germans," said the spymaster Sir John Cecil Masterman, "but often and in many cases the deception of people on our own side."

The Twenty Committee, signified by "XX," for double-cross, supplied the agents with information. It was formed in January 1941, and its members included representatives of all the relevant agencies that would contribute to its mission: GHQ Home Forces, the War Office, Air Ministry Intelligence, MI6 and MI5. The committee was headed up by Masterman, an academic in civilian life. Tall and donnish, Masterman was a cricketer at heart. He'd had a high-flying career in the late 1920s with the cricket bat — which he wielded from a left-handed stance, though he bowled right-handed at a "medium pace" — for teams like the Free Foresters and the Harlequins. A former provost at Worcester College, Oxford, Masterman was also an author of crime fiction: one of his books, the crackling murder mystery *An Oxford Tragedy*, featured a Sherlock Holmes–like detective "of European reputation." The spymaster's novels revealed his interest in what he called "pre-detection" — that is, how "to work out the crime before it is committed, to foresee how it will be arranged, and then to prevent it!" It was the criminal equivalent of what the double agents were being asked to do: to imagine and construct an event before it happened and to predict against every possible response to that event. And then to game those responses, too.

Masterman's last gift was that he knew what people wanted: the only way to get all the heads of departments to attend his meetings, he decided, was to offer them a freshly baked bun, something almost unobtainable in wartime London. At more than 226 weekly meetings of the XX Committee, the attendance was a perfect 100 percent.

Nineteen forty-one had been a year for experimentation in the double-cross system, which meant not only churning out dozens of plots but coming up with a philosophy of espionage: what worked, what didn't and why. The year 1942 was supposed to be the flowering of that philosophy, but most of the operations simply didn't pan out. Plan Machiavelli, for example, involved the passing of confidential charts of minefields off the east coast of Britain; the Serbian double agent Tricycle transported the plans, but the Germans ignored them. Plan Guy Fawkes was a fake mission to attack a food dump in Wheatstone, England, in order to build up the sabotage credentials of British-controlled operatives by sending authentic newspaper clippings recounting their deeds to the Germans (this was formally known as "double-cross sabotage," and Plan Guy Fawkes was the first example of it during the war). After long negotiations with Scotland Yard, the operation was given the green light. But the intelligence officers had trouble rousing the two elderly men who were guarding the dump, which delayed the planting of the incendiary devices, and then the officers were almost collared by an annoyingly efficient bobby. In Plan Brock, MI5 plotted to blow up Nissen huts in Hampshire for the same reasons that motivated Fawkes, but the Norwegian compass that had been left as evidence was stolen by some local thief, and a flock of sheep wandered too near the explosion site, nearly causing the planners to abort. Even when deception plans made sense, they were tricky to pull off. And even when they were executed, the enemy might not believe them, or might ineptly ignore them.

As Pujol was shown the ropes, it was felt inside the British High Command — and within the XX Committee itself — that the leaders of the deception operations were playing it too safe, afraid to reveal too much to Hitler, which was the risk of any truly ambitious deception plan: the nefarious plots cooked up in London could reveal as much about the Allies' war plans as they did the Germans'. The XX Committee, it was widely believed, had deteriorated into a bunch of nitpicking censors, cutting the information to be passed down to the least dangerous level (called "tonic" or "chicken feed") and vetoing everything that involved significant risk.

Many observers worried that a group of men who were having trouble blowing up a couple of Nissen huts in lonely Hampshire wouldn't be ready for far more ambitious missions. "How should we feel if the whole of the double cross system collapsed," Masterman worried, "before it had been put to the test in a grand deception?" At one point, the Home Forces even suggested to Masterman that the dozen or so double agents be abandoned and their operations shut down.

Pujol's first great challenge in joining the deception effort in England was the state of the deception effort in England.

There was at least one promising indicator within the system, however. Juan Pujol had been a risk, a walk-in; earlier in the war, the British had made an even more unorthodox bet that was beginning to pay off. The wager was on human capital. Highly eccentric human capital, to be specific.

When war was declared, the British intelligence services went on a hiring binge. There simply weren't enough experienced secret service officers to go around; one branch, the Naval Intelligence Division, went from fifty staffers in 1939 to more than a thousand by 1942. And to fill the offices of MI5, MI6 and the other outfits involved in the double-cross campaign, the British made a conscious decision to leave tradition behind: they recruited not from the usual sources — the colonial services in India and Burma, and the British military — but from the universities and the intelligentsia. This search for warm bodies led to some memorable job interviews. Bickham Sweet-Escott, an applicant to MI6's Section D (for "Destruction"), the group that specialized in sabotage, was told by his interviewer, "I can't tell you what sort of job it would be. All I can say is that if you join us, you mustn't be afraid of forgery, and you mustn't be afraid of murder." He signed up and found the explosives expert he was working with was a former boxing promoter and test pilot who spoke in bizarre rhyming couplets. Writers seemed to be special favorites of the intelligence branches, especially those who pumped out thrillers: Geoffrey Household, the author of the minor classic *Rogue Male,* was sent to Bucharest, where he alarmed his office mates by drinking too much and "playing casually with detonators." A Force, the Middle East deception unit, featured a chemist, a merchant banker, a music hall illusionist, a screenwriter and a handful of painters and other artists. "We were complete amateurs," said Christopher Harmer, a British lawyer turned spy-runner, "not much more than overgrown schoolboys playing games of derring-do."

For years, the intelligence services had been the home of clubbable young society men and veterans of the Indian colonial police force; "eggheads" were looked down upon and rarely hired. Now the British government began signing up academics at a furious clip: historians, linguists and classicists for the spy services, and mathematicians and scientists for analytical jobs like codebreaking. Oddballs, such as the almost unfathomably brilliant Alan Turing, became the order of the day. Turing bicycled to work at Bletchley Park, the headquarters of the cryptanalysts who produced the famous Ultra intercepts, wearing a bulky gas mask to avoid pollen. Earlier, he'd converted all his money into silver ingots, in preparation for a Nazi invasion, then dug a hole in a nearby forest and stashed the bullion there. (After the war, he failed to find it again.) Bletchley Park became a cross between an arts commune and a Bloomsbury party. When Winston Churchill toured the facility, he told its director, "I told you to leave no stone unturned to get staff, but I had no idea you had taken me literally."

The spy services were less overtly eccentric, the private lives of officers hidden behind good pedigrees and dark Savile Row suits. Tommy Harris was a successful art dealer with a specialty in Goya. His fellow spy Anthony Blunt was an art historian. Kim Philby considered his best officer to be Paul Dehn, an entertainer who "bubbled and frothed like a trout stream" and would later write the screenplay for *The Spy Who Came in from the Cold*. Many of these men had no intention of working in intelligence after the war, and so they didn't feel that one bad idea would ruin their career. Pujol, who was a kind of refugee of the imagination — uncomfortable in Franco's straitjacketed society — fit right in.

Many of the men who eventually led the deception effort against Hitler were outsiders, with a strong element of veteran intelligence men thrown in to provide balance (and who immediately began to complain about the strange people down the hall). A number of staffers in MI5 — including some Jews and homosexuals — would have found themselves in concentration camps had they been raised in wartime Germany; certainly the casual atmosphere that reigned, with ideas "whizzing up and down the corridors," wouldn't have worked at Abwehr headquarters in Berlin. It was a different mindset, another world. With the enemy poised opposite its shores, England didn't have the luxury of playing conservatively, and the British felt that intelligence was one area where they had an almost inborn advantage.

When Pujol arrived, the double-cross initiative was just beginning to sputter to life. Anachronisms like Lieutenant Colonel Lumby—the man who'd burned a sensitive file when it got too bulky—were shipped off to less important spheres and bright young men were brought in to lead the effort. Tommy Harris was one of them.

In their tiny office on Jermyn Street in St. James's, Juan Pujol studied his new partner and was instantly struck by Harris's intensity: "He smoked like a chimney and the fingers of his right hand were almost chestnut colored as he never put out a cigarette until it was about to burn him." Pujol thought Harris a kindred spirit. Kim Philby once described the atmosphere in certain British intelligence agencies as fostering "a fresh riot of ideas." That was true about the office on Jermyn Street. In Harris, Pujol found a more calculating and far-seeing version of himself.

The two men were enigmas even to those who knew them best. In Harris's looks there was a whiff of mystery. One intelligence officer called him "a casting director's ideal choice for a desert sheikh or a slinky tango lizard." But there were hidden depths behind the good looks. "There are many questions about him which are and will probably remain unanswered," wrote the MI6 officer Desmond Bristow. "It is true to say that I knew Tommy Harris well; on the other hand, there is part of him I perhaps knew then, and know now, but did not and do not wish to believe." Andreu Jaume, a family friend of the Harrises who now lives in the spy's house on Mallorca and has been researching a biography of him for years, has never been able to wrap his mind around the man. "He's like a runaway figure for me. The more I pursue him, the more he eludes me."

Harris was thirty-four at the time he met Pujol, the only son of an observant Jewish art-dealer father who had married a Spanish woman from the southern city of Seville. Tommy's grandfather and his great-uncle on his mother's side had, in the 1800s, revived the art of the toreador by appearing in the bullring dressed in the costumes of El Cid and other Spanish heroes; they kept horses in stables at their Madrid home and became famous as the "gentleman bullfighters." His father, Lionel, opened an art gallery specializing in Spanish greats like El Greco and Velázquez in London's fashionable Conduit Street. There his business flourished. Dukes, foreign dignitaries and members of the royal family would come by and chat with Harris about the latest Spanish trends in chiaroscuro.

Before the war, his son Tommy, a "brilliantly intuitive" artist, joined his father in the gallery. Tommy Harris would travel the English countryside, getting himself invited into mansions and Edwardian castles and charming the resident dowagers into selling him their treasures for a song. Tommy married an English girl, Hilda, and their home, at Chesterfield Gardens in London, became a salon steeped in art, alcohol and good food. "During my occasional visits to London," Kim Philby wrote, "I had made a point of calling at Tommy Harris's house," where he lived "surrounded by his art treasures in an atmosphere of haute cuisine and *grand vin*." The house next door was owned by the chairman of Sotheby's, who often dropped by. Rothschilds rubbed elbows with Bond Street art dealers and half-soused earls. When war came, the basement served as a bomb shelter, with London swells sleeping off the champagne and canapés in the semidarkness. Upstairs, a strange constellation of future spies came together, drawn by the warm light of Harris's hospitality. Guy Burgess, Anthony Blunt and Kim Philby all gossiped and networked at Chesterfield Gardens. (The three, along with Donald Maclean, had already switched their allegiances to Moscow, forming what became known as the Cambridge spy circle, a revelation that would shock the British spy establishment in the early 1950s — and cause Tommy Harris much heartache.)

Harris loved champagne and wild parties, but there was always a part of him that remained shuttered and off-limits, accessible only through alcohol or painting. His art was striking and often jaggedly intense. A reviewer of his work in a London newspaper wrote: "These paintings do have an intriguing, disturbing vibrancy. Stabbing brush-technique; our old friend 'the nervous line' hepped up to hecticness."

But whatever his inner tensions were, early on it became clear that Harris was the right man to guide his new recruit through the labyrinth of the spy game. "Pujol's genius was Latin but the plan was Anglo-Saxon," a Spanish journalist would later say. It was true enough. Pujol contributed cunning and a sense of style, Harris strategic brilliance and order.

Together these two men sat down in a small office in London and endeavored to defeat the Third Reich, largely through the use of their overheated brains.

8

The System

THE DOUBLE AGENT SYSTEM inspired a raft of metaphors to explain it: it was like an orchestra, with "first violins" playing the main theme, "second violins" supporting them, and the conductor — in this case, J. C. Masterman, head of the XX Committee — blending the dissonant chords of sabotage, political disinformation, rumors and physical deception into a single symphony that was then broadcast to the Germans. Or it was a cricket side — a description favored by the sport-mad Masterman. There was only one crucial difference between the game and espionage, he argued: "our best batsmen . . . might be past their best or even deceased before the date of the final game."

But neither orchestras nor cricket teams involve the one thing that made spy operations click: artifice. In fact, the thing the double-cross effort resembled most was the Hollywood studio system. The double agents were the actors, the public face of a huge undertaking designed to entrance an audience. Their case officers were their managers, and there was in fact heated competition among people like Tommy Harris to get their agents big roles in upcoming operations. MI5 was the studio, developing projects and doling them out to the right actor, tailoring the message to that agent's image with the Germans. (Like many Hollywood stars, Pujol could never be allowed to break character or his career would be ruined.) There were scriptwriters — MI5 literally thought in terms of long-form narratives — and stories in which imaginary characters were introduced and then killed off at the right moment. The British army had "production teams" that supported the agents with fake wireless traffic, with the assets referred to as "Lighting, Scenery, Costumes and Property." They even wrote "scripts" and chose actual troops to serve as extras and provide crowd noise. When they wanted to simulate an amphibious landing, for example, the sounds of a real landing were taped on wire recorders and played back during the actual battle.

Reviews, as in classic Hollywood, were important. The Allies had the Bletchley Park codebreakers, which meant that MI5 could listen to their critics in Berlin. If a report was relayed to Germany's Foreign Armies West, then to Tokyo and Sofia, Bulgaria, and Istanbul, or if a fleet of Luftwaffe bombers was repositioned based on an agent's flash message, that particular agent and script were judged a hit. The ultimate critic, of course, was Hitler himself, who signed off on only the most important Abwehr messages, indicating that he'd seen them and absorbed their content.

As in Hollywood, money mattered. The amount of cash each agent cadged from the Germans indicated how seriously he or she was taken. (Over his career, Pujol would exceed every other MI5 agent many times over, earning $1.4 million [at today's value] and single-handedly bankrolling much of the double-cross system with his "earnings.") Finally, the spies were given code names when they entered the system: as Issur Danielovich became Kirk Douglas, so did an underfed Welshman named Alfred George Owens become the dashing agent known as Snow.

Pujol was the promising new face who'd arrived from the boondocks of Lisbon. But he needed to be trained in the system. As they sat in their bare-bones office in Jermyn Street, breaking for meals at the Martinez Restaurant in Swallow Street, where they could indulge in authentic Spanish dishes, Pujol and Harris began to untangle the sprawling espionage machine that Pujol had so far kept only in his head.

Harris bent over a desk as Pujol talked, entering into a new logbook the numerous minute details of the imaginary subagents that the Spaniard had created. The fake subagents were given their own individual code name. The first agent became "J (1)," for "Juan's Agent One," and Harris opened a new file for each so that their imaginary lives could be recorded and no mistakes made. Pujol and Harris drew up a "character study" for all twenty-seven agents Pujol would eventually summon up, "realistic enough to create a clear picture in the minds of the recipients," noting their every quirk and flaw. To flesh out the lives of these fictitious men and women, British intelligence employed a location scout, an officer whose job it was to drive around England writing down bits of local color for them to use in their travels: ice cream shops for them to stop in, hotels near military encampments for them to stay. Everything else was up to the spy and his case officer. Harris and Pujol had to choreograph every movement of every member of their network: their KLM pilot-courier, for example, couldn't be represented as being in Lisbon when a letter from a different subagent claimed he was in London. It was a whole universe that needed to be constructed and rigorously maintained.

The thirty-eight messages Pujol had sent from Lisbon were sorted and catalogued, as well as the German responses. From now on, all of Pujol's outgoing messages would be printed on pink paper, and all the incoming German messages would be on green. Harris finalized a delivery method for future texts: he and Pujol would write and encode the outgoing messages, then send them to Section V of MI6 in London, where they would be placed in a diplomatic bag and taken to Lisbon. Risso-Gill, the man who'd brought Pujol in from the cold, would have an agent deliver them to the poste restante box, where the Germans would pick them up. The Abwehr was encouraged to believe that the letters were still being delivered by the imaginary KLM pilot Pujol had recruited months earlier.

By April 27, 1942, everything was ready to go, except for one last piece of business. Pujol needed a new code name. Arabel was the name the Germans had given his network, but of course MI5 needed a new moniker. When Pujol had arrived in England, an MI6 officer had dubbed him Bovril, the meat extract that the English had turned into a hot drink. But now that Harris had taken the measure of the man, the name no longer fit.

Double agents were usually shifty or revoltingly needy, cornered into working for their enemies because of money trouble, homosexual blackmail or vanity. They were often bad spies and worse human beings, and their controllers usually gave them disparaging names, perhaps as a way of distancing themselves from the craven lot. There was Agent Careless, "an extremely indiscreet and truculent fellow." There was the Snark, a Yugoslavian maid of no real account who once hatched a plan to have an enemy eaten alive by rats in order to get information from him. There was a pair of newlyweds and their dubious friend code-named the Savages. The list went on: the Weasel, Cocaine, Slave, Washout, as well as the Worm and BGM (Blond Gun Moll), a Cretan woman and low-level spy who carried a gun in her handbag "and knew how to use it." (It was said she'd once used the pistol to kill a man, though another theory said she'd actually thrown him off a roof.) Only a select few were given honorable names that suggested a real interest in the person.

But Pujol fell in the latter category. Because he struck MI5 as "the best actor in the world," he was rechristened Garbo, after the actress. Like his namesake, Pujol seemed to have an unapproachable core that remained elusive no matter how long one studied him. The code name might also confuse the Germans into thinking that Garbo was a woman, giving Pujol an extra layer of security.

To turn Garbo into a full-fledged Abwehr star, Harris and Pujol began to fill their Berlin-bound messages with "chicken feed"—basic military information, accurate, but of little value. Access to the truth was the great advantage that Pujol had gained by entering the double-cross system; he'd make no more mistakes about wine-drinking Scots. Every week, if not every day, the XX Committee sent a fresh batch of material that could safely be woven into Garbo's sprawling narratives, encoded and sent across to the Germans. This was known in the service as "buildup": the Abwehr would slowly be convinced that Garbo had access to better and better information, most of which checked out. Some of the letters were sent directly to Madrid with a London postmark, to prove Garbo was really living in the British capital.

Garbo's "agents" were now roaming all over the country, and their reports read like a spy's Baedeker of small towns and harbors: "The beach here is mined. There is a very large gun in Singleton Park, but I could not find out if it is for A.A. [antiaircraft] or coastal defenses . . . Several large hangars. 15 barrage balloons—A.A. placed to the north and west of the aerodrome. Many sentries . . . The small port of Irvine is now being used for assault barges. I saw ten anchored."

The correct handling of the delicate secret inks was a major area of concern. On November 11, 1942, the Abwehr spy-runner in Madrid, Federico, wrote instructions for the latest inks:

> You moisten a sheet of paper for a few minutes in a bath of plain water until the paper is well saturated. Then get rid of the surplus water you then put the sheet on to glass so that it should adhere completely to the surface without forming air bubbles. On this moistened sheet you put another dry sheet which must adhere completely to the first. On this second sheet the secret text must be written with a hard pencil well sharpened and pressing fairly hard on the paper without breaking its surface. Then one must take off the dry sheet and the writing will appear on the first sheet in transparent form.

Many of Garbo's letters were sent to cover addresses in Lisbon and appeared to be normal correspondence between friends or family members; the real message, of course, was between the lines in invisible ink. For this, Pujol and Harris had to invent a host of fake civilians to cover for their fake agents. One such family — two brothers and their wayward sister "Maria" — wasn't particularly happy.

> My dear Maria
>   Obviously, as an affectionate brother, I hate to think of you being ill, but my other reason is purely a selfish one. Perhaps you have forgotten what Mother is like when one of her precious children is ill . . . These last ten days . . . have been sheer hell for me . . .

> My dear Maria —
>   I have been asked by the family to write you the Xmas letter . . . I cannot say that I am feeling in a particularly festive mood yet but I dare say it will come . . . I am going to do the decorating this year, not that I particularly like doing it, but I have had enough of people falling off ladders like Joe did last year when he spent the rest of Xmas lying on a sofa with a sprained ankle and concussion.

Pujol and Harris had to keep straight the workings of their fake English family and the other civilians, adding to the soap opera's complexity. Vacations, birthdays, illnesses, shared gossip — it all had to mesh perfectly.

Fortunately for Pujol, "the greatest burden of the work" — thinking up the information to put across — "had been removed from his shoulders" when he came to London. Yet Harris made it clear that Pujol was still an essential part of the operation. He wrote, "It is . . . true to say that Garbo personally played a very material part throughout . . . He was allowed to supervise and help develop the unique and fanciful espionage organization which had been the creation of his imagination." Pujol, in Harris's portrait, "jealously examined the development of the work lest we should choose to pass material to the enemy . . . which should result in discrediting the channel . . . We could not have desired a more able or clear-sighted critic." Pujol's role in making Garbo into a force would become more evident as the game became infinitely more complex.

In those early days, Garbo's network of agents had to be "recruited" and then distributed around England and across the globe, giving Garbo the ability to report on almost any Allied military operation. He began inventing spies at a fast clip, the biggest coup being Carlos, a rich Venezuelan student in Glasgow who showed talent as an agent-runner himself. Carlos even brought aboard his own brother, who hated the Americans because "according to him [they] have killed the most sublime thing in his country," namely, its Spanish heritage. Then came Agent J (3), a senior official at the Ministry of Information in London. Tommy Harris pushed to add this character to Garbo's portfolio — they needed a big fish, and this oblivious chap was it. Pujol supposedly did some translation work for the official, and the two bonded over Pujol's memories of the Spanish Civil War and the bureaucrat's Republican leanings. The ministry official was a loyal subject of his majesty the king, an unconscious collaborator "suited for the passing of high-grade information of a political or strategic nature." Garbo now had a pipeline to the heart of British decision-making.

The second objective in these early days was to peer into Hitler's brain. That is, to reverse the telescope that the Abwehr thought they'd trained on England and look into the heart of the war machine in Berlin, without the Germans knowing it. This was done by listening carefully to what information the Abwehr was requesting, and pushing its officers to reveal their secrets. As the eyes and ears of the German forces, the Abwehr often sent signals about future operations before a panzer ever roared to life or a destroyer changed course in the Baltic Sea.

In the autumn of 1940, the Abwehr asked its spies about food depots in England, even demanding to know the price of bread and milk. Why would the Germans care about how much grain the English had stored in Devon? There was no question of starving the island into submission. British analysts came to the conclusion that Hitler was thinking about how to feed his army once it had conquered England, which told Churchill and his ministers that the Germans were still contemplating an invasion. Yet by the late summer of 1941, the tenor of the questions changed. The Abwehr stopped asking about food depots and began telling their agents to lie low and stay safe. The invasion of England was off. These questionnaires from Berlin were almost as good as having a mole in the Reich Chancellery.

The reverse telescope also revealed what obsessed Hitler on any given day. It became clear, for example, that the Führer was deeply concerned with the threat to Norway, close to his northern border and an important transshipment route for raw materials from Sweden, including iron ore. Throughout the war, the Führer kept hundreds of thousands of badly needed troops in the remote northern countryside to guard against invasion there. This gave the XX Committee something to threaten Hitler with: almost every major invasion deception included some feint toward Germany's northern neighbor, which kept those troops in place and away from the real battle zones. "If these two conditions exist," wrote Sir Ronald Wingate of the London Controlling Section, "namely apprehension and plausibility, then deception can turn what was a vague fear in the enemy's mind into a certainty." Norway was like a bogeyman that the Allies kept whispering about, while dragging a chain across a floor now and then, as Hitler, eyes agape, put one more lock on the door.

Tragically, this reverse telescope method failed when it came to the Americans. The risk-taking double agent known as Tricycle, a

Serbian playboy, received a questionnaire from his German handlers before he went to the United States on August 10, 1941. Buried in the notes were questions about one naval installation in particular: "Exact details and sketch of the situation of the State Wharf and the power installations, workshops, petrol installations, situation of Dry Dock No 1 and the new dry dock which is being built." The place in question was Pearl Harbor.

In the spring of 1942, Federico rattled off a series of disturbing questions to Garbo early in his London stay. In one letter Madrid asked: "Can you get hold of a gas mask? Give technical information about the canister. Against what types of gas is this a protection? What information can you give us about the manufacture or storage, in the coastal areas or inland, of protective materials to be used against any type of chemical warfare?" The implications were grim: clearly the Germans wanted to know how to render the crystals in the masks ineffective.

Harris sprang into action. MI5 ordered British scientists in the Gas Warfare Department to produce a fake chemical compound for the Germans. When the batch of "3¾ oz of Plain Nut Charcoal, Grading 8-18, Volume activity 17" arrived from the lab, he and Pujol packed it in a tin of Andrews Liver Salts and mailed it off to the Lisbon cover address that had been designated for parcels. The phony crystals sent German scientists on a wild goose chase, trying to find gases to overcome them.

Along with the phony compound, Garbo composed a letter filled with news of his subagents, questions about buying a wireless and requests for money for his expanding network. Then he added: "I have been passing through a long period of nervous strain . . . You do not know how homesick I sometimes feel for my own country. You cannot imagine how miserable life here is for me since I arrived . . . My Catalan character does not adapt itself to casual friendship more so when it concerns Spaniards who talk through their ass and compromise one for less than nothing."

Garbo was dabbing a few more paint strokes on his self-portrait, which revealed an isolated man, tetchy but absolutely committed to the Nazi cause. Garbo would do anything for the Reich, and his integrity could only be questioned at the risk of setting him off into a violent explosion. More and more, Federico and Kühlenthal came to accept this fragile hero, and even to be moved by him. He was a better Nazi than either Federico or Kühlenthal. He'd risked his life for the Führer — what were they doing besides swilling *cerveza* in the cafés of Madrid? The letter, and the phony crystals, struck home in Madrid. Federico immediately upped the payments to Garbo and began to write longer and more frequent messages, giving MI5 a deeper understanding of the Abwehr's thinking.

For all his genius on the page, Garbo couldn't be contained purely on paper. Occasionally, MI5 needed to prove that he was real. Bent over their desks in Jermyn Street, Pujol and Harris came up with his first real operation, a little caper that would allow Garbo to "pass from the notional to the factional." It was called Plan Dream.

Dream was a currency scheme. It was illegal to transfer money from England to pro-Axis Spain, making it difficult for Spanish businessmen in London to send money home. Taking advantage of this, Garbo told Federico that he'd come up with a way to pay his expanding network of agents, all of whom were clamoring for funds. A syndicate of Spanish fruit merchants in London wanted to send 30,000 English pounds back to Madrid. They'd contacted an assistant military attaché, a man named Leonardo Muñoz, in Spain's London embassy, to see if he could massage the deal.

So far, this was all true. The facts had been fed to the XX Committee by an informer and later passed on to Garbo, who began turning this tawdry real-world scheme into confirmation that he was alive. He told the Abwehr in Madrid that if they would pay 3 million pesetas to Muñoz, as representative of the merchants, the merchants in London would in turn hand over 30,000 pounds to an MI5 agent, posing as an official of a "big British insurance company" with funds frozen in Spain. The agent would then hand the money to Pujol, who would use it to pay his operatives. No currency-stuffed suitcases would have to be smuggled across borders. Garbo planted a letter on Muñoz before he traveled back to Spain, with a message in invisible ink, giving the Abwehr the order to go ahead with the transaction. The passwords were creaky but serviceable: when Muñoz showed up, he was to be told, "I have a message for you from Mr. Wills." If Muñoz answered, "Do you mean Douglas Wills of London?" his identity was confirmed. He was to be given the pesetas, no questions asked.

Muñoz went to Spain, met with the Abwehr, gave the correct password and got the money. The Spanish merchants then paid 30,000 pounds to the MI5 officer, netting the agency more than $1 million in today's money, a princely sum that was funneled straight into the double-cross operation. And the physicality of the caper — the Spanish diplomat, the wads of money, the secret letter — firmed up Garbo's image nicely.

Though hugely lucrative, Plan Dream was a mere tune-up. It would also very nearly cause Garbo's downfall, a twist many months in the future. But in the summer of 1942, a much larger operation came into view: Operation Torch, the Anglo-American invasion of North Africa. It would be Garbo's coming-out party.

9

The Debut

THE MOTIVE BEHIND TORCH was as much political as military: Stalin was pushing Roosevelt and Churchill to open a second front to relieve the tremendous stress on his troops fighting and dying on the Eastern Front. The Americans — and the Soviets — voted for an amphibious landing in occupied Europe, code-named Sledgehammer, but Churchill objected that it was too soon for a continental invasion: the men and materiel weren't yet available. When 3,500 mostly Canadian troops were killed, wounded or captured in the disastrous invasion at Dieppe, France, on August 19, 1942 — what the Germans mocked as the "ten-hour second front" — the British point was made. The Allies turned their eyes to North Africa.

With a major invasion scheduled, the Allies naturally sought to disguise it as best they could. A deception operation, code-named Solo I, was devised to make the Germans believe that the invasion was coming in Norway, not North Africa. Hitler's well-known obsession with a possible invasion there meant that the fjords and cities were stacked with highly rated divisions. If those troops stayed in Norway, it would make life easier for General George S. Patton, who would lead his men into Casablanca while two other invasion forces struck Oran and Algiers.

"The job I am going on," wrote Patton, "is about as desperate a venture as has ever been undertaken by any force in the world's history." More than a hundred American ships carrying elements of the U.S. 2nd Armored, the 3rd Infantry and the 9th Infantry, units that had never seen battle before, would sail straight from Chesapeake

Bay to Casablanca, evading packs of German U-boats on their way, then storm the beaches and take the fortified city. Marshal Pétain, the Vichy leader in France who controlled the Casablanca forces, ordered his troops to resist any invasion at all costs.

An attack force was assembled. Factories began mass-producing the newest Sherman tanks, while American Grumman F4F Wildcat and Douglas SBD Dauntless fighters were combat-loaded aboard the flattops, or aircraft carriers, that would take them to Casablanca. More than 107,000 British and American troops massed for the attack. "If the assault failed, it could produce disaster," the deception planner Dennis Wheatley wrote. "2000 miles from home, there would be no Dunkirk." Torch was planned for November 1942.

Several months earlier, in the summer, Garbo started to maneuver his network to cover the invasion. Deception was a chess game; one had to put one's assets in place long before attempting the fatal move. The problem for Garbo was that his Agent No. 2, "William Gerbers," the man who'd spotted the fake convoy to Malta, was perfectly positioned to see the departure of the *real* task force that would be heading to French North Africa. "For him to remain there and fail to notice the preparations and the final embarkation would have blown not only the agent, but Garbo's whole network," Harris worried. And if Garbo suddenly moved Gerbers to another part of the country just before the invasion geared up, it would look suspicious. Pujol and Harris conferred. There was nothing else for it: No. 2 would have to die.

Garbo informed Madrid that he was worried about No. 2's health. He was so concerned that he pretended to travel up to Liverpool to have a look. He found the agent's "wife" frantic and Gerbers himself in bed with a mysterious illness. Tommy Harris had consulted a physician to make sure the clinical details that Garbo sent to the Germans were accurate. Garbo arranged for No. 2 to be moved to a hospital for an operation, but he told the Germans that his Liverpool agent would be out of commission for the foreseeable future. Garbo managed to replace this single agent with three others (none, however, in the Liverpool area). With this stroke, an operative was removed from the real embarkation point, and two more — Agents No. 3 and No. 5 — were shifted to Scotland, the *fake* embarkation point. Pawns on a chessboard, Garbo's agents were being maneuvered for the final payoff.

Garbo began "spotting" Scottish and Canadian troops conducting training on the west coast of Scotland, near Troon and Ayr, which told the Germans that Norway could be the target. "Although I cannot confirm the rumor that 1 million troops were passing through Ayr . . . I see that there exist major concentrations of troops and commandos there," Garbo wrote. His subagents caught glimpses of mountaineering drills and winter equipment. "There were also about the town [of Moffat] very large stocks of antifreeze." When the soldiers left the hoods of their jeeps up, the agent glanced down and "saw" labels attached to the radiators: "All radiators to be drained before embarkation. Antifreeze mixture not to be used in vehicles until orders are given by Chief Transport Officer." These humble details pointed north, away from Casablanca.

The Germans made it clear to Garbo that they felt an invasion was coming: "Second front! Very important!! It is of the greatest importance that you should intensify all your efforts to try to get extensive information and transmit it to us quickly direct here by air mail, on concentration of troops and material, motorized units, aviation and air fields." Federico ordered him to put agents in Wales and on the Isle of Wight, to look for telltale clues. So Garbo hurried "them" off, and they sent back word that a double strike, against both France and Norway, was likely. Then, on October 11, Garbo informed Madrid that "No. 6 tells me that rumors are circulating among journalists that the objective will be Dakar." Dakar was in West Africa, halfway down the coast, many hundreds of miles north of the true targets, Casablanca and Oran. Garbo immediately qualified the news by telling Madrid that the war correspondents were in the pocket of the War Ministry, and thus Dakar was probably a false target. He was creating a smokescreen composed of many gray shades.

As the invasion approached, the XX Committee pushed Garbo up to a new level of prominence. They had to sprinkle enough truth in his messages to keep the Germans from suspecting him of disloyalty. One of his agents was allowed to "see" one of the actual convoys leaving the river Clyde for French North Africa on October 27. Garbo quickly flashed the sighting to Madrid. Four days later, he sent another bulletin: more troops were being loaded onto battleships, and the camouflage was in Mediterranean colors: "None of the troops with Arctic uniforms and equipment embarked as they are still here." Garbo was beginning to suggest that Norway was a feint. The invasion was heading toward Africa. Finally, the pièce de résistance: while visiting with his Ministry of Information source, Garbo claimed he sneaked into the unsuspecting man's office and stole a look at a "Most Secret" file titled "Policy — French North Africa." "It was impossible for me, in the few minutes available, to get more details. Nevertheless, I am convinced . . . that they are preparing propaganda which would come into force at the moment of an attack against these places."

Garbo had "found" the target. On November 1, 1942, he banged out a letter warning the Germans that the Allies would hit North Africa. It was precisely the intelligence the Germans wanted from their top spy. That message would give them the upper hand at Casablanca and Algiers — the landing areas for the invasion — and hundreds if not thousands of Allied lives would be lost. But MI5 ensured that Garbo's letter took days to pass through the British censors, so it arrived in Lisbon on November 9, one day too late. It proved Garbo's worth without costing any lives.

On the eighth, American forces had stormed ashore at Casablanca after pounding the French Vichy batteries with their naval guns. General Patton had led his troops ashore under withering machine-gun and sniper fire, his green soldiers so rattled that one shot down a British reconnaissance plane while others frantically dug foxholes to protect themselves from mortar fire and artillery rounds. The Wildcats that took off from the aircraft carriers that Garbo had "covered" strafed the Vichy battalions. Within seventy-two hours, Casablanca was in Patton's hands. The Allies had slipped a stiletto against the underbelly of Hitler's empire.

When Federico finally opened Garbo's letter of November 1, here in his hands were all the details of a major Allied invasion, written *a week* before it happened. The Germans were crestfallen, but hugely impressed: "Your last reports are all magnificent," Federico wrote.

Plan Solo was an unqualified success. When Hitler learned about the invasion, he marveled, "We didn't even dream of it." It was a high accolade. For the first time, deception had cloaked the plans of a major strategic victory. As German analysts dug through the sheaves of telegrams, coded letters, wireless traffic and reconnaissance reports and rumors that had preceded the invasion, looking for the clues they'd missed, a single fact stood out: Agent Garbo had seen it coming.

As the American battalions left Casablanca and headed toward Tunisia, chasing the German genius Rommel and his Afrika Korps, a small item appeared in the death notices of the *Liverpool Daily Post:* "GERBERS. November 19 at Bootle, after a long illness, aged 52, WILLIAM MAXIMILIAN. Private funeral. (No flowers, please.)"

Now that the convoys had long departed from Liverpool, the imaginary Gerbers had been allowed to die in peace. MI5 had placed the notice so that Garbo would have proof to send Madrid. Not only that, he reported to the Abwehr that he'd consoled the grieving widow ("the poor girl is very broken up"), slipped her an envelope filled with cash, told her what William had really been up to and then managed to recruit the widow to spy on the Liverpool docks in place of her dead husband.

With Pujol quickly rising to the top of the double agent game, Araceli was getting ready to join him. They were still very much in love. From Lisbon, Araceli wrote her husband: "Think about me a lot but don't burst your brains arranging for me to go over there. You know how I love you and the joy of finding myself at your side makes me think of everything as very easy; you know that I obey you blindly and now more than ever, and will do everything that you have told me in all your letters."

Araceli finally arrived in England in the late spring of 1942, carrying her ten-month-old son, Juan, in her arms. She was seven months pregnant with her second son, Jorge. The London she saw and heard through the window of the British secret service car was no better than bombed-out Madrid — all blackened ruins, food queues, austerity drive posters and air raid sirens instead of the glittering capital she'd expected. "She was alone with a new baby, away from home in a city she didn't know," says Araceli's daughter, Maria, "and her husband was working fourteen-hour days with Tommy Harris." Soon Araceli's nanny quit and she found it hard to replace her; Araceli struggled to make meals out of the strange British ingredients available in the shops. When Pujol did come home, exhausted from living the lives of twenty-seven other people, he didn't want to socialize with the Spaniards in London, afraid that they'd betray him or sell him out. Night after night, the intensely sociable Araceli, who craved both high and low forms of intellectual stimulation, was forced to stay at home. In many ways, Araceli had taken an even bigger leap than her husband and gotten by far the worst end of the deal. Juan was out saving the world with his new partner Tommy Harris, living his boyhood dreams with real battleships and real dictators. She, once his inspiration and his equal, was a housewife trapped behind blackout curtains, listening to the Glenn Miller Orchestra play "Moonlight Cocktail" on the wireless while bombs smashed into nearby streets.

The young woman who'd wanted adventure and love, "to talk, to reason, to discuss," found herself in a place more confining than the tiny hometown of Lugo she'd escaped years before. She hated London almost from the start, and that was soon to prove a problem for MI5 and Pujol at the moment they could least afford it.

Garbo was one of the XX Committee's rising stars, along with Brutus, a Polish air force officer, and Tricycle, the Serbian playboy Dusko Popov. They had each intoxicated the Germans in their own way. But J. C. Masterman, head of the XX Committee, saw that the field of spies was becoming overly crowded. As the Allied generals and political leaders began to talk about D-Day, he needed to depend on a few well-trusted agents whose stock was high in Berlin and not muddle the message with cut-rate operatives who would only detract from the main players. He suggested that the XX Committee "'liquidate' some of our agents, both for greater efficiency and for plausibility." An "execution subcommittee" was assembled, and agents began to be killed off in both gruesome and ordinary ways. No one was actually executed, of course, only their noms de guerre. The way was cleared for Garbo and a handful of others to lead the D-Day deception.

Garbo soon won another badge of honor, this time from the Abwehr, a privilege reserved for their most important agents: permission to use a wireless radio. Harris obtained an 80-watt German-built set that had been seized from an Abwehr spy en route to South

America. Madrid sent the cipher plan and codes: call signs for every day of the week, alternate frequencies in case the primary one didn't work, a cipher table and code groups. Harris found an MI5 staff member named Charles Haines who'd taught himself Morse code. Haines installed the radio at the Crespigny Road safe house where Pujol was living. Garbo sent Madrid the location of the set, in case one of its direction-finding radio teams picked it up. On March 7, Haines tapped out the call code for the first time. By August 1942, all reports were being sent by radio, with up to twenty messages flashing out every day in sessions sometimes lasting a full two hours. Problems did crop up — monitoring stations as far away as Gibraltar picked up the suspicious traffic and reported it to British authorities — but soon Garbo had a direct link to the Abwehr in Madrid.

Garbo and the operator did all the enciphering and deciphering of the messages themselves. Garbo would first translate the message into Spanish. "The convoy left Dover with three destroyers and two cruisers" became *"El convoy partió del Dover con tres destructores y dos cruceros."* Then he would chop up the Spanish message into groups of five consecutive letters: "ELCON VOYPA RTIOD . . ." He would then consult the cipher table supplied by the Germans. For each letter, the table gave a substitute. "E" became "K," and "ELCON" became "KCYDM." Haines would then put on the headset with its thin steel band, adjust the black enamel earpieces, flip the power switch and wait for the tubes to warm up behind the vented black steel of the casing. Once the tubes were glowing and the machine was ready, he would send Garbo's call code. Soon Haines would hear a distant tapping in the ether, the Abwehr responding from their radio station just outside the Madrid embassy. Haines would send "KCYDM" and the rest of the message would follow.

The German operator, listening intently on the other end, would jot down the coded letters and, referring to the same table that Pujol had used to create the cipher, reverse the process. The result would be a piece of paper with the original message in Spanish being handed to Kühlenthal, the real leader of the Madrid Abwehr. From there the report would enter the bloodstream of one of the most remarkable, contradictory and odd spy services in the history of intelligence gathering.

10

The Blacks and the Santa Clauses

A T THE BEGINNING of World War II, the two main spy agencies in Germany — the Sicherheitsdienst, or SD, and the Abwehr — formed the biggest and one of the best-financed spy networks in the world. They had thousands upon thousands of agents spread out from Aden to New York to Zanzibar, often working under the auspices of legitimate companies like I. G. Farben, the maker of Bayer aspirin, and Lufthansa, the national airline. Their spies lurked as far away as the unmapped Goiás region of central Brazil; two of its agents froze in the upper reaches of the Khyber Pass in Afghanistan, on assignment to connect with the Fakir of Ipi, a Pashtun revolutionary and sworn enemy of the British empire. They hired deaf-mutes to read the lips of suspects in a popular Berlin restaurant and operated a dozen spy schools, the best of which, in Hamburg (which was responsible for overseas operations), soon became one of the finest in the world, so rigorous that in the entire course of the war it graduated only two hundred agents. A typical exercise in an Abwehr school might feature a major stalking through thickly forested terrain while his students followed:

"What is that?" he would ask.

"A sheep."

"What?"

"A white sheep."

"No. You have to be more exact in your reports. What you must say is that at 1643 hours on 28 September 1944 on the right side of the road from Vienna to Breitenbrunn you saw a sheep that was white on the side that faced you."

The technical departments were, as might be expected of the Germans, first class. The Abwehr (known as the Santa Clauses, because of the gray-haired men who ran it) employed twenty master engravers and artists who reproduced the intricate ornamental backgrounds on passports. Its rival agency, the SD (known as the Blacks, because of their uniforms), kept a small team of men busy working over boiling vats, producing special batches of paper in the small hamlet of Spechthausen, northeast of Berlin. When a foreigner turned in an expired passport anywhere in the Third Reich, it was secretly passed from hand to hand until it reached Berlin, where every stamp and bit of typography was studied and copied. The slightest mistake could mean the difference between life and death. For example, the staples in a typical Russian passport of the 1940s were prone to rust, leaving red marks on the paper. But a passport carried by one unlucky Abwehr agent showed no rust. The German technicians had failed to notice this detail and had stapled the passport with nonrusting chromium-plated wire. Another agent was found in a Soviet military uniform that was an exact duplicate of a real one — except the Abwehr's tailor had sewn the shoulder tabs onto the sleeve, while their Russian counterparts always left them loose. Their fates are unrecorded, but were most likely grim.

Wilhelm Canaris, the head of the Abwehr, was a deeply intelligent strategist, a punishingly hard worker (partly because his home life was so miserable) who hated the sight of military epaulets and crisp SS uniforms. He was "very brilliant and lively, and as talkative as an old lady," an animal lover who doted on his pet dogs, going so far as to rent them their own hotel room when he traveled so they could sleep in a bed and not on the floor. His rival and uneasy friend Walter Schellenberg, head of the SD, thought Canaris an anachronism in the Reich, a kind of ghost from imperial days: "In many ways, he was what might be called a mystic."

Schellenberg was the more ruthless of the two. His staff car was equipped with a short-wave transmitter with a range of twenty-five miles, which kept him in constant touch with his staff officers. In his richly decorated office there was a battery of telephones that could link him to the Reich Chancellery in seconds, high-tech microphones concealed in the furniture and walls, electrified iron bars across the windows to prevent escape and an advanced alarm system that would bring squads of black-uniformed SS men running if anyone attempted to enter Schellenberg's office without permission. Worked into the beautiful mahogany desk itself were two submachine guns that Schellenberg could activate with the press of a button; they were engineered so that if a visitor approached his desk, the gun barrels would swivel and follow them.

Canaris and Schellenberg were both modern men. But in trying to supply the German leadership with objective information and rational analysis, they were confronted with a culture of medieval mysticism, a strange Aryan voodoo that permeated the upper reaches of the Third Reich. Heinrich Himmler, Reichsführer of the SS, was a serious student of the black arts. Himmler believed himself to be the reincarnation of the eleventh-century monarch King Heinrich I and wished, when the Nazi victory was complete, to replace modern conveniences such as airplanes and trains with a hardy breed of "steppes horses," which would supply the Reich with all its transportation needs. The Reichsführer was constantly surrounded by spiritualists, conjurers, seers and fakirs. To divine the whereabouts of Mussolini during his imprisonment by Italy's Badoglio government, Himmler put up forty of the most accomplished magicians in a richly appointed villa, fed them the finest food and wine available in the Reich's storerooms and informed them that the first seer to come up with Il Duce's exact location would be given 100,000 marks. (The conjurers, most of whom were plucked off the streets and dressed in rags, agreed among themselves to take their time arriving at an answer, so as to enjoy the Reichsführer's hospitality to the fullest.) There was a running joke among the SD's top ranks that, in order to find out when the Allied invasion of Europe was coming, Hitler was going to summon a coven of witches and magicians. The joke was not allowed to circulate beyond SD headquarters.

To assemble their sprawling organizations, the SD and the Abwehr began looking for men as World War II approached, just as the British had. First the new recruits had to pass a loyalty test. In one of his speeches, Himmler declared that an intelligence agency "must found itself upon a race, upon a people of the same blood." This was Aryan boilerplate, but later in the speech he dictated not only who should staff the service but what its work product should reflect. Not objectivity or imaginative brilliance, but "unconditional obedience . . . certainty of German strength and the final German victory."

If London culled its operatives from the universities and their arts and sciences faculties — and more generally from among the intelligentsia and cultural elite — the Germans took a very different tack. They recruited staunch bureaucrats, military careerists and scions of old Prussian families. Far from pursuing eccentricity and daring, as the British had done out of necessity, the Abwehr and the SD chose men who were loyal and dependable. They didn't want communes or coffee klatches for arts faculty; they wanted a combination of an export-import firm and a military division. Efficiency trumped eccentricity.

Germany's attitudes toward spies were even more toxic than they were in England in the early part of the war. The SD manual distributed to intelligence officers admitted this up front: "The Germans consider espionage to be work for criminals and adventurers." Military officers from ancient Prussian families who'd served the country for centuries regarded intelligence officers not only as beneath them but also as interlopers out for their jobs. The German army "ostracized officers who dealt with spies on the ground that association with these deceivers had tainted them."

Hitler hated secret agents. He claimed he would never shake the hand of one. When two spies were killed in a failed mission, Hitler was grieved that they had been good German boys. "In the future, you will use Jews or criminals for missions of that kind." Part of the German disdain for espionage came from Hitler's own sense of his infallibility. Time and again, his generals and spy chiefs had advised him against offensive action and been proven wrong. When the Führer was considering an attack on Holland and France, General Franz Halder, the head of the army's General Staff, wrote in his diary: "No one among the staff thinks that the offensive has the slightest chance of success." They were, of course, proven wrong. Before the attack on Czechoslovakia, the Abwehr's Canaris told Hitler that the Czech defenses were formidable and that the panzer divisions would not be able to crack them; Hitler ignored him and won. When the SS was rampaging across Poland, Canaris warned his chief that the British and French were poised at the German border near Saarbrücken with 110 divisions against the Germans' 23, and that the enemy was going to invade. Hitler brushed him aside, and the invasion never came. It was the Führer who, often alone, again and again saw through the enemy's bluster to its hidden intentions.

Hitler regarded himself as a genius surrounded by bureaucrats who were "dumb as a carp," winsome intellectuals, eggheads and cowards. Either his men exhibited the "sparrow-like brain of mediocrity" or they talked defeat. He steered only by an inner light, and as the war went on he was increasingly shielded from any report that conflicted with what he wished to be true. When the SD's Schellenberg compiled a carefully researched report on America and its awesome capacity for making war, it was returned with this comment: "Everything you've written is pure nonsense. You'd better see a psychiatrist." When he did the same thing a year later — report truthfully on an enemy, the Soviets this time — Hitler blew up, ordering that the analysts quoted in its pages be arrested and charged with defeatism. "He closed his mind against the truth," Schellenberg said, "but thought he could draw important conclusions from . . . random observations."

And yet at the same time Hitler was a voracious consumer of the intelligence reports that reached his desk, and he constantly asked for more and better information. He gave Canaris an unlimited budget and took the reports that reached him seriously — as long as they didn't contradict one of his core beliefs. When his megalomaniacal tendencies were not at play, Hitler used intelligence well.

In the early months of the war, the Abwehr was focused on France, considered to be Germany's most formidable military opponent on the Continent. Canaris poured resources and men into Paris, but London was kept off-limits. Hitler believed that, once he overran the Continent, he could negotiate a peace with Churchill. "I don't want any wretched spies creeping about in England," he told his staff officers, "and jeopardizing my plans."

That all changed in the summer of 1940, when Churchill's obstinacy and the RAF made it clear that England would never surrender. The chief of the German army's Operations Staff, General Alfred Jodl, demanded Canaris get a network up and running in London. "Send them into England as quickly as possible. The landings may take place as early as September 5, but not later than the 15th. We need these wretched people in England well before then." The original aim of the German intelligence effort in Britain was to lay the groundwork for an invasion. When Operation Sea Lion — the German assault on the island fortress — was finally abandoned, its double agents switched their attention to the Allied war effort. And then, particularly, to the coming invasion of France.

It takes years to develop a well-founded and flourishing spy network in an alien country, and Canaris didn't have that kind of time. The delay in inserting agents had left him exposed. This led to a gold rush of agents into England and the countryside that at times became a slapstick adventure in how not to insert a spy. For example, the Belgian Four were sent to England in the late summer of 1940 by minesweeper and dinghy, arriving on the Kentish coast. The original purpose of their mission, to gather information for Operation Sea Lion, was no longer valid, but the spies were sent anyway. Two of them understood English only if spoken very slowly. Another didn't speak it at all. When they landed, one of the spies hooked up an aerial on a bush and sent word: "Arrived safely, document destroyed. English patrol two hundred meters from coast . . . No mines. Few soldiers." He signed it with his real name, Waldberg. Only a few hours into his mission, he sent his second message: "Meier prisoner, English police searching for me, am cornered, situation difficult." The Abwehr had failed to give their agents even basic information about life in England, such as the fact that one should not wander into an English pub and ask for a glass of cider at nine in the morning. When Meier did just that, the pub owner reported him and he was arrested. The other three were soon rounded up. All but one were hanged that winter on the scaffold at Pentonville Prison.

Its high attrition rate made the Abwehr's success stories rare. It was one reason Garbo was such a valuable agent: there were so few others like him. His competition was either dead or working for the Allies.

But there was another reason that Garbo ascended so fast in the German intelligence world. Canaris considered Spain his spiritual home and General Franco his brother and pet political project. The Abwehr chief had been Hitler's liaison with the Spanish fascists, arranging for a military aid package worth 5 billion reichsmarks and assembling plane convoys to ship 14,000 Spanish troops, along with their artillery guns, from Morocco. When it became necessary to choose a station for spying on England, Canaris selected Madrid to head up this all-important mission. Spain became the keyhole into England and the Allied mind.

For this sensitive post Canaris chose Wilhelm Leissner, a naval officer turned publisher who'd moved to Nicaragua after World War I. Canaris brought him back, reenrolled him in the German navy, gave him the rank of commander and packed him off to Madrid as head of the "Excelsior Import and Export Company," dealers in zinc, mercury and cork. The old-fashioned front for the Madrid station reflected its boss. A stolid, old-school navy man who wore high starched collars and funereal suits, "he looked like the man in the old ads selling pomade for moustachios," of which he had one, a fine Teutonic handlebar. A dynamo when it came to paperwork, Leissner lacked the suppleness of imagination required to see into the intricacies of wartime Britain.

That was left to Karl-Erich Kühlenthal, the man who'd "discovered" Pujol and who was grooming him for bigger things. Kühlenthal was the son of a distinguished German officer and diplomat who'd risen to the rank of general and had served as a military attaché in Paris and Madrid. His wealthy family was related to Canaris, who'd shepherded the young man through the intelligence services and, when Kühlenthal was thirty-five, expunged the one thing that could have doomed him in Hitler's Germany. In his MI5 file, the British noted an anomaly: Kühlenthal was "a half-blood Jew." Canaris had him legally declared an Aryan in 1941, but the conversion didn't sit well with Kühlenthal's peers. The Madrid spymaster was aware that any slip-up could mean a demotion or being sent to the Eastern Front. "It is known that [he] is trembling to keep his position so as not to have to return to Germany and serve in a workers' battalion," said an informer. "He is therefore doing his utmost to please his superiors." It was no wonder Kühlenthal had dubbed Juan Pujol's network Arabel; in Latin the name means "prayerful" or "answered prayer."

Kühlenthal was consistently rated the best mind in the enormous Madrid station: MI5 described him as "a dangerous man, one of the most efficient German intelligence chiefs in Spain." But looking through the reverse telescope from London, Tommy Harris believed he'd spotted the man's Achilles' heel. "His characteristic German lack of sense of humor, in such serious circumstances as these, blinded him to the absurdities in the story we were unfolding." That is, Kühlenthal couldn't conceive of someone actually creating a Garbo; he was so extravagant he *had* to be real. Tommy Harris had worked and socialized with people like Garbo; his salon before the war was crawling with weirdoes and misfits. The outrageous was fairly normal in his world. But not in Kühlenthal's. From Harris's point of view, the Germans were culturally and institutionally handicapped when it came to deception, because they'd closed their minds to the irrational.

By late 1942, Garbo had won over Madrid. But that was only the first step. The key decisions, of course, would be made 1,200 miles away in Berlin. And it wasn't just Kühlenthal who was searching for a way into the Allies' mind. Hitler himself was becoming more and more obsessed with what was happening in London. He complained that his intelligence service couldn't even provide him with the names of the opposition in Parliament; he'd been reduced to reading the *Guardian* and *The Times* to find out who Churchill's political adversaries were. "We are separated from England by a ditch thirty-seven kilometers wide," Hitler said, "and we cannot find out what is happening there!"

Nevertheless, he had his own ace in the hole, a slim, cold aristocrat named Colonel Alexis von Roenne. Roenne was the descendant of an old family that had once owned vast tracts of land in Latvia, awarded to them by Frederick the Great for their service in the Prussian wars. Roenne was devoutly Christian, patriotic, often haughty to his peers and subordinates, "impossible to make friends with," a perfectionist with a zeal to save Germany from its enemies. Trained as a banker, when war came Roenne had volunteered for the highly regarded Potsdam Regiment and was wounded on the Eastern Front. After recovering from his injuries, he'd joined military intelligence, where he'd advanced quickly by modernizing the service's information analysis, in part by developing the so-called *Feindbild,* an evaluation of enemy forces pieced together from every available source into a constantly evolving portrait of the Allied armies.

If Kühlenthal was a kind of huckster, Roenne was the real deal, a ruthlessly objective filter of the reams of confidential information that came across his desk. He'd commanded the "big table" during the German invasion of France and had correctly predicted the key episodes of the blitzkrieg. When Hitler was contemplating the attack on Poland, Roenne went against the Abwehr by saying that "the Western allies would protest a German attack [on Poland] but would take no military action." This caught Hitler's eye, as did Roenne's accurate analysis that the French army was vastly overrated and that the Maginot Line wouldn't hold. By 1942, when he assumed the top intelligence job at Foreign Armies West, responsible for all intelligence relating to the battle against the British and the Americans, Roenne had the Führer's full confidence. Roenne wasn't a mystic or a brown-noser; in fact, he considered himself a knight of ancient Prussia. His family had won battles for Frederick the Great while Hitler's ancestors were being used as cannon fodder. He refused to tell Hitler what he wanted to hear.

The colonel was installed in German army headquarters in Zossen, about twenty miles south of Berlin, sheltered in a reinforced A-roofed bunker, protected from Allied bombs by layers of concrete. The Abwehr gathered the intelligence and Zossen analyzed it. It was the brains of the High Command: teams of photo analysts spent their days studying blurry black-and-white pictures shot from five thousand feet, rubbing elbows with exhausted codebreakers and the soldiers who manned the fixed intercept posts, which listened in on telephone and wireless communications. Those intercepts give one indication of the breadth and depth of German surveillance: the agency responsible for wiretapping, the Forschungsamt, had six thousand employees, many of whom spent hours crouched over their desks in rented rooms around Germany, monitoring the daily lives of suspicious persons. The staffs of the listening stations would write "Z reports" on brown paper — the official color of the Nazi Party — and forward them to analysts, who received 34,000 domestic and up to 9,000 foreign messages daily over the war years.

Anything relating to the military situation in the West flowed to Roenne: reams of diplomatic cables, secret letters from double agents like Garbo, Allied magazines and newspapers, wireless traffic and purloined documents came in from all across Europe. Roenne's analysts pored over each message in detail, checked the new information against the cards in their enormous files, then suggested revisions to the *Feindbild*. The reviews of the spy reports were sometimes harsh: "worthless," "swindle," "absolutely blooming idiotic," along with the pungent "full of shit." Roenne would evaluate the day's harvest, then write daily reports that were sent to commanders in the western theater, with another copy going to Jodl, the army's chief of operations and its liaison with Hitler. If Jodl thought a message was important, it would be placed on the Führer's desk.

When Roenne had first become head of intelligence for Foreign Armies West, he'd naturally gone to Canaris to ask about German spies in England. The answer surprised him. "The fact," Canaris boasted, "that we have any V-men at all in Britain, and have had several for as long as three to four years, is undoubtedly the most remarkable feat in the history of espionage . . . We have succeeded in sustaining them so well that we are receiving even at this stage . . . an average of thirty to forty reports each day from inside England, many of them radioed directly on the clandestine wireless sets we have operational in defiance of the most intricate and elaborate electronic countermeasures." He was describing Garbo's network, and only a few others, all run by double agents. They were the eyes and ears of the German High Command inside the enemy fortress. And they were all controlled by England.

In one of the drawers of his desk at Zossen, Roenne kept a small map of Europe. Periodically he'd take it out, his clear gray eyes slowly tracing the rocky coastlines and mountain routes of the Continent, imagining the Allied divisions, the convoys, the supply trucks moving toward Norway or departing from Southampton. Just as Garbo and Harris were probing the mind of the German High Command, Roenne was trying to picture where the Brits were placing their armies and how many American soldiers were dawdling at that moment in Piccadilly Circus.

And, of course, what it all meant.

11

The Rehearsal

T HE DECEPTION GAME was based on a series of arcane techniques, many dating back to the time of Sun Tzu or before, which had been only slightly refined for modern warfare. The fact that the basic methods were well known to the operatives on both sides didn't stop them from being used and reused constantly; even a chess grandmaster who knows the Sicilian Defense by heart will still fall victim to a particularly ingenious or convincing variation. There was the classic bluff, telling a false but highly detailed story to cover a real operation; the bluff was the common coin of every nation's espionage arsenal and the basis for most of Garbo's schemes. Then there was the rarely tried, forbiddingly intricate and gaspingly dangerous double bluff ("We should never resort to it unless in absolute despair," the British spymaster Sir Ronald Wingate gravely opined), in which an agency put forth the details of the real operation and hoped the enemy would come to believe, partly because of the scheme's sudden appearance in their hands, that this was in fact a false cover story, planted by their opponents, which would convince the enemy to look elsewhere for the attack. If the double bluff failed, of course, the entire game plan had been exposed to the enemy and disaster awaited. There was the fine art of "coat-trailing," offering up one's own agent to the opposition in hopes he'd be recruited, thereby planting a mole deep in the enemy's ranks. And the "breakoff," also known as the "get-out," was the name given to one of the most important maneuvers in all double-cross operations: explaining to the enemy why the fake story didn't turn out to be accurate, in such a way that he doesn't lose faith in your agent — or in his own spy-runners.

Pujol had intuited many aspects of the game even before coming to England, simply by using his own highly developed sense of guile. But now he had to hone other skills, and scale them up to global range, using the worldwide assets of the British empire as his tools. One of the first things he was asked to master was how to make something — in this case a 23,000-ton aircraft carrier — disappear.

In December 1942, a request came in from the XX Committee to "cover" the repositioning of the HMS *Illustrious*, the last flattop patrolling the Indian Ocean. The enormous ship was being routed to more urgent war duties, but the Admiralty wanted the Germans to believe it was still lurking near the Horn of Africa. Garbo was given the job. He dreamt up a report from Agent No. 3 in Glasgow, who "spotted" three aircraft carriers in the waters of the river Clyde in Scotland, one of which was the brand-new HMS *Indefatigable*. (Actually, that ship had been launched just a week earlier, on December 8, but would need a year of fitting out before it would enter active service.) Agent No. 3 made friends with an officer of the crew who let it slip that the carrier was soon to sail for the Indian Ocean, "with specially equipped aircraft for tropical flights." After a suitable delay, which would have given the *Indefatigable* time to sail to the Horn of Africa, the radiomen of the *Illustrious*, still off the African coast, began to send messages identifying their ship as the *Indefatigable*. The Abwehr's agents picked up the traffic and reported it to Berlin. The *Illustrious* then went quiet and sailed north for its new assignment.

The switch had been made. Intercepts from isos found that the Germans and Japanese now believed that there were *two* aircraft carriers in the Indian Ocean, the *Indefatigable* and the *Illustrious*, when in fact there were none. Garbo had made a carrier disappear and another — which hadn't been commissioned yet — appear.

Soon after, Garbo faced a sudden crisis. In a message marked "Urgent," Federico ordered him to give the Germans the departure times of trains out of London to the south and southwest of the country. Ten lines were specified: Canterbury–Dover, Dover–Deal and Deal–Sandwich among them. Federico indicated that there were more trains that the Abwehr had its eyes on; further requests would follow in the near future. The request lit up the switchboards in the intelligence and defense ministries. Why would the Germans want to know when the Dover train left Canterbury, down to the exact minute? It was a puzzle, and Harris, Pujol and MI5 had to tease it out before they could reply. What was the significance of the south of England? Was something being planned — acts of sabotage, a bridge blown up for a spectacular mass murder?

Finally, an officer in the Ministry of Home Security figured it out. He did this by thinking not about what the Germans were planning to do, but what the Allied Bomber Command was already doing, night after night in the air above the occupied countries. Since late 1942, the RAF had initiated a policy of "train-busting," a specialized form of attack by "intruders," often single-engine Hawker Typhoons, whose expert pilots prowled the skies looking for steam locomotives streaking through the lowlands of Belgium and France. When they found one, the pilot would swoop down and open up on the train — loaded with armaments, food and other vital supplies — with explosive shells. "I saw my cannon shells hitting the locomotive," one aviator said after such an attack. "There was a big flash and clouds of steam." The fighters sometimes flew so low that debris from the exploding trains blew skyward and ripped holes in their wings; others, veering away from German antiaircraft fire, cut through telegraph lines and returned to base with the wires embedded in their radiators. The operation played havoc with enemy supply lines: the RAF was blowing up engines pulling twenty or thirty cars of badly needed goods. The RAF pilots — especially from the hard-flying 609 Squadron — became heroes in the British press.

What this lone analyst figured out was that the Germans wanted revenge for the train-busting, and they weren't going to limit themselves to supply routes. Federico's request could only mean that the Luftwaffe was going to go after passenger trains, and the fliers needed the exact departure times to coordinate the strafing runs. Guy Liddell, head of MI5's counterespionage division, wrote in his diary: "The Germans' tactics are apparently to shoot up the engine and then the passengers if they are foolish enough to get out."

Garbo was caught. He could easily have walked into a railway station and picked up the timetables, but doing so would mean that innocent civilians would die. It was strictly against MI5 policy to provide the Germans with any information that could lead to direct military action, especially against civilians. But how could he say no and keep the Abwehr's confidence?

After delaying for weeks, Garbo finally told Kühlenthal that the timetables were unavailable, so he was sending the times for January (which would already be slightly outdated), warning that "my experience when traveling has been that the trains nowadays do not go with the same regularity as before." He had provided schedules recent enough to satisfy the Abwehr, but imprecise enough to save English lives. The Luftwaffe was never able to mount the revenge attacks.

All the while Garbo kept the Abwehr on edge with his demands and outbursts. When reporting bomb damage from Luftwaffe attacks, he fumed: "It displeases me very much to have to do this work as my blood boils when I have to hear nonsense about our attacks. I have done it this time as you asked me to give you the truth about the morale of the people and to find out something about the effects of our bombing." He was providing reams of information — locations of air bases and ships — but as far as he could tell, the Germans weren't acting on it. Why weren't Luftwaffe bombers attacking the ports and blowing the destroyers out of the water? "I have been able to estimate that possibly from the highest spheres my mission has not been appreciated as it should be, and though the matter has earned your spirited enthusiasm it has become apparent to me that in Berlin they have shown themselves skeptical with regard to my work." Like a petulant lover, he seemed to want Berlin to love him as much as Madrid did; MI5 knew that the real power lay in the German capital. Kühlenthal wrote back hurriedly, blaming bureaucracy: "We beg you not to be impatient if the objectives indicated have not been bombed because this is outside our control here."

Garbo's influence was growing. His dispatches began showing up in messages out of German outposts in Stockholm and Sofia and as far away as Istanbul and Tokyo. The Abwehr shipped him an improved type of secret ink in cotton-wool balls, disguised as medicine. German and British scientists were engaged in a constantly evolving chemical war: invisible ink vs. reagent. As the British concocted new and more exotic compounds (from methylene blue to "tetra base") to uncover the secret writing in letters, the Germans responded by in-

Juan Pujol as an infant, with his mother, brother Joaquín and sister Bonaventura.

The young dreamer, dressed up in a harlequin costume for Carnival.

Pujol (upper right) as a young man with family and friends.

Pujol (center) and older brother Joaquín (left) in a light moment.

Posing with a friend (left) and Joaquín.

The ambitious, alluring and volatile Araceli.

A poised and confident Pujol before the
desperate years of the Spanish Civil War.

GARBO

Date 31.10.44.   TRANSLATION.

POLITICAL QUESTIONNAIRE.

a.   What is the opinion in high political circles with regard
     to the Russian advances in the Balkans, in the Baltic
     countries and in Finland?   What do they feel about the
     Communist movements in Italy and France?

b.   Are there any indications that the Soviet Union are trying
     to form an alliance with Japan?

c.   Is there within high political circles or in independent
     political circles, or amongst the American public itself
     an anti-Communist atmosphere?   Who are the most open
     exponents?

d.   To what extent have differences arisen between the U.S.A.
     and Great Britain with regard to their mutual relations
     with Russia?

e.   We are interested to have details with regard to points
     dealt with at the Quebec Conference and the results of
     this Conference.

f.   Is a meeting between Roosevelt and Stalin expected after
     the last conference which took place in Moscow?   Or can
     it be assumed that before the end of the year there will
     be a meeting between Roosevelt, Stalin and Churchill?

g.   What is known about the aims of the United States with
     regard to the French Colonies?

Translation of an Abwehr political questionnaire
sent to Garbo.

Pujol in his uniform as a
lieutenant in the Spanish
Republican army.

The inimitable Colonel David
Strangeways during the war.

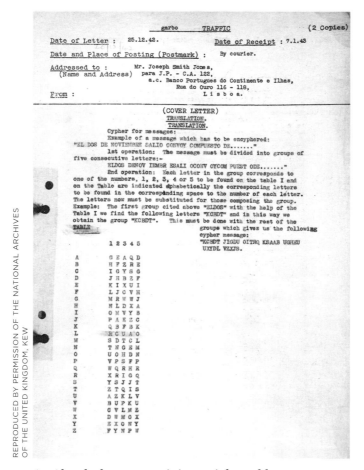

An Abwehr letter containing a cipher table.

Tommy Harris in his days as an aspiring artist and art dealer.

A self-portrait of the young Tommy Harris in Spanish costume.

Garbo's famous June 9, 1944, message that declared the June 6 landings a feint. His German code name — "Alaric" — is clearly visible at the upper left.

Pujol after the war, when he was living in Venezuela.

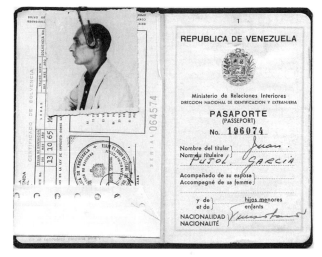

The former spy's Venezuelan passport.

Pujol with his wife, Carmen Cilia, daughter Maria Elena and son Carlos, in Venezuela.

D-Day veterans surround Pujol on the fortieth anniversary of the landings, 1984.

The man known as Garbo (left) viewing a monument to the Normandy dead.

venting more subtle formulas, including one whose secret ingredient was hemoglobin. For that formula, the spy had to cut his finger and use drops of his own blood to make the ink.

Along with the ink came a higher-grade cipher in a series of seventeen miniaturized photographs. This was a closely guarded asset, and Kühlenthal asked Garbo to "prevent it at any time from ever falling into the hands of the enemy." Harris considered this a breakthrough, "the most important development in the case so far." The Germans had recently switched to a new ciphering technique, which the geniuses at Bletchley Park had been unable to break even after weeks of effort. The photographs sent to Garbo allowed the British to penetrate the new code "within a very short time." Later, there would be still more advanced ciphers. "Denys Page tells me that the information supplied to him about Garbo's code was of the utmost value," Guy Liddell wrote. "Before he received this code he was working entirely in the air and says that it is quite doubtful whether he would have ever got on to the right lines."

It was all excellent buildup material for the spy. But the topper that spring was the cake job.

In March 1943, Garbo excitedly told the Germans that his Agent No. 3 had gotten a glimpse of an RAF "aircraft recognition handbook," filled with drawings and technical data on the current air fleet. The book belonged to a noncommissioned officer in the air service who was down on his luck. When Agent No. 3 casually mentioned that he'd like to have the book as a souvenir, the NCO said he might let it go for the right price. No. 3 asked Garbo how much he could offer, and Garbo asked the Germans. They came back with the rather exorbitant price of 100 pounds, about $5,200 in today's dollars. No. 3 drove a hard bargain and got it for three pounds.

But how to get the bulky thing to Madrid?

Other messages had been inserted into the bindings of books and bunches of fruit, and one "left [the] last days of January with letters camouflaged in the stomach of a dog." (The dog was a toy in the shape of a Scottish terrier.) For the RAF handbook, Garbo hit on an idea: he would wrap the book in grease-proof paper and bake it inside a cake. He got the widow of his deceased "agent" William Gerbers to make the concoction and then wrote in chocolate icing: "With Good

Wishes to Odette" — the two *t*'s in Odette were the prearranged signal that the message was genuine. The cake was sent by the diplomatic bag to Lisbon and delivered by a secret service officer. In invisible ink, Garbo wrote on the cover letter: "Inside the cake you will find the book on aviation which was obtained by 3 . . . I had to use several rationed products which I have given in a good cause . . . If it does not arrive too hard it can be eaten . . . Good appetite!"

On July 1 at 2121 hours, Garbo read an incoming message: "We have received the cake in perfect condition." Kühlenthal was delighted with the caper. The book was authentic — though MI5 had removed all the up-to-date information on the planes, so it was practically useless. A year later, an MI5 informer reported that when Canaris, the head of the Abwehr, was touring Spain, Kühlenthal was "the star turn at this meeting . . . He told a great number of Garbo stories, among them the story of the cake." The Madrid spymaster ended it by saying that "he had an agent in England who was also a cook, who made cakes which were unpleasant in taste in spite of the fact that their contents were excellent."

Each double agent had his specialty. Agent Tricycle, the dashing Dusko Popov, was exceptional at what might be called physical espionage. He was dispatched to foreign capitals to meet Abwehr agents face-to-face, and proved very good in the moment, when one had to outthink a Gestapo officer who might kill you if your next answer was wrong. Garbo, on the other hand, was known for his imagination and daring. "I would never have had the nerve," said the intelligence officer Christopher Harmer, "to allow any of my agents to be as audacious as he was." The cake job was a small example of the theatrical flair that would soon come into play in a major crisis.

MI5 would later be given a quantifiable estimate of just how valuable Garbo's services were to the Third Reich. An internal message from Madrid to Berlin contained this startling line: "[The] activity of Arabel" — i.e., Garbo — "in England constantly at the price of his life was just as important as the service at the front of the Spanish members of the Blue Division." It might have been a bit of hyperbole on Kühlenthal's part — puffing up his best boy — but the Spanish Blue Division had sent 45,000 volunteers to the Eastern Front over the course of its service. They'd fought bravely at Novgorod and frozen to death while fighting at Leningrad. By the war's end, 4,594 members of the division had been killed and 8,700 wounded.

So Madrid had set Garbo's worth at 45,000 soldiers. But what is a relationship if it isn't tested every so often? In June 1943, Garbo decided to flex his muscles in an incident that made headlines around the world.

The vital air link between Portugal and London had remained open that summer of 1943. The British Overseas Airways Corporation flew planes from Poole Harbor in Dorset to Cabo Ruivo, near Lisbon, and a second route from Sintra in Portugal to Whitchurch in Somerset. The London-bound planes left Portugal daily, the eyes of ten thousand refugees looking longingly on their silver fuselages as they headed north. The two routes were crucial, giving British intelligence a link with the spy capital and maintaining the leading air connection with Europe (there was a nighttime flight from Scotland to Stockholm, but the route was more dangerous and the schedule more erratic). Luftwaffe fighters ruled the airspace over Europe, and sometimes attacked the aircraft; a burst of machine-gun fire from a Messerschmitt 110 once left a bullet hole in the hat of a Swiss diplomatic courier. But Flight 777A kept flying, often with a cabin populated by spies and top-secret envoys.

Until June 1, 1943. A camouflaged DC-3 named the Ibis was flying a roundabout route to London over the Bay of Biscay, hoping to avoid the Luftwaffe. Suddenly a *schwarm* of eight Junkers Ju 88s from the Kampfgruppe 88 fighter wing, based in Brittany, appeared in the blue sky and began making strafing runs, the bullets thudding into the DC-3's fuselage. The Ibis desperately tried to evade the German fighters as they blasted away with their wing-mounted guns, but on the third pass, the passenger plane began to smoke, then crashed into the bay in a ball of flame, killing everyone aboard.

The incident made headlines because of who was on board: Leslie Howard, the British star of Broadway and Hollywood, who'd played Ashley Wilkes in *Gone With the Wind*, reportedly bedded Tallulah Bankhead and Myrna Loy and moonlighted for MI6. LESLIE HOWARD IS LOST IN AIR LINER SHOT DOWN BY NAZIS, London's *Daily Mirror* screamed. Before boarding the flight, Howard had been trav-

eling across Portugal and Spain giving lectures on the modern cinema while secretly meeting with anti-Nazi activists and firming up
support for the Allies.

Garbo couldn't let the incident pass. One of his imaginary subagents could have been on that plane, and his KLM pilot-courier
could have been flying it. He sent a blistering message to Federico
demanding to know what the Luftwaffe was thinking. The Portugal–
London planes were never attacked again.

Pujol was growing confident enough in his abilities to outsmart the
Abwehr that he and Harris began to amuse themselves by dreaming
up cryptic messages to drive their opponents batty. After the "death"
of William Gerbers, Garbo claimed to have discovered a cache of
notes made by the operative just before his illness struck. Garbo examined the scribblings and "decided that they were certainly anno-
tations made during the course of the agent's espionage travels." But
the code was unknown to him; perhaps the Germans would have better luck?

Pujol and Harris must have cackled with delight as they batted
ideas back and forth in their little office in Jermyn Street, one-up-
ping each other with fiendishly tantalizing cryptograms. First they
decided to compose the "notes" in German, since Gerbers had come
from a Swiss-German family. Some of the messages they cut off just
as they were getting interesting: "*Grosse olbek zwischen Birkenhead
e —,*" which meant that large *olbeks* had been spotted near Birkenhead — but no German-English dictionary lists the word *olbek*. They
hinted in another that the British battleship *King George V* was being
fitted with torpedo tubes when in fact it had none. Harking back to
his Lisbon days, Pujol drew up detailed diagrams of airfields, sketching in everything from the exact position of unidentified aircraft to
the location of enormous hangars. But he failed to say where these
airfields actually were.

"It is true to say," Harris admitted, "that the only virtue in passing
on these notes was that they were a satisfactory leg-pull." Pujol had
infected the normally serious Harris with the joy of the flimflam.

Despite the fun and games, Garbo's first serious attempt to create a
D-Day deception ended in abrupt failure. Plan Bodega was a "most

complex and elaborate" scheme to create an imaginary arms depot in the very real Chislehurst Caves, in the southeastern suburbs of Greater London, and to lure Federico to England to inspect them. In the spring of 1943, Garbo put forth the story that his Agent No. 4, a "Gibraltarian waiter," had gone to London looking for work in one of the posh hotels frequented by diplomats and tycoons. There it was hoped he'd be able to eavesdrop on after-dinner conversations between gentlemen enjoying their Port and forward the news on to Berlin. But the Ministry of Labor had instead sent No. 4 to work in a quarry, in the belief that "all Gibraltarians should have a natural aptitude for tunneling" (because of the many sieges of the island fortress throughout history, which required the natives to dig passageways for supplies and arms). The waiter grudgingly "accepted" the excavation job, thinking he might be able to discover some unknown underground depots. But what he found surpassed his wildest hopes.

Pujol and Harris were deep into spy-fiction territory as they told Federico that No. 4 had been marched down to the London Underground and put to work digging extensions of its tunnels. What the operative found out was this: the British were connecting their subway lines to the enormous Chislehurst Caves, where arms had been stored during World War I. "Immense quantities of small arms munitions" were being shipped by train from armaments factories in the Midlands, switched to secret small-gauge tracks and forwarded on under the feet of unsuspecting London pedestrians to the caves (which were actually empty of all armaments and served as public air raid shelters). This was all going on away from the eyes of the Luftwaffe, with remote-control electric trains that required no personnel, running silently beneath the streets of Soho. After months of digging and investigating, Agent No. 4 "reported" that he had stumbled on nothing less than the network that would supply the D-Day regiments. By finding out when the work was expected to be completed, he could give the Nazis the date of the invasion. And by detecting where the tunnels led, he could tell them where the operation would be launched. From that, the Germans could deduce the target.

Those were the questions that troubled Hitler in his sleep, that he would have paid millions for. And Garbo was offering the answers on a platter.

Garbo himself offered to take Federico through the tunnels. MI5 operatives started searching for an arms depot where Federico, after being led into a tunnel and bamboozled into thinking he was walking through the London Underground, would have his blindfold removed. "He would . . . have been allowed to return to Spain from where he would undoubtedly have proceeded to Berlin to report on his extraordinary adventure, full of praise for Garbo's astuteness and ability, and conscious of the importance of the underground depots."

The codebreakers at Bletchley Park began picking up traffic on Garbo. Madrid was forwarding the entire texts of his messages about the Chislehurst Caves on to Berlin. Hopes rose.

Then Garbo made a mistake. In a twelve-page letter sent by courier, he laid out a plan — supported by blueprints that No. 4 had managed to smuggle out — to dynamite the tunnels leading to the caves. "It was explained that by blowing up one of the trains whilst in the main tunnel by means of a time bomb the tunnel itself would collapse and thus the stores would be entombed at the vital moment when they would be required."

Harris and Pujol waited. They knew the plan would be catnip for Hitler: if the Germans could blow up the tunnels, D-Day would have to be canceled or scaled back. The only thing better than predicting the invasion was stopping it before it ever happened.

Then the answer came back from Madrid: a firm no. It soon became clear why. MI5 had made a crucial miscalculation. Over the past year, Garbo had become such a luminary in Madrid — with both Federico and Kühlenthal hitched to his star — that the suggestion that he turn to bombing tunnels was met with a cold chill. Blowing up the Chislehurst train would mean transferring control of Garbo away from the Madrid station to Division II, the Abwehr agency responsible for "sabotage and special tasks." Kühlenthal and Federico had found, groomed, paid and staked their careers on Garbo. Why would they now give him up to another division? MI5 hadn't counted on the intense rivalries inside the German intelligence agencies, a matter of life and death for men like Kühlenthal.

As more messages arrived from Madrid, it became clear that two other factors were at play: Federico had no desire to come to London. If he was caught en route, he'd likely face long months in a brutal interrogation center, and possibly the hangman's noose. He would let Garbo go it alone. And the Abwehr's specialists at Zossen, south of Berlin, had gone over Garbo's excitable twelve-page letter with a fine-tooth comb and found it wanting. Too much opinion, not enough detail.

A lesson had been learned: the Abwehr in Zossen was not the Abwehr in Madrid. Zossen's agents were tougher, more analytical, less susceptible to Garbo's special brand of intrigue. It's unknown whether the cave proposal ever reached the desk of the gray-eyed Roenne at Foreign Armies West, but his highly trained officers had shot down the scheme. Plan Bodega was pure Garbo, wildly colorful, Jules Verne–like in its scale and depth of detail, its talk of winding tunnels and a secret world underneath London. But it hadn't worked.

Imagination simply wasn't going to be enough.

III

THE FAR SHORE

12

The Dry Run

I N 1942, THANKS TO Operation Torch in North Africa, the heroic Soviet fighting at Stalingrad, and the Allied air raids on German cities and targets in the industrial region of the Ruhr, the Allies were beginning to turn the tide of the war. The next step would be the opening of a second front with an Allied invasion of Europe. It was originally planned for 1943, but at the Casablanca conference in January it became clear that the men and materiel — landing craft, supply ships and especially the thousands upon thousands of American troops that would storm the beaches — wouldn't be available for the epic battle that would be necessary to take back France and begin the long slog to Berlin. Churchill and Roosevelt set the tentative date for invasion back to May 1, 1944.

If it became known that there would be no D-Day in the next twelve months, Hitler would be free to pull troops and panzer divisions out of Western Europe and bring them to bear on the Eastern Front. In order to keep the German divisions away from the crucial battles in Russia, Hitler had to be made to believe an invasion was not only possible in 1943, but imminent. Every great drama requires a dress rehearsal, and in the spring and summer of 1943 Garbo and the entire deception community took their places for D-Day's dry run. It was called Operation Cockade.

The very capable Lieutenant General Frederick "Freddie" Morgan was given command of the operation as chief of staff to the supreme commander, responsible for planning the cross-Channel invasion and all its preliminary missions. The goal of Cockade, his first major assignment, seemed straightforward. Morgan had to lead "an elaborate camouflage and deception scheme extending over the whole summer with a view to pinning the enemy in the West and keeping alive the expectation of large scale cross-Channel operations in 1943." There were three main elements to the plan, each with a code name. Wadham was a phony attack on Brittany, on the French coast; Tindall was a phony attack on the Norwegian coastal city of Stavenger; and the linchpin to the plan, Starkey, was "a major amphibious feint" on the Pas de Calais in France. Starkey had two objectives: to lure the Luftwaffe's planes out of their hangars and destroy them in the air above Calais, and to convince the Germans that the second front was being opened in France. There was also a provision in Cockade's original outline to turn it from a feint into a real invasion if the German defenses looked exceptionally weak. Should the conditions look promising, the Cockade armies could pour across the beaches and head for Paris.

The scale of the initial plan was impressive: 15,000 sorties to be flown by Allied fighters; 6,000 bomber sorties by medium and heavy bombers over the projected landing zones, in both night and day operations; thousands of British and Canadian troops to be massed in the embarkation and assembly areas on the English coast to fool the Germans into believing they were boarding ships for the invasion; two R-class battleships, enormous, 624-foot-long craft originally ordered for World War I and bristling with 13-inch-thick armor and powerful 15-inch guns to pound the concrete-reinforced batteries along the Pas de Calais coast; 12 destroyers to protect the battleships across the English Channel; and squadrons of seaborne commandos, royal marines and paratroopers to drop from the skies in case the invasion turned real. The planners hoped, in the best-case scenario, for fourteen days of intense aerial combat, an "Armageddon-of-the-Air," where the Luftwaffe would be shot to pieces in a series of high-altitude dogfights.

An operation of this size and complexity would depend in no small part on double agents. On one of the Wednesday meetings of the XX Committee, the deception planners asked if Garbo could lead the operation. Cockade would be his chance to prove he was ready for the real D-Day. Could he do it? Tommy Harris agreed with the request and hurried back to Jermyn Street, where he and Pujol furiously began adding new subagents and repositioning existing ones, placing them where they would do the most good. Cockade would be the largest and most ambitious deception operation in the war up to that point, a test of everything Garbo and the entire intelligence community had learned over the previous two years.

As an agent working for the Allies, Pujol remained in a certain amount of physical danger as the war went on. The Germans were known to kidnap suspected double agents and bring the more valuable ones to Berlin for questioning and execution. Hitler's intense dislike of spies was reflected in the *Nacht und Nebel* (Night and Fog) directive, issued by the German High Command at the end of 1942, which stated that two types of prisoners in the concentration camps — resisters and spies — had to wear coats with black letters — N over X over N — scrawled on the back. These unfortunates were to be executed without word of their fate being sent to their families. Even the *way* they were killed was cruel: when spies were brought to the guillotine, they were condemned to have their necks placed on the block facing up, so they could see the blade fall.

In case of a surprise German invasion of the island, MI5 had a plan for the double agents: they would be shipped to northern Wales and hidden from the Gestapo. In charge of the plan was Cyril Mills, one of the men who'd met Pujol when he first arrived in England. Since Mills was the son of Britain's answer to P. T. Barnum, the plan was called Mr. Mills's Circus. Appropriate code words were used for the Circus plan. "I have now completed arrangements for the accommodation of the animals, the young and their keepers, together with accommodation for Mr. Mills himself," wrote one officer to headquarters in April 1941. The plan itself was hardly sentimental. "If there is any danger of the more dangerous cases falling into enemy hands," wrote Tar Robertson, who was in charge of double agents, "they will be liquidated forcibly." The British were themselves not above killing spies: Scruffy, a Belgian ship steward, real name Alphons Timmerman, showed up in Gibraltar and was processed through the Royal Victorian Patriotic School and caught — in part because he'd asked that his wages be sent to his mother. Two things gave him away: a line in an Ultra decrypt that mentioned him and the ingredients for making secret ink that were found in his luggage. Timmerman was sent to the dreaded Camp 020, where the interrogators broke him down and he confessed. Then he was executed. His death notice was published as part of a plot to see how the Abwehr would react.

There were others in far more danger as Cockade ginned up. If deception was a chess game, the pawns and the knights were living, breathing human beings who sometimes had to be sacrificed.

The people of France, the British agents of the Special Operations Executive who'd infiltrated Paris, the French partisans, even the Germans, were all waiting for the invasion in the spring and summer of 1943. The seaside town of Le Portel, near the large port of Boulogne in northern France, was typical of the occupation experience. Le Portel's history goes back to the fourteenth century, and for many generations the lives of its inhabitants have been connected with the sea, but only rarely with war. The town's fishermen went out in their wooden boats to fish for herring and mackerel in the Atlantic, suffering the tragedies inevitable to any working harbor. On October 14, 1881, for example, seventy-one of the town's men launched their boats in the morning and never returned; they'd been swept away by a storm. Sea widows raised their children with the help of their neighbors. The town was close-knit and proud, considering their fishermen a cut above the ones in nearby Boulogne.

On May 25, 1940, the black and red Nazi banner had snapped in the wind of the belfry in Boulogne for the first time when Le Portel came under German occupation. Days later, the town sent fishing boats to Dunkirk, where the British Expeditionary Force was in danger of being wiped out. The fishermen of Le Portel plucked exhausted British soldiers out of the water and onto the chipped decks of their fishing smacks and headed for England; some boats ended up at the bottom of the Channel, their hulls pierced by the bullets of strafing Luftwaffe fighters. Back in Le Portel, the town's clocks were changed to "*l'heure allemande*" (German time), two hours ahead of the normal time, and a curfew kept the fishermen and their wives inside after 7 p.m., on pain of imprisonment. Mines were laid on the beaches the Portelois had enjoyed for generations, bread and meat were rationed, and passes were required to travel anywhere outside the town limits.

When tobacco ran out, the townspeople put dried grass in their cigarette papers and smoked it; clay took the place of soap. The Portelois
were a tough breed. They persevered — and prayed for deliverance
from the occupiers.

The town's citizens knew just how difficult an Allied invasion
would be. Some of them had been shanghaied off the streets and
forced to pour concrete for blockhouses and level the ground for new
roads that the panzers would roll down when D-Day came. They'd
watched at nearby Cap d'Alprech and Fort de Couppes as two enormous gun batteries were built to blast any ships that dared approach
across the Channel. The locals had done what little they could to resist — allowing the wagons filled with concrete to accidentally tip
over every so often, slowing the work and driving their German over-
seers wild with frustration.

In that summer of 1943, as Operation Cockade got under way, Le
Portel and the rest of France were tense, expectant. Rumors of liberation regularly swept through the partisan ranks and unsettled the
populations of the small towns. The planners of Cockade knew this.
They understood how much they were risking in raising the hopes
of the occupied territories: "The effects of these operations will be to
heighten to flash-point expectations of relief before the winter," read
a confidential Allied report on Cockade, "and then at the very onset
of the winter to disappoint" them. But the operation was the first step
in retaking Europe, and it was pointed directly at Le Portel.

By August 2, 1943, Garbo was working full-time on Cockade. His No.
7 "went" to southern Wales on a reconnaissance mission and stumbled on regiments where there shouldn't have been regiments. He
also "heard" rumors of something called Exercise Jantzen. He could
only conclude that something big was being planned against the
coast of Brittany. Agent No. 1, who happened to be in the area on va-
cation, came across the same mysterious regiments training for what
was rumored to be an invasion. To keep the Germans keyed on a possible invasion of Norway, Garbo reported that he'd heard of the Russians advancing toward the fjords and took the extraordinary precau-
tion of traveling himself to Scotland to "confer" with No. 3 and see
for himself what was going on. Pujol stayed in London, of course, but

Garbo gave a detailed report of his trip. When he reached Glasgow, he reported some worrying things: commandos rappelling up and down the local cliffs; new camps rising next to existing airfields, obviously meant to house airborne troops who were rumored to be on their way; a noticeable increase in RAF insignia seen on soldiers in town; new cranes appearing, presumably to prepare for the arrival of sizable shipments of supplies.

Back in London, Garbo said he found No. 1 waiting anxiously for him. All signs pointed to an imminent invasion of southern France. No. 1 alerted the Germans directly by secret-ink letter sent from Winchester: "All the northern part of Southampton Common has been taken over by the military and has been surrounded with barbed wire. There are sentries everywhere. Among the trees I saw tents camouflaged dark green and I think that there are many vehicles for I saw some maneuvering on the road and possibly guns, as I caught a glimpse of one which was being repaired by some soldiers. I heard soldiers being drilled."

When No. 1's letter reached the Germans, the Abwehr was startled to find that it had been "striped" — British censors had swept the letter with five brushes wired together, each dipped in a different developer to unmask different inks. Fortunately, the particular chemicals didn't reveal the invisible writing (intentionally, of course, since it was MI5 who had done the striping). But it was worrying: the British censors in Winchester were clearly on alert, searching for spies near the Cockade ports. Then the British government took the extraordinary step of censoring all letters bound for the Iberian Peninsula, Sweden and Switzerland, places "where the enemy was known to be operating cover addresses." Every letter going to suspect locations was striped. It was an enormous undertaking: in the first week alone, the censors tested 22,000 pieces of mail. But it was the kind of thing the British would implement on the eve of D-Day, so it had to be done for Cockade. The Abwehr warned Garbo by wireless about the crackdown and ordered that no subagent's letters were to be sent from the towns where the invasion forces were gathering.

Garbo recruited a new imaginary agent to bulk up his Cockade reporting: she was an employee of the Ministry of War, the nerve center for any invasion plans. Having established his reputation as a ladies' man early on in Lisbon, he now gleefully "bedded" this plain-faced secretary, too dowdy and timid to attract many male advances. "This makes her all the more accessible to mine," Garbo crowed to Federico. "Already she is delightfully indiscreet." The Germans must have chortled at this stereotype in action: the Mediterranean playboy irresistible to frigid English women. Garbo's new admirer, however, was costing him a fortune: "You must let me know whether I have carte blanche with regard to expenses incurred in her company, for it is natural that whenever I take her out I have to invite her to dinner and drinks and give her presents. I am certain that with this girl I can obtain information . . . She doesn't care two hoots about my being married and rests in the hope that I can get divorced."

As the fake invasion, now scheduled for September 8, drew nearer, Garbo grew worried. "It appears that the situation has become worse," he wrote Federico. Agent 4 (a) scouted the port at Dover and "reported" back: "Large scale preparations for attack are coming to a head. Assault barges concentrating Dover and Folkestone. There is talk of large aerial attack and bombardments over the Channel intended to destroy your defenses and at the same time to facilitate large concentrations of barges and small boats there." That was the bait for the Luftwaffe, intended to lure them out to open skies where the RAF would send their planes burning into the English Channel. Garbo's bulletins continued: "Agent 1b in Portsmouth reported: Many invasion barges have arrived by road. Also in anticipation of heavy raids the AA and National Fire Service had been reinforced, being moved from other places. There are numerous corvettes and destroyers in the harbor." And another: "About 70 assault craft for transporting troops are in Hamble river. Convoys of Canadian troops and armored vehicles are continually arriving. Predominant insignia dark blue square."

Garbo's fake subagents were pointing the Germans toward the port of Southampton in southeastern England. It was the likeliest jumping-off point for the invasion on Pas de Calais. Then they cut off communication: they'd dropped the strongest hints they could, and now it was time to let the Germans draw their own conclusions. All mail from the agents stopped, and Garbo reported that the British were hunting for his men. Finally the authorities expelled all foreigners from the area — in actuality, not just in a Garbo message. Something big was obviously coming.

Operations like Cockade were incredibly complex, equivalent to stage-managing an epic action film, with thousands of soldiers from different armies, stationed from Glasgow to Dakar, and involving the planting of rumors as far away as Rio de Janeiro and Tokyo. Bombers flew raid after raid over Calais to soften up the defenses. Landing craft were built and delivered to the embarkation ports. Fake tank carriers, known as Bigbobs, and dummy troop carriers, known as Wetbobs, were placed in the waters of British ports. Forty thousand tents were erected in assembly areas in Portsmouth, Dover and other port cities, to give the Luftwaffe's reconnaissance planes the impression that soldiers were going to be pouring in shortly. Notices were slapped on the walls of the London Underground telling commuters that visits to southern England were now illegal. Furious hotel owners — it was the height of the summer holiday season — were actually forced to call their guests and cancel all reservations. Guards on key roads stopped anyone carrying cameras or telescopes. Mobile telephone-eavesdropping units prowled the streets of Canterbury and Brighton, listening in to ordinary conversations. If you told your Aunt Nelly about the handsome Canadian sergeant you'd met at the pub the night before, you might hear a knock on your door minutes later.

The public was allowed, intentionally, to see certain things: landing craft pulling into Richborough and Rye harbors, for instance. Fifty new wireless stations were quickly erected, and the amount of traffic the German monitors picked up in southern England spiked (it was coded gibberish, meant to look like doubly encrypted, opaque messages). Gliders disappeared from airfields in the north and reappeared on ones in the south. It was all timed and plotted to sync up with the reports coming from Garbo and the other agents.

Luftwaffe planes went back to Germany or occupied France with their belly cameras full of crisp photos showing crowded ports and new camps bulging with decoy tents. The skies over the Pas de Calais erupted in machine-gun fire as Luftwaffe fighters fought duels with the RAF; British pilots shot down 45 enemy aircraft while losing 23 themselves. In the nine days before the operation kicked off, the RAF flew 6,115 sorties, their fighters and bombers diving through antiaircraft fire, to give the impression that Calais was being readied for the Big One. German and British gunboats dueled in the choppy English Channel, shooting torpedoes and raking each other with machine-gun fire.

The media was roped in with leaks engineered by the black-propaganda agents. Soon the BBC was broadcasting reports like this one: "The liberation of the occupied countries *has* begun . . . We are obviously not going to reveal where the blow will fall." The news traveled all over the world. The French Committee of National Liberation told its members that the first step in their liberation "may come any day now." The United Press crowed that "zero hour for the assault on Western Europe is approaching." Even the Archbishop of Canterbury was drafted into the effort. During one of his sermons, he asked believers to pray for the soldiers and sailors who would soon be fighting and dying to liberate Europe.

The dream of Cockade — if all went well, a real invasion and a quick strike into France — was exactly what Pujol wanted. "I had the power to advance the date of the end of the war," he said. He hoped not only to save Allied lives, but those of German soldiers as well. Pujol was finally at the center of the fight for the ideals he'd believed in since childhood. "There are three kinds of people," he wrote later, "those who make things happen, those who watch things happen, and those who wonder what happened." Pujol now counted himself firmly in the first category.

The stage for Cockade was set. But would the audience come?

13

An Intimate Deception

A S HE CLOCKED MIND-NUMBING hours in the office alongside Tommy Harris, working out the almost infinite complexities of his portion of Operation Cockade, Pujol ran into an unexpected and troubling problem. After two years in England, Araceli was showing signs of mutiny.

Many of the men in MI5 had domestic difficulties. Tommy Harris and his wife, Hilda, had legendary, knock-down drag-out fights after drinking bouts. Guy Liddell's wife, Calypso, had run off to America with his four children; Liddell learned of their destination only when he glanced at a publicity photo heralding the *Queen Mary*'s docking in New York and noticed his offspring waving from the deck. Dudley Clarke of A Force, the undisputed genius of Allied deception, was a lifelong bachelor who'd once fallen in love with a Russian aristocrat named Nina and agreed to take part in a currency-smuggling operation the "distinctive Slav beauty" had devised; it nearly cost him his freedom, and did cost him a large chunk of his money. But even in this less-than-traditional crowd, Araceli was a special case. Pujol knew that, when roused, she could be as volatile as nitroglycerin.

Araceli had had her fill of wartime London, a grimy, difficult place to live. In the early months of her stay, the capital had burned nightly; people in the suburbs would go outside to watch "the huge red glow of the distant flames," as one Londoner remembered, during which the air could reach 1,800 degrees Fahrenheit. Death was a constant presence. One evening, a woman was stepping out her front door to walk her white Scottish terrier when a Luftwaffe raid began. After the all-clear signal, her body was "found lodged on top of a telephone box at the bottom of Dault Road, over a hundred yards away." Corpses were everywhere — pieces floating in the Thames or deep in cellars, found rotting days after the German planes had left. After a bombing raid, the air had a nasty texture: the smell of cordite from the ack-ack guns, phosphorus from the German bombs, burnt timbers, sewage, masonry dust released from buildings hundreds of years old, the charred sap of trees with their bark blown off — "dust, dirty water, the cabbagey smell of gas," recalled one Brit who spent the war in the capital, "a whole concoction of smells that in those days you associated with newly destroyed buildings." Glass from windows crunched underfoot, and shrapnel hissed menacingly from the piles of collapsed brick. Londoners learned to fear the "bomber's moon," the clear nights with a full orb in the sky, which attracted the Luftwaffe like hornets. Every night was crisscrossed with the beams of four thousand searchlights, many of them mounted on mobile trucks, that guided the British antiaircraft gunners. There was nowhere you could look in London to escape the evidence of war.

The newspapers were hard to stomach, especially for parents of young children such as Araceli. "One by one," the *News Chronicle* reported about the aftermath of one air strike, "the tiny victims were recovered. A dark-haired baby boy in a blue knitted bedjacket and a fair-haired girl in pink. Others just as they had been dressed and tucked in for the night. They were identified by the little labels tied to their ankles."

Araceli navigated this blasted landscape as a stranger, an exile. Her husband was one of the key operatives in the war, but she couldn't tell anyone this, couldn't even wear a "sweetheart badge," the small lapel pin — a regimental badge or miniature RAF wings — that told other women your boyfriend or husband was doing his part. Neighbors watched from behind their curtains as the telegram boy from the post office turned down their street on his noisy motorcycle, engine thrumming, everyone silently praying the messenger wouldn't stop at their door — in his pouch was a telegram from the War Office, informing the family their son was dead or missing in action. Araceli, whose husband returned home every night from his mysterious work, couldn't share any of this with her neighbors, and couldn't tell of the enormous sacrifice they'd made to be here.

The marriage came under increasing stress. "Many tense moments" marked the relationship as Garbo got deeper and deeper into the deception effort. On June 22, 1943, Guy Liddell, MI5's director of counterespionage, recorded a worrisome development in his diary: "There has been a crisis in the Garbo case. Mrs. Garbo is extremely homesick and jealous of Garbo who is completely absorbed in his work and has consequently to some extent neglected her. Her one desire is to go back to her home country. She thinks that as the whole of Garbo's network is notional we have no further use for his services."

It was an easy inference to make. Why couldn't MI5 just imitate Garbo's distinctive voice and let her and Pujol return home? But Cockade would prove that Pujol was the essential guardian of Garbo's voice, and his ideas and his tenacity in creating the character were invaluable. Araceli's request that MI5 release her husband was rejected out of hand.

The break came on the night of June 21, 1943. Araceli had arranged to attend a dinner at the Spanish Club with fellow expats she'd recently met. The luminaries of Spanish London would be in attendance, including the staff of the embassy. Araceli was looking forward to dressing in her finest outfit, feasting on some Spanish delicacies and perhaps drinking a glass or two of champagne. She desperately needed a night out. But Pujol said no, the danger was too great. The Spanish embassy was a well-known nest of pro-Nazi sympathizers, and he couldn't risk even the tiniest indiscretion.

When Araceli heard the news that she'd be staying home another night, she exploded. The two argued "rather violently." Unable to stand being in the same house with her, Pujol fled and called MI5 from a local phone box, saying that if Araceli called making outrageous threats, they should just ignore her. Araceli did call Tommy Harris, her rival, the man who'd replaced her as Pujol's partner, and screeched into the phone at him:

I am telling you for the last time that if at this time tomorrow you haven't got me my papers all ready for me to leave the country immediately — because I don't want to live five minutes longer with my husband — I will go to the Spanish Embassy . . . As I haven't got any further with threats, even if they kill me I am going . . . I know very well what to do and say to annoy you and my husband . . . I shall have the satisfaction that I have spoilt everything. Do you understand? I don't want to live another day in England.

Araceli was threatening to expose Garbo. The incident reverberated all the way to the top of MI5 — even before Churchill was briefed. "She ought really to be locked up and kept incommunicado," growled Guy Liddell. "But in the state of the law here nothing of the sort is possible."

MI5 had to get Araceli under control. The man tasked with overseeing the double agents, Tar Robertson, hurried over to the Pujols' home to "read her the riot act," but Araceli stood her ground. One agent suggested she be told that MI6 had intercepted a message from the Gestapo to one of its sleeper agents in London, telling him "to make contact with Garbo," an ominous sign that could mean a planned hit on her husband. Another analyst suggested that MI5 call the Spanish embassy and warn them to be on the lookout for a crazy woman who was "anxious to assassinate the ambassador." But this would complicate matters by getting the police involved in the drama, "which would be a bore." Sending Araceli back to Spain was considered too, but Liddell couldn't trust her not to talk there, especially now that she hated MI5 and Pujol equally.

One can only imagine Araceli's theatrics. Months before in Madrid, she'd scared the Abwehr agent Federico half to death with her performance as the distraught wife, and then she'd only been *acting*. Now she really was at the end of her rope. Harris, whom Araceli certainly perceived as her rival, called her "highly emotional and neurotic," even "unbalanced." More likely, she was just desperate to go home.

British attitudes toward emotional women in wartime were far from sympathetic. "Causing a scene" wasn't just bad form, it was endangering morale through pure selfishness. When people's husbands were dying on the front lines or in the skies above London, missing home didn't justify screaming at an MI5 officer. But Araceli surely went much further than screaming. "In contrast to her husband," Tommy Harris wrote, "Mrs. Garbo was a hysterical, spoilt and selfish woman."

MI5 had to come up with a plan. Pujol himself masterminded it. During a meeting with Harris, he laid out a bold course of action for preventing his wife from betraying the cause. Harris was taken aback by the "rather drastic" scheme; it was more diabolical than the fake assassination idea. It's clear from reading the case notes that Pujol was shocked and embarrassed by what Araceli had done, and he wanted to put an end to the threat she posed once and for all. To do so, he decided to use everything he'd learned about deception and intrigue and turn it against his wife.

Liddell laid out the plan: "It is now proposed that Len Burt should take a letter to Mrs Garbo after 5pm when the Spanish Consulate would be closed, telling her that her husband had been arrested and asking for his pajamas, toothbrush, etc. Tomorrow, if she appears to be in a repentant mood, she will be taken to see Garbo either in a cell at Cannon Row or at Camp 020." Before she arrived, MI5 would give her the disturbing news: earlier, they'd brought Pujol to see their chief, who'd informed the Spaniard that his mission was being terminated. The chief then demanded that Pujol send a final communiqué to Federico, making some excuse as to why he was breaking off contact. An outraged Pujol had refused and demanded to know why he was being deactivated. Liddell had told him it was because Araceli had apparently gone out of her mind and threatened to expose everything. At that insult to his wife, Pujol had "completely lost his temper," tried to attack the MI5 head and his fellow agents and, all in all, "behaved so violently" that he'd been arrested and thrown in jail along with various spies and malcontents headed for long prison stays or execution. Pujol had sabotaged his career — maybe his life — to defend Araceli's honor.

Camp 020 was a grim place, a former asylum for shell-shocked World War I troops, ringed by a barbed-wire fence. It was filled with prisoners undergoing harsh interrogations and ruled over by Lieutenant Colonel Robin "Tin-Eye" Stephens, a man of violent prejudices who strutted through the camp's hallways grumbling about "loathly Germans" and "scrofulous Bosches." Stephens despised

Spaniards especially, seeing them as "stubborn, immoral and immutable." He never removed the monocle from his right eye, through which he fixed a menacing stare at the prisoners; he was even rumored to sleep with it in place. And though it was never specified to Araceli that her husband would be hanged, that had been the fate of fourteen German spies who came through Camp 020. The place fairly reeked with menace. MI5 hoped she would repent, protest her husband's innocence and admit that "the whole crisis has been due to her stupidity."

It's no wonder that Harris thought Pujol's plan drastic. Araceli would be led to believe that her tantrum had earned her husband a possible death sentence. Harris, no friend to Araceli, asked Pujol if he was sure he wanted to put her through it. Pujol didn't flinch. "He took full responsibility for all possible reactions which his plan might produce on his wife," Harris wrote. MI5 agreed that Pujol would have control of the operation and could change tactics at any moment if he thought the scheme was going south. "Had it failed," Harris wrote, and had Araceli found out that it was Pujol who'd thought up the plan, it "would have ruined forever his matrimonial life."

The scheme was quickly put into action. An MI5 agent delivered the note about Pujol's arrest to Araceli. She immediately fell into a "hysterical outburst" and refused to get her husband's pajamas and toiletries. Then Araceli phoned Harris, as Pujol had predicted she would. Harris relayed the story of her husband's arrest: the meeting with MI5's commander, Pujol's refusal to write the breakoff letter to Federico, the violent struggle and the clank of the jail door.

Araceli heard him out and, calmer now, replied that Pujol "behaved just as she would have expected him to. She said that after the sacrifices he had made, and her knowledge that his whole life was wrapped up in his work, she could well understand that he would rather go to prison than sign the letter we had asked for . . . She was convinced he had behaved in this way to avoid the blame . . . falling on her." Pujol had predicted his wife's reaction precisely. Now to see if she would take the bait.

As badly broken down as the marriage was, as lonely and neglected as Araceli felt she was, she clearly still had deep feelings for Pujol. "In tears," she told Harris that MI5 was wrong to arrest her husband, that Pujol would give everything for the Allies, including his life. She begged him to release Pujol. Then she hung up.

Success. But Araceli wasn't finished. A few minutes later, she called Harris back, now "in a more offensive mood," and threatened to take her two children and disappear into London's back streets. Next she phoned Pujol's wireless operator, Haines. The startled officer reported that Araceli was "apparently in a desperate state, and asked him to come by the house in thirty minutes." If MI5 had thought Araceli wasn't capable of stratagems as maniacal as her husband's, they were wrong. Alarmed, Haines rushed over to the Pujols' house.

There he found a frightening scene: Araceli in the kitchen, incoherent, the house filled with the rotten-egg smell of gas. Apparently MI5 had driven her to suicide. Haines shut off the gas and picked Araceli up off the floor. Luckily, she was still breathing.

No one close to her believes this was a suicide attempt. "Was she capable of pretending that she wanted to kill herself to make a point?" asks her granddaughter, Tamara. "Absolutely. Would she really have done it? With her two children in the house? Absolutely not." Liddell agreed. "This was clearly a bit of play-acting for [the agent's] benefit." Araceli had one-upped the British spooks with a little drama of her own. But in staging it, she had underestimated Pujol.

Haines tried to calm Araceli down, but that evening she tried the gas trick again. MI5 was forced to station an agent to watch over her all night, to see that no harm came to her. The next morning, Tar Robertson arrived and listened to Araceli plead for her husband's life. It would seem that the incident was over and that Pujol's plan had worked. Araceli was repentant and had been "weeping incessantly for hours." Harris demanded she sign a document promising never to try to leave England again, and to leave Pujol free to do his work. She signed it. With the document in MI5's files, Pujol could now, as per his agreement with MI5, call off the final and most painful act.

But he didn't. Knowing how tough and wily Araceli was, Pujol wanted to drive his point home. Perhaps he wanted to punish his wife, too. She'd nearly sunk Garbo and put the lives of thousands of

Allied soldiers at risk. So he decided to give her a day she'd never forget.

The finale went ahead. Araceli was loaded into a Black Maria — a secure police van — and brought to Camp 020. She was blindfolded and led into the interrogation center, where Tin-Eye Stephens was waiting for her in his Gurkha Rifles uniform. The blindfold was removed and Araceli found Tin-Eye glaring at her through the monocle, most likely with visible disgust. He turned and led her to Pujol, who'd been dressed in the clothes of a common prisoner.

The spy was now in control. As Araceli sat in front of him, weeping, Pujol asked his wife, "on her word of honor," whether she'd gone to the embassy to reveal his secrets. (He knew she hadn't, thanks to the MI5 agent posted by the embassy door.) She told him no, it had all been a cry for attention. "She promised him that if only he were released from prison, she would help him in every way to continue with his work with even greater zeal than before." Then Pujol broke the bad news: he was to stand trial the next morning. The chief of MI5, the man he'd tried to attack, would meet with her tomorrow at the Hotel Victoria to give her the verdict.

The next morning, Araceli met with the chief — played masterfully by an intelligence officer named Cussen — who told her that she "had only avoided being arrested by a hair's breadth." As for Pujol himself, MI5 had decided on mercy. He'd be allowed to continue his work and return home. But Cussen emphasized that any repeat of her threats could jeopardize his stay in England and perhaps his life. "Thoroughly chastened," Araceli went home to wait for Juanito to come back to her. He was released that night, his prison stay marked by the beginnings of a thick beard, which made him look "rather like Lenin."

Harris found the whole affair fascinating, a glimpse inside the private life of the voluble but secretive man he'd worked with elbow to elbow for two solid years. To see how well Pujol had read Araceli, and how he'd neutralized her outbursts with a plan that relied on all the tricks of the spy trade, was to Harris truly impressive. It confirmed "that the conclusion which Garbo had drawn before putting the plan into operation had been correct."

But MI5's Guy Liddell saw another side to the episode. "I gather that [Pujol] is somewhat shaken by his experience of the last forty-eight hours," he wrote in his diary for June 24, "and that although the plan was of his own making it was one of the most distasteful things that he has had to do in his life." Pujol knew that Araceli was really homesick and miserable, while he was having the time of his life living out his boyhood dreams. There'd been rumors of trouble in their marriage — Guy Liddell at one point refers to a naval officer "for whom some considerable time ago [Araceli] formed an attachment," though there is no further mention of the officer in the records.

Yes, Araceli had been outrageous. But her pain was real. And instead of taking her side, Pujol had tricked her so that he could continue his personal war with Hitler.

Pujol never spoke about the incident and never wrote down his version of the events. The motives for his icy resolve remain unknown. But perhaps, along with his anger that Araceli was risking the lives of thousands of men with her dramas, he was indignant that she'd violated that part of himself that he'd long considered almost sacred: his imagination. Just as Operation Cockade was playing out, she'd tried to tell people that his greatest creation, Garbo, was a fake, to suggest that the British could pull the character's strings and speak with his flamboyant voice as well as Pujol could. She'd tried, in effect, to separate Pujol from Garbo.

In response, he'd played Araceli like a violin. They might have started out as equals in deception, but by now he'd surpassed her in every way. His mastery of the game was complete, even when he used it against someone he loved.

14

Haywire

IN THE SUMMER AND early fall of 1943, Operation Cockade's planners, along with Pujol and Harris, began to experience what John Masterman called a "gnawing anxiety" in their collective gut. It became clearer and clearer in those months that the planners had underestimated what it took to get commanders and thousands of soldiers in far-flung encampments organized into an invasion force, albeit a fake one. Plans began to be whittled down, resources withdrawn. On June 17, the Joint Planning Staff crossed out a provision in the plans that would allow Cockade to become a real invasion if the defenses looked weak. From then on, it would be a pure deception exercise, all bark and no bite. Four days later, the Royal Navy protested that using the powerful R-class battleships for a fake invasion was unacceptable. What if they were hit by the coastal batteries and sunk in the English Channel? The propaganda victory for the Germans would be huge. The idea quietly went away.

Reports came back that most of the American officers who were supposed to be involved in the invasion weren't even aware that such a thing as Cockade existed. The U.S. Navy, which was supposed to be supplying ships and personnel, told the planners that they couldn't so much as talk to them until two weeks before the fake D-Day, and none of the units they donated to the effort had any amphibious training, making them essentially useless. And no one realized until August, a month before Cockade went operational, that the plans called for a formidable naval convoy to leave the East Coast of the United States in support of the feint. That idea, too, was scrapped in frustration. The planners went looking for one of the U.S. Navy units that would supposedly cross the English Channel on September 8 and found that it hadn't been at its given encampment for over two years, and the unit couldn't even be located in time to be asked to take part. The leader of the operation also found himself at sea: "Will someone kindly tell me what I am to say," General Frederick Morgan barked to his subordinates, "when I am to say it, and to whom I must say it?"

A closer examination of one of Cockade's main aims — to lure Luftwaffe planes out of their hangars — would have revealed that it was well-established Luftwaffe policy to hold back its pilots until *after* the expected D-Day, and kill the regiments as their trucks and jeeps clogged the roads inland. Even if the Germans believed the invasion was real, there was a good chance that no Luftwaffe planes would be available to shoot down. The basic research behind Cockade was flawed.

The high of Operation Torch, the invasion of North Africa, dissipated and all the old prejudices about deception returned. It was a waste of time. It was a waste of good diesel fuel. Privately, many in the Allied command felt that it was ungallant and its results hard to measure.

If deception, in its structure, was like the Hollywood studio system, its vulnerabilities were more like an ecosystem's: each event impacted every other event across a wide area. If the physical deception faltered or a rumor was poorly placed, the reputation of the double agents suffered, and vice versa: bad work flowed throughout the system, corrupting everything. Something that happened at an embassy in Ankara could make one of Garbo's messages obsolete. In Cockade, several networks — mostly involving the hardware needed to back up the narrative — were going bad, causing the survival of the ecosystem itself to be called into question.

The notoriously fickle British weather failed to cooperate. Rain and storms meant canceled sorties, and the Luftwaffe was unable to send reconnaissance planes over to verify the buildup. Churchill was unhappy. "I cannot feel," he wrote after seeing the plans, "there is enough substance in this . . . Even at some inconvenience, a much larger mass of shipping should be assembled." The prime minister's note resulted in a small fleet of twenty vessels suddenly becoming available; they were quickly formed into a second prong of the attack to head out from the Solent eastward toward Beachy Head, to give the raid additional heft. But it was too little, too late.

From every quadrant the evidence built up that a deception operation of this magnitude might simply be beyond the powers of the Allies. "A mounting wave of desperation rose" over Cockade. The press was pumping expectations too high. "An unofficial source states that the Allies will move against Germany by the autumn," the United Press reported in late August, "and the race for Berlin is on with Anglo-American forces poised to beat the Russians. Signs multiply that the Allies may land in Italy and in France within the next month."

Even Pujol was growing frustrated. To get a message approved for sending to the Germans, he and Harris had to go through a byzantine process. First the planners provided the double agents with a number of "serials," individual stories that were to be broadcast to the Germans, including target dates when the information had to go out and the real-world incidents connected to the story (say, the fact that two minesweeping flotillas would be leaving Dover on September 1). This way, the planners could storyboard the entire deception operation and hand out pieces of the narratives to different agents for transmission to the Abwehr, who the Allies hoped would take the bits and weave them back into the master narrative. Contradictions and false starts could be eliminated before they happened, and a coherent image created out of thousands of flashing lights.

It sounded brilliant on paper, but only on paper. "The difficulties with which we were confronted were enormous," Harris wrote. The problem was rewrites. Harris would take the serial for the day and compose a rough message. He'd hand the message to Pujol, who would make changes to reflect the character he'd built up over so many months, then translate the revised version into Spanish. The message would then have to be translated back into English before being sent on to the planners, who would make their own changes and send the text on to the service that was involved — if it was a message reporting on a minesweeper, that would be the Royal Navy. The Royal Navy might have objections: the war situation was fluid, and the scenarios envisioned in the original serials might have changed overnight. An officer would make the navy's changes and send the message back down the chain to Pujol and Harris. Pujol would "frequently" find something wrong with the new version; for example, the navy or the deception brass wanted him to say something that Garbo would never say or that conflicted with an earlier message. When it came to Garbo's persona, Pujol was a rock: he had to protect the character at all costs. So the Spaniard would make his changes and the tortuous process would start all over again.

The normally unflappable Harris despaired. The system was "altogether chaotic," "strenuous," "exasperating." He was finding that Pujol, so relaxed and easygoing in other areas of his life, was a raging perfectionist when it came to Garbo. "If I do just one thing," Pujol said later, "I want to do it well." The process became a stream of chain letters that never seemed to end. It was like trying to write a novel in the middle of a battle that the novel was describing.

Garbo doggedly kept beating the drum of war to Madrid: "45 torpedo boats in Dover . . . Hundreds of light naval craft arriving, including gunboats, being loaded with supplies, then shipping out for disguised rendezvous points . . . All RAF leave in specified areas cancelled effective August 25th." To support his messages, frogmen and raiders on preparatory missions crawled onto the beaches at Calais, leaving letters behind seeking information from locals for the forthcoming invasion. A series of raids on the coast — called FORFAR missions — began, with orders for commandos to snatch any German soldier they saw and bring him back to England for interrogation (and to let the Germans know they'd been scouting targets). One raiding party climbed the steep beach cliffs but couldn't cut through the barbed wire they found at the top. So as not to return empty-handed, they managed to snip off a piece of the wire and carry it back to England for engineers to study. Others couldn't land because of high waves, or turned back to escape capture after spotting German patrols. The point was to make the enemy notice them, but there was no evidence that any of the FORFAR missions had ever been observed.

The planners had to ask themselves: What if we held an invasion and nobody came?

Across the Continent, anticipation swelled in the late summer of

1943. News of the fake invasion was radiating far and wide. The Chinese minister in Ankara reported back to his superiors in Chungking: "England and the United States will assume the offensive on a second front at the end of September. Simultaneous air, sea and land operations will be undertaken on the Continent." In The Hague, Hendrik Seyffardt, the pro-Nazi Dutch general, was assassinated. A grenade detonated in Lille, France, killing twenty-three German officers. Danes trampled a German soldier to death, and a train carrying Nazi troops was sabotaged near Ålborg. Belgian citizens called out to German soldiers, "Have you packed your bags yet? The Allies are coming!"

On September 7, Garbo sent a flash message to Madrid at 2033 hours: weather permitting, the invasion would take place the following morning. The message was relayed to Berlin and then on to operational headquarters in Paris. The German navy dynamited the hulls of several ships and sank them in the approaches to Calais to blunt the expected amphibious assault, known to the Allies as Operation Starkey. The Reich's divisions in France were put on alert. But the eighth dawned stormy, and D-Day was put off until the next morning. Churchill sent his blessings via telegram: "Good luck to Starkey."

On the night of September 8, airfields in England rumbled with the engines of de Havilland Mosquitoes, coughing to life in the darkness. The Mosquitoes and the heavier Wellingtons lined up on the runways, aimed at the French town of Le Portel and the twin gun batteries, code-named Religion and Andante, that lay nearby. The combat aircraft were the point of the spear of a huge air armada of 258 planes, grudgingly loaned out for Cockade. Minutes later, heavy Halifax bombers, with code names like D-Dog and K-King, revved their engines and went airborne into a cloudless sky flooded with bright moonlight. Because of the short distances to the target, the bombers carried minimum fuel and maximum bomb loads as they lumbered into the sky. The U.S. Army Air Force sent its planes aloft to 28,000 feet, while the Brits flew lower. Polish pilots pushed their planes hard; in the bellies of their aircraft were 4,000-pound "blockbusters," the largest explosives in the Bomber Command's arsenal. At a base in Cambridgeshire, Starkey claimed its first victims when a New Zealand crew aboard a Stirling heavy bomber veered off the runway and slammed into a pair of nearby houses, erupting in flames. As ground crews rushed to help, the bombs in the bay exploded, killing the would-be rescuers along with the pilot and his crew. Four planes in the air over France were raked by antiaircraft fire, others crashed with all hands killed. None of the thousands of men who took part, not the pilots or the navigators, had heard the name Starkey or knew that they were bombing in service of a phantom.

It was a warm night in the French fishing town of Le Portel. The air raid siren in the town hall in Rue Carnot took up the alarm that was spreading up and down the coast and sent its forlorn notes out through the narrow cobblestone streets. The first planes appeared overhead in late afternoon, American Marauders, and the residents heard the unmistakable high-pitched screech of 1,000-pound bombs spinning toward the earth before they smashed into the brightly colored houses. At first the Portelois thought it was an isolated incident — bombs had gone astray before and killed a few neighbors in the close-knit town of 5,500 people. But soon the darkening sky was drumming with the sounds of engines, and planes were dropping one bomb every eight seconds. As the townspeople ran to their cellars, that interval compressed until it seemed as if the world around them were exploding without end.

The streets of Le Portel turned into an abattoir. Buildings shattered, sending out clouds of choking dust, and bodies were blown apart by the high explosives. Survivors pulled the dead and wounded onto crude stretchers — shutter blinds and tabletops — and stumbled through the streets looking for a doctor as pieces of hot metal shrieked past in the night. The ground shook with each detonation, knocking people off their feet. A bomb exploded near a group of fourteen people and thirteen of them fell dead from the shock of the blast or the shrapnel; the lone survivor was found amid the corpses, catatonic, unable to move. The local priest, l'Abbé Boidin, crawled into cellars to pray with families huddled in the darkness, smoke from fires and the dust from exploded masonry making the air hard to breathe. Hours later he would return on his rounds and find the same house collapsed under a direct hit. Homeward-bound air crews as far away as the Thames could look back to France and see the flames of the burning town.

The people of Le Portel were pinned under collapsed girders and roofs; rescuers formed human chains to get them out, only to be felled by a new wave of explosives. One woman who'd been nursing a baby was uncovered under a pile of rubble. She was dead but the baby was crying in her arms. "We [were] waiting to die because this is inevitable," remembered one Portelois.

Ninety-three percent of the small French town was destroyed. Three hundred and seventy-six men, women and children were killed in one night. If there was one ray of hope in the cellars, as the Portelois listened to the high explosives splitting the air, it was that the townspeople could comfort each other with the thought that the bombs signaled the long-awaited invasion and the end of the Nazi occupation. What else could these waves of planes blotting out the moon mean if not freedom? As morning dawned fine and warm, they peered through the jigsaw mounds of rubble and black smoke toward the serene blue of the English Channel.

September 9 was a beautiful day for an invasion. A special train was engaged to bring British and American generals and top officers from London to the beaches at Kent, where they could see the thirty-ship convoy that had departed from Dungeness steam toward France, while the second prong of the attack, Churchill's twenty ships, made its way to the chalk cliffs of Beachy Head on the south coast. Chugging alongside the destroyers were Thames barges that had been roped into the invasion, as well as tourist steamers that would normally have been ferrying visitors around the waterways of London. It didn't matter that they were pleasure craft; it was mass that mattered, not armaments. From shore, you couldn't tell that the boats were empty except for their crews.

The ground underneath the generals' feet vibrated as an armada of Allied fighters thundered overhead, pointed toward the beaches at Calais. By 9 a.m., this potent invasion force was ten miles from the shore, but no Luftwaffe counterattack appeared and no enemy ship tried to intercept it. "It was an inspiring sight to see everybody doing his stuff to perfection," sighed General Morgan, commander of the entire operation, "except, unfortunately, the Germans."

When at 9 a.m. the code word Backchat came over the ships' radios, the convoys laid down a smoke cover and quickly turned tail, heading back the way they came. The planes cut slow 180-degree arcs in the brilliant sky. Operation Cockade was over.

Garbo had to explain why the invasion had never come, or risk losing the Germans forever. This was called "the breakoff." When the BBC began reporting that Cockade was only a practice run, Garbo immediately got on the radio and denied this. "I can definitely prove the lie of the ridiculous Press and Radio official news," he told Madrid. He reported that the troops who'd been turned back from the Calais shore were "surprised and disappointed" at the change in plans. To cover himself, Garbo hinted to Madrid that the invasion had been real but was called off at the last moment because of the Allies' armistice with Italy, which had been announced on September 8. The new alliance had made the war planners reconsider their second-front strategy. Other double agents were tapping out messages implying that the German defenses had simply been judged too strong and that the Allies had decided to pound Germany from the air instead of confronting the panzers on the ground. Garbo wrote: "I do not think that the British High Command have sufficient sense of humor to take their troops for an outing on the sea nor that they have such a surplus of petrol and bomb as to amuse themselves." Some nefarious plot was unfolding: "extravagant rumors" were sweeping London about what had really happened behind the scenes.

Garbo's message was a counterattack and a smokescreen all in one, but could it hide the fact that Madrid's super spy had been wrong? In their Jermyn Street office, Pujol and Harris held their breath, waiting to see if they'd damaged Garbo irretrievably. On September 13, the spy sent a packet of newspaper clippings supporting his case, and he continued to work his sources furiously. Finally, responses started flowing in from Madrid.

Garbo was safe. "Their confidence in me was absolute."

Apparently the whole charade had been minor news in Berlin. The top German war planners never believed the invasion was coming, so why get upset about a few wrong-headed reports? To his handlers, Garbo was now seemingly untouchable. "Your activity and that of your informants gave us a perfect idea of what is taking place over there," Federico gushed. "These reports, as you can imagine, have an incalculable value and for this reason I beg of you to proceed with the greatest care so as not to endanger in these momentous times either yourself or your organization." Kühlenthal backed up his star agent. Not only did the Madrid head cable the full explanation of the canceled invasion to Berlin, he also added his own emphasis. Garbo's report that the troops had been "surprised and disappointed" was strengthened to "the measure caused disgust amongst the troops." Yet if Hitler's top brass weighed the available evidence correctly and ignored Garbo's reports in the future, how would he protect the real D-Day to come?

Harris was handed new messages from Berlin to Madrid that evaluated Garbo's work: "Both reports are first class. Between 9/1 and 9/3 English minesweepers were observed in Channel off Boulogne . . . Please get the V-Mann to keep an eye on all troop movements and preparations, and also any possible embarkations, especially in eastern and south eastern England. Speedy reports on this subject are urgently desired." Garbo's reports were deemed "particularly valuable," and his messages on troop movements "of extreme importance." Even Colonel Roenne, the gray-eyed genius of Zossen, was now susceptible to Garbo's charms. The double agent had so crossed up the Abwehr that it approved a 50 percent raise for all his operatives, plus a bonus on top of that for those involved with Cockade.

Garbo hadn't just triumphed, he was now doing something no other spy in World War II did. He was slowly and imperceptibly turning himself from a spy into an analyst, even an oracle. That is, he not only fed the Germans bits of traffic, he then proceeded to tell them what they meant. With his sources high up in two key ministries, Garbo was becoming a soothsayer of Allied intentions.

The Abwehr had resisted this in the early days, complaining to Garbo about his long-winded letters full of analysis and conjecture.

Because spies were deeply despised in the German system, they were allowed only to pass along nuggets of information. But the Abwehr men weren't complaining any longer; they sought his counsel, something they did for almost no other operative in the field. Yet it still might not be enough.

For the Cockade planners, the reviews were very different. Scathing, in fact. "The movements made were rather too obvious — it was evident [they] were bluffing," said Gerd von Rundstedt, commander of German forces in the West. "The general make-up and number of agents' reports give rise to the suspicions that the material was deliberately allowed to slip into the agents' hands." From his bunker at Zossen, the authoritative voice of Colonel Roenne rang out. "The multiplicity of the at-times utterly fantastic reports about allegedly imminent operations . . . ," the aristocrat wrote Hitler directly, "reveals an intention to deceive and mislead." Roenne was, as usual, the most clear-eyed analyst of the deception planners' work.

Hitler was so unimpressed by rumors of an invasion he *removed* twenty-seven of the thirty-six divisions guarding Western Europe and sent them to the front lines in Russia, Sicily and the Balkans between April and December 1943, the exact opposite of what the Allies wanted the Germans to do. Ironically, had the Allies actually invaded France on September 9, 1943, they would have found the beaches stripped of almost all their German troops. The final report on Starkey found that the garrisons and pillboxes at Calais had been "practically denuded." The invasion would have been a cakewalk.

The Allied commanders were just as unimpressed by Cockade as the enemy was. The generals who mattered, the ones whose wholehearted cooperation would be needed when the real D-Day came, were appalled. William Casey, the head of secret intelligence of the Office of Strategic Services, the precursor of the Central Intelligence Agency, spent September 9 with General Jacob Devers, overall commander of the U.S. Army in Europe, as Cockade played out. "[He] watched and shook his head," Casey remembered. "[He] had seen it, he didn't like it and it had failed." The old mistrust of deception flared up again. If, when the real D-Day came, the enemy was as un-deceived as they had been with Cockade, the Allied armies would be chewed up on the beaches and in the coastal towns of Normandy. D-Day would be a bloodbath.

We don't know if Tommy Harris knew of the deaths at Le Portel and elsewhere. If he was unaware of the details, the case officer must have at least suspected that many people had died for Cockade. But the news was kept from Pujol; there was no operational need for him to know, and for all his toughness in dealing with Araceli, Pujol was an emotional and often tenderhearted man. "Violence is contrary to all my ideas," Pujol said years later. "There are no dead men on my conscience." There was no need to upset him and risk his sharpness for the work ahead.

Cockade had been a disaster. Men and women had died in a hope-lessly bungled cause. The *totality* that was essential to a great mili-tary illusion — men, rumors, physical deception, black propaganda, radio intercepts, all working together to create a seamless alternate reality, a vast army in the English Channel that the Germans could smell and hear — had never come close to being achieved. Cockade had been meant to instill fear, but it had only elicited contempt. The Allied deception planners sat in their offices in London and asked themselves: How did they *know?* How did the Germans figure out that Cockade was a fake? What crucial element from the play was missing? Was it the scenery, the writing or the overall theme?

The Allied planners produced an in-depth report on German re-actions to Starkey and stamped it "Most Secret." The report makes for fascinating reading. The analysts came up with five theories as to why the enemy had ignored the operation: "i) not noticing, or fail-ing to attach significance to, the preparations for Starkey until it was too late to do anything about them, ii) not being able to reinforce the Channel coast heavily owing to commitments elsewhere, iii) appre-ciating from the general intelligence background that the Allies were not in a position at the time to invade Western Europe, iv) appreciat-ing that Starkey was not likely to be more than a second 'Dieppe,' and v) learning in advance the real nature of Starkey."

In other words, *We have absolutely no idea why it didn't work.*

The report was more than a spectacular example of ass-covering; it was a statement of philosophical despair. To those few men walking around London in the fall of 1944 who knew the truth about the operation, the mystery was the most terrifying thing of all. Cockade had failed and nobody had a clue why.

15

The Interloper

O N DECEMBER 20, 1943, in a sparsely wooded forest in East Prussia, in a crude wooden hut-like building that had been thrown up using local timber, Adolf Hitler was contemplating the second front. The staff officers gathered with him were tired and anxious, even though the scrublands of East Prussia were far from Berlin, which was being continuously pummeled by the RAF and American heavy bombers. The bad news that flowed in constantly from the East and Stalingrad made the mood at Hitler's headquarters only more depressing. Winter and the rough seas of the English Channel had allowed the German divisions in France to rest, to lay mines and to build more concrete gun emplacements, but now that spring was coming, the Allies' focus would be on plans for a continental invasion. Hitler had summed up the stakes in his Directive No. 51 over a month before:

> The danger in the east remains, but a greater one looms in the west: the Anglo-Saxon landing! . . . In the east, the vast extent of the territory makes it possible for us to lose ground, even on a large scale, without a fatal blow being dealt to the nervous system of Germany. It is different in the west! Should the enemy succeed in breaching our defenses on a wide front here, the immediate consequences would be unpredictable.

Actually, they were very predictable: if the Allies secured a beachhead in France, they could drive inexorably toward the Ruhr, the industrial heartland of Germany, destroying its munitions and tank factories and crippling its ability to wage war as Allied forces headed for Berlin. It would be, as Churchill said, not the beginning of the end, but the end of the beginning.

As the meeting in the Prussian woods progressed, Hitler's staff clustered around an enormous map of Europe. Finally, the Führer announced that the invasion would come in the spring. The men nodded. Disagreeing with the Führer was not allowed, and besides, he was fantastically knowledgeable about the anti-invasion fortifications known as the Atlantic Wall. Hitler knew "the location of the defenses better than any single officer" in the German army. Now the Führer, too, studied the map. "It would be good," he said, "if we could know from the start: Where is a diversion and where the real main attack?"

To judge from that map, which described the European theater as it stood in December 1943, one would think that the Allies could choose from a handful of targets where a second front could be launched. But when one factored in the needs of the invading force, many of those candidates melted away. The Netherlands had deep ports and lay closer to the Ruhr than France, but its coast was beyond the range of the RAF's fighters; Allied tanks couldn't negotiate its sand dunes, and the Germans could open the dikes and flood the lowlands at any sign of invasion. Denmark was ruled out because it was too far from Allied supply lines and the factories along the Rhine. In the end, there were only two real potential targets: Normandy and the Pas de Calais.

The Pas de Calais had clear advantages: it offered the shortest distance to English shores, just twenty-one miles from the port at Dover. Once taken, it would offer a direct line to Germany's heartland: southeastern England is closer to Düsseldorf than Düsseldorf is to Berlin. But in its rightness lay a snare: the Germans had placed their best divisions and their heaviest gun emplacements there. The Atlantic Wall at Calais, bolstered by 16-inch guns stripped from German warships, was deemed impregnable. Attackers would arrive by sea and find thousands of tracers pouring down from the cliffs and panzer divisions rolling up to blast the Sherman tanks back into the water. And the ports at Dover and Folkestone, across from Calais, were too small to allow for the massive outflow of everything from potatoes to mortar shells that would be needed immediately after the first regiments took the coastline.

In the end, the Allies settled on Normandy, 160 miles southwest of Pas de Calais. The beaches there were less heavily guarded. Normandy lay within range of the P-47 Thunderbolts and P-38 Lightnings that would keep the Luftwaffe off the incoming battalions. There was only one panzer division, the 21st, guarding the region, while Calais had five. Decent draws led away from the beaches, and a workable set of roads existed farther inland. But surprise was the first and clearest advantage of choosing Normandy. For the invasion to work as planned, the secret had to be kept.

To deceive Hitler, the D-Day planners couldn't depend on the occult battiness of Himmler or on Hitler's own "inner voice," which had caused him to take tremendous risks in the invasions of Poland and Holland. The upper reaches of the Third Reich were still awash in mysticism and denial: when Hitler read a lengthy report on food shortages in Russia, he wrote across the top: "This cannot be." But this monomania applied far more to offensive operations than to defensive ones. For Hitler, his ego was not so much bound up in the prediction of where the Allies would land as it had been in whether he could take Poland against the advice of his generals. The essential decisions didn't depend on his daring or courage; they were, in effect, *technical* questions. When it came to addressing the second front, he was far more apt to look at the available evidence dispassionately, to seek counsel and change his mind based on actual intelligence reports, than he had been when debating the German invasion of France.

This was both a blessing and a curse for MI5 and double agents like Garbo. It meant that Hitler was providing an opening for their information to get through and influence him, so long as it could be convincing. But it also made the German process of deciding from where the invasion was coming more democratic and objective, which meant that the real invasion point was going to be harder to hide.

The information about D-Day went out to the fewest possible Allied officers. Those let in on the plan were called "Bigot," and when they spoke to each other they used green scrambler telephones. When ten Bigot officers went unaccounted for during a preinvasion mishap, a feverish search was mounted until every body was recovered. The radio operators who sent the traffic relating to D-Day were told not to talk in pubs or even in the latrines.

Few gave the invasion plan much chance of success. Amphibious landings in support of an invasion had a bloody reputation earned over many centuries. Kublai Khan's attacks on Japan in 1274 and 1281 failed because of storms and bad ship design; the Spanish Armada's attempt to land an army on British shores in 1588 was wrecked by storms and a ferocious naval battle; the huge British invasion force at Cartagena in 1741 was defeated by a much smaller Spanish contingent; and Gallipoli in 1915 and 1916 had become a byword for disaster. True, the British had managed three successful landings in World War II — North Africa, Sicily and Salerno — but all three had been against unfortified positions. When the Allies attacked the heavily defended coast at Dieppe in August 1942, the invasion had failed at the cost of thousands of lives.

Casualty rates were predicted to be 90 percent. The Allies hoped, in the best-case scenario, to land five divisions in France during the first twenty-four hours; the Germans had fifty infantry and eleven armored divisions waiting for them. When Sir Alan Brooke, chief of the Imperial General Staff, laid out the details of the attack, code-named Overlord, he ended his presentation this way: "Well, there it is; it won't work, but you must bloody well make it." General Sir Hastings Ismay wrote to a field marshal: "A lot of people who ought to know better are taking it for granted that Overlord is going to be a bloodbath on the scale of the Somme and Passchendaele." In early 1944, Churchill wrote, "I see the tides running red with their blood, I have my doubts . . . I have my doubts."

While the Allies worried over the very concept of a cross-Channel invasion and Hitler contemplated his maps, wondering where it might fall, a secret battle was being waged in London as to how D-Day could be disguised from the Germans. The basement of Whitehall was filled with people writing and rewriting the "story" that would be told to Berlin. The plan would eventually be code-named Bodyguard, after Churchill's famous declaration: "In wartime, truth is so precious that she should always be attended by a bodyguard of lies." But in late 1943, the composition wasn't going well.

In the offices of the London Controlling Section underneath White-hall, Controller of Deception Johnny Bevan and his staff — including the portly, clubbable writer Dennis Wheatley, the man who'd been there in the bad old days with his file-burning chief Lumby — worked over the master deception plan in the winter of 1943. Bevan's staff looked at each aspect of the proposed operation from every angle, trying to decipher how it would play out in the minds of the Germans, how it could be fitted into the mosaic of the overall deception, and the best way to execute it.

The staff wrote paper after paper, subsection after subsection, with titles such as "Factors against the possibility of disguising the purpose of the expedition" and "Possible means by which the truth about our intentions may become known to the enemy." Bevan read the papers and sent them back covered with comments, demanding more and more detail, more realism. He was furious if his officers assumed something would go well. There were interlocking cogs in the machinery — if one scheme failed in Turkey, another in Norway could go haywire — and Bevan wanted every possible disaster accounted for. Perhaps Starkey still haunted him. Perhaps the American soldiers he saw sauntering in the streets of Whitehall, their lives in his hands, had unsettled this nervous but kind man. Whatever the reason, with each draft the Bodyguard plan grew longer and darker.

Gradually, Dennis Wheatley came to realize that "it had become a hopelessly depressing document . . . virtually informing the Chiefs that the chances were ten to one against the cover plan . . . succeeding." The novelist read his superior the riot act and finally convinced Bevan the plan had to be changed. The staff whittled it down from twenty pages to three. The chiefs of staff accepted it "without a murmur."

Churchill, one of the driving forces behind the scheme, was excited. "The plan has to be just close enough to the truth to seem credible to Herr Hitler, but will mislead him completely." Bodyguard would earn the Allies "a thin extra edge that could mean the difference between a glorious triumph and a bloody debacle . . . If we pull this off, it will be *the greatest hoax in history!*" By December 1943, the plan was up and running. The great departure from Operation Cockade was a simple one. This time, there *was* an invasion coming. They just had to disguise two facts about it: where and when.

Reduced to its essentials, Bodyguard laid out what the Allies wanted the Germans to believe before D-Day — that there would be a fake double-pronged attack, a spring assault on Norway and a summer invasion of the Pas de Calais. The divisions needed for an invasion of Europe, however, were understrength and the production of landing craft was behind schedule, so that "no large scale cross-Channel operations would be possible until the late summer." July 15 would be put forward as a likely D-Day. The Norway feint would be known as Fortitude North, and the Calais ruse would be Fortitude South.

The intelligence agencies began to divide up Bodyguard and put it into practice. By January, when Eisenhower took over planning for D-Day, his staff realized that the double agents "were proving themselves to be by far the most effective channel for controlled leakage." They would be the tip of the spear, with Garbo and Brutus — the Polish airman — in the lead. The entire deception operation would pivot off a few men and their case officers.

From their little office, Pujol and Harris began to advertise how far the Allies were from being ready for invasion. On January 5, Garbo told Madrid, "I have read in the English press commentaries on the alleged belief in German official circles that the offensive against the Continent will begin within the next 15 days. If this is the belief of our High Command you can affirm to Headquarters immediately that no danger whatever exists in this period." He'd spotted a new type of American landing craft propped up at Albert Dock in Liverpool on January 15 and sent a sketch, but there was only one vessel, hardly a sign of impending apocalypse. On January 21, he wrote: "Conversation with a friend. He considers that the Anglo-American offensive against the Continent, should this take place, would not happen for a long time." The other double agents were also blitzing the Germans with stories of late-arriving troops and snafus. "Labor troubles in the United States," Tate — Wulf Schmidt, MI5's first double agent — reported on January 20, "have curtailed production of invasion barges to such an extent that the dates of future operations may be affected." Brutus chimed in three days later: "There is an opinion held amongst us that Montgomery will probably, as in Egypt, train all the troops all over again." The Abwehr's sources reported that artesian wells for troop encampments were being drilled in Kent, something no army would do unless it was planning for a long stay.

But the messages from London weren't getting through. The Germans radioed Garbo that their analysts were seeing a spike in reports of increased activity. Something major was being planned. The Abwehr sent Garbo a string of highly detailed questionnaires on the invasion force: "News from various sources speak of preparations being in full swing for operations of great importance at a very near date from those islands. I await with urgency and the greatest interest your reports." January 14: "For tactical reasons one must assume that the danger centers for future operations are Devon, Cornwall and the south coast between Weymouth and Southampton." That was exactly right; those were the real embarkation areas for D-Day. "Numerous reports of the alleged postponement of the invasion," read a March telegram from the German embassy in Lisbon, "are, in the opinion of this Abteilung [department], to be regarded as systematic concealment of the actual plan."

Garbo remained above suspicion, but the Germans were picking apart the deception plan in real time. And it wasn't hard to understand why: the ports and harbors of southern England were filling up with an array of landing craft. So many planes were crowding the airfields that people joked that you could walk from one end of England to the other on the wings of fighter planes. Everywhere there were soldiers. "They came by land, by train, bus, truck, or on foot," wrote the historian Stephen Ambrose. "They formed up by the hundreds in companies and battalions, by the thousands in regiments, to march down narrow English roads, headed south. When they arrived in their marshaling areas, they formed up by divisions, corps, and armies in their hundreds of thousands — altogether almost 2 million men." They brought with them nearly 500,000 vehicles, 4,500 cooks, thousands upon thousands of tents and tons of bulky equipment.

• • •

The army brass did their best to disguise the new arrivals: gravel paths were laid in their camps so that the Luftwaffe couldn't snap pictures of new trails through the English grass; wire netting shielded the tanks and jeeps from curious eyes; MPs patrolled the "sausages," or camps, to prevent thirsty soldiers from mixing with the locals in nearby pubs; and campfires were forbidden, even though the English countryside was still covered with morning frost. But London at any given time had half a million soldiers from sixty different nations thronging its bars and cabarets, and they'd brought with them so much equipment that the running joke among the British and American soldiers was that the only thing keeping England from sinking into the sea were the silver barrage balloons tethered to the land.

Everyone involved in trying to hide this enormous army felt the pressure rise at the beginning of 1944. Pujol was becoming increasingly consumed by his creation, Garbo, as the operation grew to a fever pitch. Some days he composed and sent four or five messages, the longest running to 8,000 words, in addition to the 1,200 wireless messages he wrote during the war. "The work Tommy Harris and I did was hard," he wrote. "It meant having to solve complex problems and make difficult decisions." Harris watched his partner closely; Pujol couldn't be allowed to burn out before the final chapter. "His entire existence remained wrapped up in . . . the work," Harris wrote.

Pujol was able to escape the war for only a matter of hours. He and his family were evacuated at one point to the country town of Taplow, in Buckinghamshire, and put up at a hotel by the Thames. The idyllic place seemed a world away from the torn-up capital, and it was filled with twenty-five fellow refugees, among them a redheaded Jewish girl who asked Pujol to give her Spanish lessons, a Czech couple and a vice consul from the Spanish embassy. There were parties in the evening, and Pujol never missed one; he craved light conversation and, especially, dancing. "In my youth I was considered a good dancer," he said, and now he took up the paso doble and the foxtrot with a vengeance, striking his heels on the hotel's wooden floor to the delight of everyone.

But Pujol couldn't tell his fellow guests his real reasons for being in England or reveal his anxiety about the mission.

By 1944, the Abwehr was an imperfect organization, often at war with its rivals, the Sicherheitsdienst, or SD, and even the military it advised. But it had sixteen thousand agents spread all over the globe and it was adept at many areas of the spy game. "What evidence there is," Masterman wrote, "goes to show that the Germans were at least our equals in all the arts connected with espionage and counterespionage." In the justly famous Venlo Incident in 1939, the SD had convinced British intelligence that a group of disgruntled German officers in the Dutch border town of Venlo were planning a coup against Hitler. When two SIS agents went to meet with the plotters, the Brits were captured and Hitler was handed a gift-wrapped excuse for invading Holland, as the SIS's presence in Venlo proved that the Dutch were no longer neutral. The brilliantly executed plot haunted British spymasters for years. Even if the Abwehr was flawed at the top, it couldn't miss the signs of the greatest invasion in history, signs that would be everywhere to see in the harbors of England and the back alleys of Lisbon.

To detect the invasion, the Germans had to be barely competent. To disguise it, the British had to be illusionists of genius.

Garbo especially was under the gun. He'd expanded his operation in the south and southwest of England in the previous months, bringing in new "recruits," from Welsh Aryans who "hated the British like death" to a rabid Greek communist to saboteurs and fascists, all to prepare for D-Day. The Germans knew that something was happening in Southampton and Devon, and would expect their star agent to let them know exactly what that was, down to the regiment insignia and number of tents.

Garbo continued to put across the party line. After a discussion with his friend the minister, he wrote Madrid that the official believed that Germany would be brought down by air power, not land attacks. Garbo's lover, the homely secretary, confirmed the view a few days later. "She emphasized one point above all, which was that the Anglo-Americans will not start the offensive until they have everything absolutely ready." But how could Garbo continue pretending that nothing of real interest was going on in England when it was crisscrossed by his agents? As good as he was, even Garbo couldn't cloak a continental invasion force in complete darkness.

One person in particular was bothered by Operation Fortitude. He was a small, imperious and elegantly turned-out man by the name of David Strangeways. The name fit: Colonel Strangeways was an unorthodox man who rubbed many of his peers the wrong way. "Much disliked," said one fellow soldier; "an impossible and insufferable *enfant terrible*," remembered another (although both admitted they secretly admired Strangeways). The colonel hated bureaucracy with a passion and would simply ignore procedures if he thought they were wrong-headed. When a historian interviewed him years later, he was unapologetic: "'I was not a much loved person,' he admitted cheerfully." David Strangeways had an internal compass that was as strong as Montgomery's or Patton's. When, after he'd left the service, he became an Anglican priest, he developed a theory that no sermon should last more than eight minutes. Although a wonderful speaker, Strangeways never exceeded that time limit, something his flock in the parish of Ipswich grew to admire.

Born in 1912, Strangeways was the darkly handsome son of the founder of a prominent research hospital. He'd read history at Trinity College, Cambridge, and joined the Duke of Wellington's regiment in 1933, serving in Malta before seeing his first action at the retreat at Dunkirk. Stranded on the shore with the German army advancing behind him, disaster only hours away, Strangeways spied an abandoned Thames barge floating near shore. He ordered his men to strip off their uniforms so the water wouldn't weigh them down and swam with them out to the unwieldy vessel. Using the sailing skills he'd learned as a boy, he got them safely back to Portsmouth, where the mayor and a group of photographers were waiting to greet returning troops. The quick-thinking officer emerged from the hold dressed in the barge's curtains. Strangeways was mentioned in dispatches for saving his men.

In 1942, he'd had his first taste of intrigue. Strangeways was chosen to deliver the deception plans for Operation Torch — the North

African invasion that Garbo had cut his teeth on — to the generals in Cairo, by way of Gibraltar. In his luggage he carried a copy of the deception planner Dennis Wheatley's latest potboiler, with a letter inside from Wheatley to a friend, filled with bits of gossip about the forthcoming invasion that the Allies wanted passed to the Germans. MI6 knew that Gibraltar hotel employees on the payroll of the Abwehr often rifled through the luggage of British arrivals. Strangeways carried out the little scheme, and the information made its way to Berlin.

The dapper officer came into his own when he began to work under Dudley Clarke, the mastermind of Allied espionage, in the Middle Eastern campaign. Clarke was the fountainhead of deception thinking, a genius who had, in the opinion of one of his officers, "the most all-containing brain of any man I ever met." Blond, small and well dressed, with a "gently booming voice" and eyes that sparkled with secret delight, Clarke became a legend in the Middle East before moving on to the European theater. Many of the concepts that the XX Committee used — the importance of timing, the need for a story to feed the enemy — Clarke had developed in the wild days in Cairo, where he'd placed his office below a brothel so that no one would notice all the officers coming to his address. "He was certainly the most unusual Intelligence officer of his time, very likely of all time," said David Mure, one of his staff officers. "His mind worked differently than anyone else's and far quicker; he looked out on the world through the eyes of his opponents." Clarke had a near-photographic memory, keeping the details of half a dozen complicated plots in his head at once. Under his leadership, the deception outfit known as A Force had become an innovator and a technical marvel: it scoured the Middle East and built a library of 1,200 different kinds of paper for forgery purposes; it collected nearly every revenue, metal, rubber and embossed stamp used by the Nazis; it could reproduce the signatures of the most important German officials and maintained a huge index file that could tell you where General X was on any given day. Like the modern-day FBI, it could re-create a burned or shredded document. It could even dye a man brown so that he might pass as an Arab.

David Strangeways was one of Clarke's best students. After studying at the feet of the master, he was dispatched to Tunisia, where he dreamed up a series of cunning and successful plots to outwit the best German commander, Erwin Rommel.

One of the keys to the success of the Allied spy operation was a certain double capacity in the men who worked inside it. Juan Pujol could have become one of the world's great swindlers had he chosen to, a Ponzi schemer or a gigolo, but instead he yearned to do good. Those qualities rarely go together: con men do not want to save humanity, and starry-eyed humanists could not fake their way past the best minds in the German intelligence service. David Strangeways had Pujol's kind of doubleness: he was a brilliant strategist who was lethal in battle. In other words, he was a tough ground-level commander who had thought deeply about deception and how it could be woven into a kinetic war.

Strangeways did it all, in Tunisia and elsewhere: he formulated the plans, picked the operatives to carry it out, oversaw the signals and physical deception, watched the Germans respond in real time and even fought in the battles that resulted. He'd done deception from beginning to end. No one in the European theater had the same experience. The Middle East was like a laboratory of deception where Strangeways could experiment and work out his theories to the end.

The battle for Tunis exemplified this. In the winter of 1942, the British First Army and the American II Corps were closing in on the capital from the west. Strangeways directed the Germans' attention to the south by passing traffic through a fake Abwehr agent code-named Cheese, supposedly a Syrian of Slavic heritage who was in reality an enterprising British lieutenant colonel named William Kenyon-Jones, who, against the express wishes of the British signal corps, had an amateur wireless set built from spare parts in Cairo and had won the trust of the Abwehr's Athens station with his weirdly accurate reports. With Cheese sending out fake updates and with a few dummy tanks positioned in the south next to real ones, giving the Luftwaffe the illusion of a major armored movement, Strangeways hoodwinked the Desert Fox, Rommel, into believing the Allied armies were where they weren't.

But the capital, Tunis, still hadn't been taken. Strangeways jumped into an armored car and dashed off to the smoking city, still echoing with the machine guns of the last of Rommel's holdouts. When Strangeways arrived at German headquarters, he shot his way in, blew open the safe and confiscated the secret codes, confidential documents and cipher machines before the Germans could dispose of them, then rounded up the remains of the French colonial police and restored order in the city. Wheatley, putting on his novelist's hat, claimed that Strangeways was "the first man into Tunis" that day. While that might have been an exaggeration, the Allied infantry did march into the city the next morning and found "the capital virtually under [his] control." The notoriously difficult Field Marshal Bernard Montgomery was so impressed with the dashing young officer that, when Monty was called back to England to take part in D-Day, he brought Strangeways with him to head up his deception outfit.

Strangeways arrived in London around Christmas 1943. Wheatley remembered his first sight of this odd, brilliant man. "He was . . . so beautifully turned out that, even in battledress, he looked as if he had stepped straight out of a bandbox." But the European theater he'd just entered was different from the Middle East: sprawling, enormous and very political. Plans took months to be approved and implemented. Each agency had its own bureaucracy. If you needed the Royal Navy in on a scheme, you had to spend weeks just getting to the right person. The power relationships were as complex as any government's, and Strangeways was outranked by almost everyone he needed for Fortitude.

But Strangeways didn't care how many stripes you wore on your sleeve; he was notorious for trampling in people's private domains and overruling people he had no right to overrule. In fact, he seemed to enjoy needling his superiors. "He thought he *was* Monty," said one officer.

Operation Fortitude had taken the best minds in London months and thousands of man-hours to put together. Everyone had signed off on it. But Strangeways, the newcomer, took one look at the scheme and decided it was complete rubbish. "Put it this way. The plan had been made by people who had been in England and had never been out doing any practical deception work. That is, deception work which was combined with military activity." Strangeways could practically see a well-lubricated Dennis Wheatley coming back from a heavy lunch in his silk-lined jacket and working this thing up before his afternoon nap. It was a plan conceived in an office without windows. It wouldn't do.

At a famous meeting of intelligence heads, Strangeways stood and held up a copy of the Fortitude plan. He announced the plan was useless and proceeded to slowly tear it up in front of the men who'd written it. "It gave maximum offense," reported one officer. "What was said about Strangeways hardly bears repeating."

This was in February 1944. D-Day was scheduled for May 1. The men who'd planned Fortitude weren't amused. "Everybody was furious. This bumptious so-and-so, who does he think he is?" But because Strangeways had the backing of Monty, Britain's most powerful military commander, the deception planners had to at least listen to his ideas. Then they hoped to bury them.

Major Roger Fleetwood Hesketh was the sole intelligence officer of Ops (B), the deception operation embedded within SHAEF, Eisenhower's Supreme Headquarters Allied Expeditionary Force, and he numbered among the minds who'd formulated Bodyguard. He was a former barrister and a gentleman, "the beau ideal of an English country squire," whose twelfth-century manor, Meols, was regarded as the most haunted house in the country, while also boasting "one of the best claret cellars in England." One could hardly have found a more confident and well-entrenched member of the British establishment. As Strangeways was set to deliver his new deception plan in early February, Hesketh assured his officers that the scheme would be no more than warmed-over Bodyguard, with "a few new ideas" thrown in to save face. In the battle to create the deception plan for D-Day, the old guard, not this arrogant ponce, would prevail.

One day soon after his pronouncement, the revised document arrived at Hesketh's office. He read it through silently, then handed it to an MI5 officer and liaison, Christopher Harmer.

"What do you think?"

Harmer paged through the plan, reading with mounting astonishment. "It was a revelation," he would later say.

He looked up at Hesketh and gave his verdict.

"I can't believe we will ever get away with this."

16

The Ghost Army

MANY ALLIED OFFICERS believed that D-Day could not be "covered." It simply defied logic. The thing was too big and too visible. The British general J.F.M. Whiteley, who'd helped plan D-Day, told his friends he wouldn't wager a pound sterling on the success of the early version of Fortitude. One American intelligence officer, Ralph Ingersoll, called the idea of misleading Hitler like "putting a hooped skirt and ruffled pants on an elephant to make it look like a crinoline girl." When a member of the London Controlling Section went in front of one key group of high-ranking officers to present Bodyguard, his audience "flatly refused to believe that it would be possible to deceive the enemy" before D-Day. Then there were those who simply didn't *understand* what was being presented to them. When a staffer laid out the plan for Calais, one brigadier general protested, "But we are not *going* to land in the Pas de Calais."

Instead of scaling down the plan in the face of these doubts, Strangeways went in the opposite direction. He envisioned a much larger and riskier deception. The colonel proposed creating an imaginary army — the First United States Army Group, or FUSAG — of one million men where none existed, and sending it on an imaginary invasion where none was planned, at Calais. The new plan's aim was to trick the Nazis into believing that Normandy was a feint and that a huge, almost totally hidden army was waiting to stage the real attack. No one had so much as contemplated such an audacious gambit.

Strangeways wanted Garbo and the others to create an army of specters, while the Allies gave it a seething, audible, diesel-fumed life of its own, using specially trained regiments of soldiers and technicians, dozens of British navy ships and hundreds of the Eighth Air Force's fighter planes and bombers. Strangeways and his men would focus on the double agents and fake wireless traffic, and other units, under Operation Bodyguard, would create an amy of special effects — taped sounds, fake explosions, fake everything, to look and feel like an actual invasion.

The scheme was fresh and bold, miles away from the attacks on humble Nissen huts that the XX Committee had been engaged in only two years before. "After the initial shock, I think everyone was a bit shamefaced that they hadn't thought of it themselves," said the intelligence officer Christopher Harmer. A British historian would later describe Strangeways's approach as "true to the tradition of English eccentricity; the sort of thing that Captain Hornblower or [Sherlock] Holmes in fiction, or Admiral Cochrane or Chinese Gordon in fact, would have gone in for had they been faced with a similar challenge."

Creating this army out of thin air would normally take weeks if not months of committee meetings and strategic papers and negotiations between the army group and the signal corps, what Strangeways called "awful, ghastly staff procedures." He was having none of it: "All I did was to go to the Chief Signal Officer and say, 'Can you do this?' He said, 'Of course we can.' I knew him well, he knew what I did, and we never discussed anything about 'Why.'" *Why* was not a welcome question in the lieutenant colonel's world; *why* was the exclusive domain and property of David Strangeways. His men soon learned not to ask it. "We got away with murder," Strangeways recalled wistfully. "But it was all for the cause."

Juan Pujol never met David Strangeways, may never have heard his name. But he now had a planner whose vision was as fearless and broad-beamed as his own.

As the last-minute changes were made, five double agents took the lead. Brutus, the Polish airman, would be essential in passing to the enemy the false Order of Battle, the list of divisions readying for the invasion of France. Tate was a Danish spy, real name Wulf Schmidt, who'd parachuted into England in September 1940, been caught, thrown in prison, turned, and given his code name because he resembled the popular music-hall comedian Harry Tate, famous for his tag line, "How's your father?" He would pass information to the Germans on the American armies departing from the States for action in

Europe. Treasure was a high-strung Frenchwoman who once double-crossed MI5 because she believed one of its operatives had killed her dog; she was put out to pasture, but the secret services kept broadcasting in her name. Treasure would inform the Abwehr that Monty had been named commander of FUSAG, conditioning the Germans to the idea of Brits leading Americans, and vice versa, which would play a large part in the phony army's operations. Tricycle was the daring Serbian Dusko Popov, who would smuggle fake plans for the cross-Channel invasion into Lisbon and straight into German hands. Garbo was the first among equals. He would send countless "reports" from his network of "agents" spread far and wide.

To ramp up for Fortitude South, the fake attack on Calais, Garbo began sending his imaginary agents to the target cities and towns all over the south and southwest of England, the jumping-off point for the "attack" on Pas de Calais. In February, Agent 7 (2), the retired Welsh seaman, went to Dover; 7 (4), the Indian poet called Rags, was assigned to Brighton; the traveling businessman, 7 (5), was installed in Devon; and the treasurer of the fictitious Brothers in the Aryan World Order, known as 7 (7), made his way to Harwich. Agent No. 4, the waiter from Gibraltar who'd failed to lure Federico to the Chislehurst Caves, was sent to cover the 3rd Canadian Infantry Division in Hampshire. Agent No. 7 (3) journeyed to far-off India, but most of the phantom spies were lodged in possible embarkation points along the eastern and southeastern English coast. Garbo's "sources" inside the Ministry of Information and Ministry of War were also waiting, ready to be exploited. As far as the Germans knew, Garbo could now not only capture battle orders where they originated — London — but also detect them in the movements of men and materiel where the orders met the realities of the field. The fake Allied Order of Battle became all-important. What army was threatening France, what divisions and regiments comprised it, who commanded it, and where was it moving? This was what the Germans wanted to know.

When the soldiers began hitting the shore at Normandy, the attack would inevitably cause a split in the German leadership: one group who believed it was the real cross-Channel invasion, and another, persuaded by Garbo and his comrades, who believed it was a feint and the real blow would come at Calais. If Garbo could convince a core of true believers, they would act like mini-agents themselves, pushing the plan invented in London. Garbo had to convert these men, then give them the tools to win the battle within the German war machine.

Contrary to popular perception, the days after the invasion of Normandy — the beaches that the Allies referred to as the "far shore" — would be just as critical as D-Day itself. Most armies attacking a thinly fortified coast are able to gain at least a foothold on the beach by the sheer magnitude of the forces they bring to bear; the American, Canadian and British troops would far outnumber the German defenders on that first day and should be able to claim the first few yards of territory. Colonel Roenne had confirmed this when he took his Mercedes for a five-day tour of the Atlantic Wall in late October and early November 1943. It was clear to him that the Allies could land an invasion force almost anywhere they chose away from the heavily fortified harbors. It was in the days *after* the landing, when the D-Day forces would be most vulnerable, that success or defeat would be decided. The Allies would try to bring hundreds of thousands of men, tanks and supply trucks, howitzers and first-aid kits ashore, while the Germans would mass their forces to try to pinch off and destroy the exposed position of the Allies. Even Rommel conceded the point: "The enemy will probably succeed in creating bridgeheads at several different points and in achieving a major penetration of our coastal defenses. Once this has happened, it will only be by the rapid intervention of our operational reserves that he will be thrown back into the sea."

The Germans had been preparing for the cross-Channel invasion for two years, and they had ten armored divisions held in reserve for the counterattack. Eisenhower worried in particular about the German Fifteenth Army, with its three panzer divisions, camped just miles from the coast of Calais. MI5 estimated that if Garbo could prevent a single division out of that reserve from moving toward the beaches at Normandy for a full forty-eight hours after D-Day, the extraordinary time and effort that had gone into his character would have been worth it. One division for two days. That was the marker. Ten days was considered the absolute limit for the deception's lifespan.

Garbo himself wanted to achieve more. His hatred for Hitler had only increased in the past few months, as the war decimated regiments and whole cities at an appalling rate. "I'm not Jewish or Polish or French," he said, "but I felt the pain of the Jews and the Polish and the French."

The Fortitude strategy for Garbo was to feed the Abwehr a stream of mostly harmless information from the south and southeast of England — the fake embarkation points — that, at the beginning, was almost 100 percent true. The occasional phony report tossed in the mix would be covered by the checkable facts surrounding it. Then, over time, the ratio of truth to falsehood would be slowly and imperceptibly altered until the reports were 100 percent sham.

Just as Garbo was preparing to build his ghost divisions, a new questionnaire arrived from Madrid: "It would be of the greatest interest to know how many armies there will be and how many have already been formed. Headquarters and names of the commanders of each Army as well as their composition, i.e., corps and divisions under command, the objectives assigned to each army." The Germans had practically invited Garbo to fill in their charts with the fake regiments.

Garbo began to send "extremely high-grade" material, up to five and six messages a day; so much traffic was flowing to Madrid that he had to largely forget about writing long letters. He relied almost solely on the wireless. Between January 1944 and D-Day, he would send or receive more than five hundred messages, a breakneck pace. The Abwehr in Madrid set up a special office to deal with the "vital information" pouring in from his network alone.

He was sketching the outlines of a huge army unfolding itself across southeast England. There was no more time for flourishes; his prose grew Hemingwayesque. "By the main road between Leatherhead and Dorking I saw hundreds of lorries and cars parked. Jeeps. I also saw there about forty tanks camouflaged with nets . . . I also saw the insignia of the Second Army on a convoy of supply lorries in transit through Oxford in the direction of London. American insignias seen: The star of the SOS, the 8th Army Air Force, ground personnel of the USAAF, the head of an eagle . . . There are two or three

American camps in the District and at least a Pioneer Corps of Ne-
groes. The Americans carried out an exercise in Port Talbot starting
25th February employing artificial smoke."

Strangeways insisted that Garbo never point the finger at the Pas
de Calais. "You don't take a great big silver salver and give it to him
on that. He's got to make the story up himself. Then if the story goes
wrong he blames himself, not you." Garbo was careful never to mention the fake target; in fact, in the thousands of messages and rumors
and psych-ops actions, *no one* was allowed to mention Calais. It was
a gaudy piece of risk-taking on Strangeways's part. What if Roenne
and the Germans didn't assemble the points of information into the
portrait that the British desired? Subtlety had proven deadly during
Operation Cockade. But if they were too obvious, Roenne and Hitler
would suspect deceit.

As he built up FUSAG, Garbo also devised a strange piece of black
propaganda aimed at the doubters in the Third Reich. On February
23, he sent a letter concealed in a piggy bank shaped like Churchill's
head. In it, he revealed he'd had a long conversation with "his friend
at the Ministry" and learned that the British government was preparing plans in case the German army deserted France in advance of a
possible invasion. The Russian advance in the East, he told Madrid,
had convinced Whitehall that the Germans might retreat to their
home soil because they knew that Stalin's forces "will have respect for
no one, they will destroy her [Germany] completely and will remove
every useful man and use him as a slave to reconstruct Russia." British intentions, on the other hand, were much more benign. "[Ger-
man commanders] know we do not wish to see a ruined Germany.
It is not our intention to subjugate the German but to destroy everything which smells of Nazism and militant conquests. I believe that it
is very possible that the German Army itself will ask us to go to their
assistance to save them from the cataclysm which is approaching."

The piggy-bank letter was a gambit to get the Germans to surrender to the British, pumping up their fear of what Stalin would do once
he reached Berlin and at the same time offering generous terms for
capitulation. The Ministry of Information was tasked with making
sure there were no reprisals against collaborators or Nazi sympathizers, which told the Germans that the Brits were intent on protecting

them, while the Soviets would presumably slaughter them like sheep. (The letter foreshadowed the division of Berlin and the first days of the Cold War.) Garbo added the startling claim that FUSAG, the enormous army that was gathering in the south of England, wasn't an invasion force but an army of occupation.

Garbo even filched a leaflet — completely fake — that was to be dropped over France once the Germans left:

Frenchmen,

German troops are now evacuating French territory. French and Allied troops are now landing by sea and air in various parts of your country.

Avoid any popular manifestations against collaborators which might give grist to riots or similar occurrences. Whatever may be the feelings of anger against the enemy or those who may have collaborated with them, or acted against those patriots who have resisted German oppression, individual vengeance may lead to disturbances . . .

France is liberated. Long live the United Nations!

Dwight D. Eisenhower.

Commander in Chief of the Allied Expeditionary Force.

Of course, in sending the letter, the "super-Nazi" Garbo mocked the idea of withdrawing from France. "I told [the minister] the German was not a man who would withdraw like the Italian, and that his losses would be paid for in blood by those who took the gains." The seed, however, had been planted.

But even as Garbo began to cast his spell, the Germans almost immediately pierced it. In March, German embassies and legations around the world received an urgent message from Joachim von Ribbentrop, the minister of foreign affairs. It ordered them to find out what the code name Overlord meant, no matter the price. The secret name of the D-Day invasion was out, a tremendous coup for the aloof Colonel Roenne, who could now scan any Allied report for the code word.

As with Cockade, the genius in Zossen was proving much more formidable than the spymasters in Madrid.

17

The Backdrop

A S THE CALENDAR ticked toward June, the Allies were moving heaven and earth — and knocking heads together at a furious clip — to make Garbo's ghost army real.

General George Patton, commander of the real Third Army, was named commander of the imaginary million men of FUSAG. He was a logical choice: Hitler regarded Patton as the Allies' best leader, and the German High Command respected his unpredictable approach to war. Patton was soon spotted everywhere around southeastern England, rallying the nonexistent troops in appearances that were heavily reported in the press. A self-described "goddamned natural-born ham," Patton professed that he enjoyed "playing Sarah Bern-hardt." His performance wasn't subtle: he would say goodbye to fellow generals by calling out, "See you in the Pas de Calais!" And when he addressed the men of the Third Army, he'd awkwardly remind them, "You don't know I'm here at all."

David Strangeways had eliminated almost all of the physical deception from Operation Fortitude, preferring to rely on the double agents and wireless traffic. But the overall Operation Bodyguard still called for an enormous stage show to fool the Germans — and lend authenticity to Garbo's stratagems. Truth and falsehood were mixed together with calculated abandon: 250 Wetbobs — five-and-a-half-ton landing-craft decoys painstakingly constructed out of a thousand separate pieces — were moored in British harbors. Security was tight: when one unlit decoy was struck by a barge on the Orwell River, the barge's captain and crew were arrested and held until after D-Day. (Bumping a decoy immediately revealed that it was a hollow prop.)

Ersatz camps were built and campfires were kept burning by crews dashing from one to the next to maintain the right amount of rising smoke. Bulldozers carved fake airstrips into farmland and crews installed fake lights and built fake wooden aircraft to rest just off the runways, even turning them 90 degrees every day to give the illusion that they'd been flown during the night. When darkness fell, car headlights mounted on makeshift carriages were pulled up and down the airstrips to simulate fighters taking off and landing. The Luftwaffe attacked some of these chimeras that shimmered in their bomb sights, and crews worked furiously to repair the bomb craters, exactly as they would have done if the airstrip was real. The set decorators also devised fake bomb craters out of canvas, one version for bright days (with heavy shadows) and another for overcast days. The work was so lifelike that several RAF pilots tried to land on the runways and wrecked their planes in the process.

An entire valley in Cornwall was dammed, flooded and lit up. The deception planners hoped that Luftwaffe night raiders would mistake the flooded valley for a harbor and send their bombs into the water. Battalions, consisting of an average of 700 or 800 men, were ordered to impersonate divisions, which comprised about 15,000 soldiers. All the accoutrements of a real division were put in place: orders were issued to the commander, mail was sent to its headquarters, and the colonel or brigadier in charge of the battalion would emerge from his tent in the morning dressed in the uniform of a major general and step into a staff car flying a major general's pennant. All his staff officers got fake promotions and new uniforms (though their pay stayed the same), and their cars were repainted with the correct decals and insignia. They drove around town, flirted with WACs, got drunk in the local bars if they were lucky, all the while wearing their costumes and advertising their presence in the area. Hospitals and warehouses made out of wire, wood and canvas were thrown up in record time to service the fake assault forces.

One of the centerpieces of the scheme was a gigantic oil-storage facility built out of old wharf jetties, abandoned oil tanks and sewage pipes scavenged from wrecked cities. It was erected on a three-mile-long piece of shoreline near Dover. The Allies requisitoned a wind machine from a British movie studio to send billows of dust across the area so that the Luftwaffe would think construction crews were hard at work. Only if you walked around the gargantuan site would you see that the huts and buildings were all abandoned and the only thing flowing through the pipes was wind.

Monty and King George VI were shown in the newspapers inspecting the mammoth facility — newspapers that were being read in the Berlin Abwehr offices soon after — and Eisenhower gave a speech at the White Cliffs Hotel in Dover for the men who'd built the depot. RAF and American fighter planes patrolled over the fake terminal, but they were under orders to let a certain number of Luftwaffe reconnaissance planes fly past it unmolested — unless the planes dropped below 30,000 feet, considered to be the point at which their cameras would detect the illusion. Those low-flying aircraft were sent flaming into the ocean. But the pièce de résistance came when the powerful German batteries at Cap Gris Nez in Calais began sending their rounds arching toward the oil facility. When this happened, the skeleton crew of British soldiers who maintained the station lit sodium flares to fool the German spotters into thinking they'd scored a direct hit and the depot was engulfed in flames.

Pigeons were also drafted into something called Operation Columbia. Boxes of the birds were parachuted into Belgium, France and Holland with messages taped to their legs identifying them as property of FUSAG. Notes attached to the crates informed the finders that the homing birds would return to England if released; the notes also encouraged the local partisans to tape messages to the creatures' legs. Many of the pigeons returned to their home stations, one with a note attached to its leg, written in German cursive: "Here is your bird," it read. "We ate the other one."

The plot extended to the bookstores of Istanbul, Bern and Lisbon. Men and women marched into the shops and asked the proprietors if they had Michelin Map 51. If the owner didn't have a copy, the customer would raise his or her voice and demand that it be ordered. Map 51, of course, covered the Pas de Calais. Entire books and technical journals were written and printed by MI5 with invasion theories pointing to Calais, then slipped past the censors and sent to Germany.

In March, Churchill visited a sham armored division, arriving in his Humber staff car and puffing on a cigar as he inspected the fake tanks made out of rubber by movie-set designers from Shepperton Studios. "A most impressive display of armor," he remarked to his guide, Major General Hollis of the War Cabinet. "Yet, so you assure me, Hollis, each of these huge tanks could be vanquished by a bow and arrow?" Hollis told him a boy with a hunting knife could do the trick. Earlier, a bull had escaped a farmer's field and charged a dummy tank — and was spooked when the thing collapsed in a heap.

Vicars in Suffolk and Kent protested against the "decline of morals" among their female parishioners, due to the influx of strapping young American GIs in the eastern provinces. One outraged Brit wrote his local newspaper complaining about the sudden appearance of hundreds of used condoms near army camps. Women wrote in, furious about the dust that American jeeps sent billowing into their freshly washed sheets and nappies hanging on clotheslines. The GIs were real, of course, as was the culture shock when they arrived: the soldiers brought with them records like "Flat Foot Floogie" and "Mairzy Doats," called any Englishman they didn't know "Mac" and received checks that were five times the pay of the ordinary British soldier. But they were mostly in the west and south of the country, where the real embarkation ports were. All those outraged letters that appeared in newspapers from the east of England were written by young intelligence officers back in London. The double agents "spotted" the letters and sent clippings to their controllers in Madrid and, eventually, Berlin.

As Pujol and Harris worked fourteen-hour days sending information — which slowly changed from all true to completely false — the Allies produced an incredible variety of devices to trick the senses before and during the invasion: flame and smoke flares dropped by aircraft onto the water, which would produce the illusion of a torpedo boat on fire; drone boats that could simulate the explosion of an assault craft; naval prosthetics — massive wood-and-canvas movie-set shells — that could turn a modest frigate into a *Colorado*-class battleship, or a sub chaser into an escort carrier. The result of the last invention was called a "Swiss Navy," a collection of fairly harmless vessels that appeared to be a significant attack force. Battle sounds were recorded on magnetic wire or sound film, simulating the noises of ironworkers building a bridge or the engine of a landing craft turning over or the roar of onrushing tanks. The Allies' library of sensory diversions could simulate raging fire, a six-hour platoon engagement, poison gas (the chemical burned the skin like mustard gas but didn't kill), the smell of cordite, an entire naval convoy (by the use of "window," strips of paper coated with aluminum foil on one side that appeared on radar to be massive ships), a fleet of aircraft (achieved by "spoof vans," trucks carrying transmitters that played the sound of engines thousands of feet above) and much more. Even the London *Times* was shanghaied into the effort: special editions were printed and left in conspicuous places, featuring altered photos that showed battleships in the Firth of Forth in Scotland.

England was sealed up tight, becoming an island fortress hostile to any foreign intruder. Coastal areas from Land's End to the northwest border of East Anglia, and from Arbroath to Dunbar in Scotland, were declared off-limits to visitors within ten miles of the shoreline. A dazzling array of physical deceptions were readied: machines for making tank tracks, dummy paratroopers that would explode when they hit the ground and torpedoes called "water heaters" that, when fired, propelled themselves to an assigned point, waited, then at the correct time ascended to the surface and played recorded sound effects. There were the "Bunsen burners," invented by the Americans, that consisted of a radio receiver attached to a loudspeaker; when dropped by parachute onto a battlefield, they flooded the area with voices or battle noises, then self-destructed after four hours. There were devices called "pintails" that stuck in the ground on impact and sent off a "Verey light" exactly like the flare that paratroop officers used to signal their troops; not to mention radios that could simulate the noise of war, chemical concoctions that could re-create the smell of war, phonographs that played snatches of soldiers' conversations or the din of entire squadrons of fake soldiers. Then there were "black propaganda" campaigns: leaflets dropped over enemy territory and subversive messages broadcast by clandestine radio stations. A series of rumors — called a "sibs campaign," after the Latin word *sibilare*, to hiss — was planted as far away as Rio de Janeiro. War gossip and false leads were spread in neutral embassies in Lisbon and elsewhere, and foreign diplomats in London were given "tips" on what was really happening with the invasion plans. Prisoners of war in German concentration camps received letters spiced with chatter intended for the eyes of the German censors.

Insignia were invented for Garbo's phantom armies: for the First Army Group it was a black Roman numeral I on a blue pentagon. Some persnickety clerk in the quartermaster general's office protested the design, saying that "the placing of black on blue violates the law of visibility," but the colors were kept. Four signal groups were set up in different parts of England to simulate the traffic of both the ghost army and the real divisions. A single wireless truck impersonated the communications of an entire divisional headquarters, sending messages to its various brigades. The Americans brought over their own specially trained unit, the 3103rd Signal Service Battalion, to roam the English countryside and coordinate the movements of the forces that "belonged" to Garbo. When Garbo "spotted" a large number of shoulder patches indicating that some troops had moved camp, trucks would emit bursts of traffic sounds from the new location.

All the while Colonel Roenne watched, and the Allies intercepted his reports to gauge the deception's impact. When the estimated number of Allied divisions rose in his intelligence reports, the planners smiled. As Garbo fed the Germans FUSAG sightings and Strangeways created Allied facsimiles out of canvas and rumors, those numbers started to increase. In January 1944, Roenne estimated that there were 55 divisions in the United Kingdom. The actual number was 37.

The unexpected, however, could never be eliminated. In Plan Gotham, merchant ships carried scores of landing craft on their decks as they sailed into the Strait of Gibraltar. The purpose was to show the Germans — who watched all traffic in and out of the strait from a dozen lookout posts along the shore — that assets were not being drawn away from the Mediterranean toward England. That would keep Hitler worried about Norway. And the landing craft were actually large inflatable decoys. All went well on one Liverpool shipment until the wind picked up, at which point any German observers gazing through their binoculars would have seen these multi-ton craft bouncing crazily on the ship's deck like so many birthday balloons.

Some of the plans never made it off the drawing board, or proved to be a dud in the field. In Operation Leyburn, intelligence officers discreetly asked authorities in neutral countries about how to protect great works of art that were stored in the Low Countries. The idea was to hint that the invasion was headed toward Holland, but the Germans didn't get it. The Americans contributed the "truly bizarre idea" of trying a Dunkirk in reverse: hundreds of small fishing smacks and other boats would gather in the ports of southeastern England as if they were preparing to bring two million men to Calais. The plan was dropped: Why on earth would the Allies use fishing boats? Other schemes worked brilliantly. To bulk up Fortitude North, the phony invasion of Norway, the Royal Air Force flew dummy aircraft from fields in Suffolk to eastern Scotland, enough to give the impression that four heavy bomber divisions were being transferred closer to Scandinavia. The British minister to Sweden innocently asked his counterparts if he could gather weather data in Stockholm and even put up sophisticated air navigation equipment. The only reason one would do such a thing was to prepare for a fleet of landing craft streaming north.

Operation Graffham quickly ramped up the pressure on Sweden. The same minister asked if the country would permit Allied aircraft to land at Swedish airfields, and demanded that "British transport experts" be allowed into the country to plan for a German withdrawal from Norway. He also requested that Allied planes be allowed to fly reconnaissance missions over the country. A commodore was sent to Sweden to meet with the commander in chief of the nation's air force. If the Allies invaded Norway, the commodore asked, would the Swedes send their troops to stop the certain mass murder of Norwegians in the internment camps? At the same time, wireless operators sent messages from Garbo's phantom divisions. A typical one read, "80 Div. request 1,800 pairs of crampons, 1,800 pairs of ski bindings."

The Germans were spooked: "Reliably reported soundings by high-ranking English Air Force officers in Sweden which aimed at the handing over of Swedish air bases for invasion purposes, may be regarded as an indication of a *small operation* in the Scandinavian area." Hitler decided to keep 250,000 badly needed troops in Norway and Denmark, when British analysts estimated only 100,000 were needed to keep the peace. That was 150,000 extra troops that wouldn't be fighting in Normandy.

Operation Copperhead was taken right from a Hollywood screenplay. On a visit south of Naples, the deception mastermind Dudley Clarke took a break from his punishing schedule to see *Five Graves to Cairo*, a Billy Wilder spy flick that incorporated actual footage from the Battle of El Alamein in its closing scenes. Starring as Rommel was the Austrian star Erich von Stroheim, who designed his own costume and studied photographs of the famous German general for hours on end. Wilder was in awe of the actor: "Standing with his stiff fat neck in the foreground, he could express with his face more than almost any other actor."

Sitting in the audience, Clarke watched in fascination. The impersonation, as over-the-top as it was, and the appearance of a British actor who resembled General Montgomery, gave him an idea. If von Stroheim could play Rommel in the film, why couldn't a British actor play the real Monty — in the real war?

Clarke knew the Abwehr maintained an observation post on Gibraltar, perched over the airfield so it could observe through a telescope every passenger arriving on the daily flights. If Monty suddenly appeared, it would mean that the British general was reconnoitering launch bases for the phony attack on the western French Mediterranean. The phony attack was called Operation Vendetta, and for months it had been critically short of assets: there were hardly any real soldiers attached to Vendetta, and hardly any attack vessels. A visit by Monty would work wonders. The hero of El Alamein was wild about the scheme, which was fairly predictable, as Guy Liddell drily noted in his diary, because it turned "on the theory that the Second Front cannot possibly start without him."

The actor who played Monty in *Five Graves to Cairo* was much taller than the real general, which made him less than ideal, and a backup imposter had broken his leg in an automobile crash. Clarke had to look outside the acting profession. After a search of the British ranks, he found the perfect double in the offices of the Royal Army Pay Corps: Lieutenant M. E. Clifton James, who could have passed for Monty's twin. James had imitated Monty once before, when a British war rally was floundering. James stepped onstage, pretending to be the famous general, and the crowd had gone wild.

James was now flown to meet Monty, to study how he walked, talked and moved his hands when he spoke; the impersonator was told to give up drinking and smoking (Monty did neither), and a prosthetic was attached to the stub of his middle right finger, which James had lost in World War I. Then, on May 26, 1944, he was flown to Gibraltar on Churchill's private plane. During the flight, James sneaked to the back of the plane and drank gin from a hidden flask, to the horror of his minders. At twenty thousand feet, the imposter was "slapped, massaged . . . and doused with cold water" to sober him up.

When the plane landed, the fake Monty was whisked off to a reception, where he dropped hints about something called Plan 303 for the invasion of France (there was, of course, no such thing). One of the invited guests was Ignacio Molina Pérez, a Spanish liaison officer and Abwehr spy. Pérez's eyes nearly popped out of his head at the sight of the resplendent general. "Eagerly he turned to the Colonial Secretary for further news while the latter with feigned embarrassment was forced to admit that the Commander-in-Chief was on his way to Algiers." Pérez left the party and was seen jumping into his car and speeding off to the town of La Línea, where he called his Abwehr contact. Finally, the fake Monty was brought to Algiers and paraded around, drawing the Germans' attention to the Middle Eastern theater, before being stashed in Cairo until D-Day launched.

The Allies also used basic economics to fool the Nazis. When they had wanted the Germans to believe an invasion of Greece was coming in 1943, the paymaster of GHQ Middle East had begun buying up drachmas by the barrel-load. The deception planners wanted to try a slightly different tack for Operation Bodyguard. They asked the British treasury to print pound notes with "British Army of Occupation in France" stamped across the front. British operatives stuck a few in their wallets, and when presented with a restaurant or hotel bill, they would pull out one of the marked notes. "Then, having allowed the person to look at it, we hurriedly snatched it back and handed them an ordinary pound note." This simple trick helped to spread rumors about the forthcoming invasion around London.

The Americans tried a subtler scheme. They'd realized earlier that sending partisans out to the railyards south of Paris to check on the effects of Allied bombing raids was costing too many lives and exposing the French resistance to the Gestapo. Now they simply checked the weekly price of oranges in Les Halles, the huge wholesale marketplace where merchants came to buy produce. If the price went up, it meant that trains were not getting through and that the bombs were hitting their marks. If the price went down, it meant that the bombardiers had to adjust their tactics. In the lead-up to D-Day, the deception planners also looked into the international fire insurance market in certain areas of occupied France. The hope was that equally sophisticated German thinkers were keeping an eye on the market for clues as to where the Allies were planning on dropping incendiary bombs, believing they would insure their targets before they struck. In February 1944, one double agent, a businessman working with British intelligence, notified the Abwehr that he'd landed a job with the Fire Office Committee, a British group that tracked insurance policies around the world. He reported that a curious thing had happened: an unnamed government agency was making inquiries about Norway, Belgium and northern France. Could it be . . . ?

Even some of the Allied agents and operatives who were creating these apparitions were half convinced they were real. "The world of make-believe in which we lived . . . was apt to engender a strange mental attitude," said Colonel Roderick Macleod, who spent months working on the Norway feint. "As time went on we found it harder to separate the real from the imaginary." Pujol felt the same way about his phantom soldiers. "I created them. They were my children."

By the early spring of 1944, the tapestry was weaving itself together from a thousand strands. The ingenious plots hatched by the deception planners were the background scenery that made the double agents' work feel authentic. But Garbo and the others were still the point of the spear, the people whom the Germans were listening to most closely. Without the Germans' confidence in Garbo, even the most ingenious plot would have been irrelevant.

By May, Roenne counted 79 divisions in England, when there were only 52. The deception gap had increased from 18 to 27. Yet that number was the result of more than the double agents' cunning. One day in the summer of 1943, Roenne had buttonholed his operations officer, Lieutenant Colonel Lothar Metz, who worked up Foreign Armies West's daily report on the Allied forces. "From now on," Roenne told Metz, "we have to exaggerate. The Operations Staff deducts a certain percentage from everything that we report. So we have to get ready for that. We have to exaggerate."

Roenne knew that Hitler refused to accept accurate estimates of the Russian forces in the East, because doing so would make it clear that the Wehrmacht was overmatched. Anyone who told the truth about the enemy was branded a defeatist and either persecuted or ignored. Roenne felt an ancient duty to protect Germany, and inflating the numbers, he believed, would serve as a hedge against Hitler's rejection of the truth. Even if the Führer reduced Roenne's manpower estimates, they would still be closer to the truth than the rosy numbers proffered by Hitler's underlings.

Metz was stunned. "Herr Colonel, I can't do that. I learned as a soldier that you must answer for what you do. It has to be true."

Roenne told his underling to think it over for twenty-four hours. The next day, Metz came back with his answer. He would do it.

The deception planners had been unable to exploit most of Hitler's psychological quirks. But here was a German officer reacting to the Führer's denial of reality by creating an illusion to compete with Hitler's illusion. Garbo's chimera was receiving an unexpected boost from inside Germany.

"Tangle within tangle," Churchill wrote. "Plot and counter-plot, ruse and treachery, cross and double-cross, true agent, false agent, double agent, gold and steel, the bomb, the dagger and the firing party, were interwoven in many a texture so intricate as to be incredible and yet true."

The route to Berlin was clear. Every single message Garbo sent to Madrid was being relayed to the German capital and then teleprinted on to Colonel Roenne's staff at Zossen. Not only that, every eyewitness report of a drunken American soldier in an English pub or a company of paratroopers spotted through a windshield was being forwarded to Berlin — and, due to Roenne's scheme, the number of soldiers was being dialed up. "The movement and regrouping of all notional and misplaced formations," Harris wrote, "the subject of the reports of the Garbo network, became the subject of the Daily Intelligence reports of the German Supreme Command, to be widely circulated in German official circles, and on which all German appreciations were subsequently based."

Garbo was winning the game. He, along with Brutus and Tate, had succeeded in creating a million-man ghost army in England where there were only empty tents and spoof vans. But that was only half the mission.

As D-Day rapidly approached, the next question became: How can we convince the Germans that the real army that will land on French shores on June 6 *isn't* real? That it is, in fact, something else entirely? Now that he and Strangeways had conjured a million men out of thin air, Garbo had to take the real American and Canadian and British soldiers, and the thousands of tanks and jeeps that were going to hit the beaches of Normandy, and make them disappear.

For a number of reasons, some of them obvious, some of them completely unforeseen, that turned out to be a much more difficult proposition.

18

The Buildup

NSIDE GERMANY, THE SPLIT in the German High Command
that Tommy Harris had long predicted was becoming a reality.
Hitler had been firmly in the Calais camp for months. But
by mid-spring 1944, he was focusing more and more on Normandy.
On March 4, the Führer pointed to Normandy and Brittany as the
most likely targets of the invasion. At a meeting with his generals on
the twentieth, he gave them the same message: watch Normandy. In
April, studying a map of the French coastline, he tapped his finger on
the rocky shore and said, "I am for bringing all our strength in here."
On May 2, the deputy of General Jodl, chief of the Operations Staff,
rang Field Marshal Gerd von Rundstedt at his headquarters, a stun-
ning mansion on the Seine west of Paris, and told him that extra men
and materiel were needed to shore up the defenses in Normandy and
Brittany. "A partial success by the enemy in the two peninsulas would
inevitably at once tie down very strong forces of OB West," the German armies in France and occupied Europe.

Roenne and Rommel, along with most of the German High Command, had backed the Calais option all along. Even an amateur war
buff could instantly see the advantages to attacking its coastline,
and the training that German officers received — with its emphasis
on logical and orthodox theory, not on deception — backed up that
thinking. But in the beginning of May, Rommel lobbied Hitler for
control of the reserve forces to bulk up the defenses in Normandy.
Rundstedt protested; he wanted those divisions held in reserve until
the main attack came. For the moment, Hitler sided with Rundstedt,
but Rommel was increasingly nervous about the thin line of defend-

ers behind the beaches that would become known as Omaha, Utah, Gold, Juno and Sword.

There was a secondary fracture in the leadership: some German analysts warned of a one-strike invasion and others believed that there would be two attacks, the first one a ruse. Hitler wavered on whether the opening attack would be a feint or the real thing. But by May, Jodl was telling the chief of staff of the commander in chief in the West that Normandy "would be the first target of the enemy." The *first* target — indicating, of course, that there would be a second, and much more powerful, assault elsewhere.

In their office, Pujol and Harris had been working nonstop to strengthen this suspicion. On April 9, Garbo radioed Madrid: "The situation as explained to me by the agents from the south coast is really alarming, enemy action is expected from one minute to the next." He begged his contacts to confirm what he was hearing. "You must make reconnaissance over the north west ports of England to ascertain whether the ships mentioned in my message of yesterday are actually there." Garbo knew, of course, that the ships would be there; he never sent a message without knowing that assets were in place.

Then, in late April, the fictitious Gibraltarian waiter known as No. 4 "sent" a letter to Garbo in London saying the 3rd Canadian Infantry Division had been issued vomit bags, life vests and cold rations. These were the last things a soldier got before being sent on an amphibious assault. The only possible conclusion? The invasion was a go.

Was D-Day here? Garbo flew into a frenzy. But Agent J (5) — the secretary in the War Ministry with whom Garbo was having a torrid affair — contradicted the reports. She claimed the movements that No. 4 had seen were just part of an exercise, practice for the real thing. A bitter conflict erupted between the two subagents, created and expertly manipulated by Garbo, who took the side of No. 4. When that operative "reported" that the 3rd Canadian had been ordered to clear an area of its camp to prepare for the arrival of second-line troops, the spymaster pounced on the claim that this was just an exercise: "This proves J (5)'s lie, because she suggested, naively, today that troops in the southern area were on maneuvers." Garbo messaged Madrid that his lover, J (5), was being hoodwinked. He warned the German High Command to prepare for a million men coming ashore in France beginning in the next few hours.

For Garbo and Tommy Harris it was a calculated risk. Would Garbo lose credibility by foreseeing a massive attack that wouldn't materialize? Or would he gain credibility by showing he was human and didn't always interpret his own intelligence correctly? The troops, of course, didn't come. Indeed, the movement that Garbo's invented subagents were seeing was part of an actual rehearsal: Exercise Fabius was the final dry run for D-Day. On May 3, assault divisions across the south of England poured into their naval support craft and each set off for a replica of its landing zone. Elements of the 3rd Canadian stormed Bracklesham Bay in West Sussex, while the U.S. 1st Infantry pounded up the beach at Slapton Sands.

A week before, during another rehearsal called Exercise Tiger, nine German patrol boats had spotted the American landing craft and attacked. Mayhem had ensued: Allied craft were raked by friendly fire, and soldiers unused to the water put on their life vests incorrectly and sank like stones. Sherman DD tanks spilled into the sea, and a transport struck by German bullets erupted in a fireball. The American troops jumped into the drink, where the weight of their combat packs forced their heads under the waters of Lyme Bay. Six hundred eighty-three soldiers died, all American, all for a mere exercise. When the survivors crawled up on Slapton Sands, more snafus caused the heavy cruiser HMS *Hawkins* to open up with live ammo, and 308 more men perished in the chaos.

It had been another black cloud over the invasion. The carnage had also harmed the deception plan. Unknown to the Brits, Hitler received reports of the disastrous exercise and, with his uncanny recall for the obscurities of coastal anomalies, remembered that the beaches at Slapton Sands closely resembled those of Normandy. The blunder reinforced his growing belief that the Allies would come ashore there.

Now Exercise Fabius, the last drill before the actual D-Day, was under way. The messages from Agents No. 4 and J (5) were part of the deception: they showed the Germans that Garbo's network was primed and ready for the invasion. When it became clear that Fabius wasn't the real thing, on May 7 Garbo sent his regrets that he'd jumped the gun; he blamed the whole thing on a twitchy operative: "4 has displayed the ability of a simpleton. I am very disgusted with him though I have not let him know this."

This was a subtle psychological trick that Garbo often used: kvetching about how idiotic his agents were, something the Abwehr men could sympathize with. It was like water-cooler talk among spymasters, and the Abwehr responded in kind. "We here, in the very small circle of colleagues," they wrote him at one point, "who know your story and that of your organization, talk so often about you that it often seems as if we were living the incidents which you relate to us, and we most certainly share, to the full, your worries." There were other ways that Garbo bound Kühlenthal and Federico to him; his discovery of secret Aryans and anti-British and corrupt ministers told the Germans what they wanted to hear: namely, that England was honeycombed with Nazi sympathizers who *wanted* the Germans to invade. Garbo presented a vision of an enemy that almost wished, and certainly deserved, to be defeated. It was all part of what the Germans called "nerve warfare."

Garbo reported to Madrid that No. 4 was a little discouraged by his great stupidity. Kühlenthal urged forgiveness: "You should give him more encouragement as, if not, it might happen that when the real invasion is about to take place he will not notify this owing to over-precaution." Everyone was on a hair trigger, looking for the first signs of D-Day. Meanwhile, the stock of Agent J (5), who'd correctly identified Fabius as an exercise, shot up. It was exactly what Garbo had wanted.

In May, the French resistance reported that Rommel had moved the highly capable Panzer Lehr Division from Hungary to France, and the 21st Armored Division had been sent to Caen, only thirty minutes from the Normandy beaches. There were rumors that other panzer divisions would follow, which indicated that the Germans now believed the real invasion was coming at Normandy. The news disturbed the invasion planners in London. Was the deception effort a lost cause? Normandy was being more and more exposed as the likely target of D-Day. The second part of Garbo's mission — the

Calais deception — had to be ramped up to distract the German High Command from the Allies' true intentions.

The chimera was ready to move.

To shift German eyes from west to east, FUSAG hit the road. The actual Third U.S. Army had been annexed to the sham FUSAG, lending it some real boots on the ground. The Third Army was then located in Cheshire, in the northwest of England, but if it was going to be part of an invasion of Calais, it had to be on the east coast, closer to the target. Instead of transferring the men and jeeps and tanks hundreds of miles — a plan that would have placed a heavy strain on commanders — the move was transmitted through the air. A squad of writers eavesdropped on the Third's signal traffic, then created new "scripts" that placed them in the east. Though the chatter was secret — and enciphered — the text in the messages was pure gibberish, laboriously created by signal operators by choosing the fourth or fifth word of a newspaper article, until IBM invented a machine that spewed out a completely random series of words. Everything was done under a tight cover of secrecy; the radio operators who sent the messages were themselves never told if the traffic was real or imaginary. Even a tiny change in their technique might give away the game to the Germans.

The Third Army's wireless network in the west of England went silent, then popped up weeks later in East Anglia, close to the eastern shore. The Allies had invented a device that allowed a single set to mimic the traffic of six radios, so that the entire division's signals could be imitated by one operator. The Germans soon picked up the traffic and placed a pin on their maps locating the Third Army in its new home of East Anglia, when the real troops were hundreds of miles away.

Troop trains and road convoys were coordinated so that the double agents could "see" the locomotives pass through real towns at the real times that Garbo reported. A card catalog was even kept showing the position of every FUSAG regiment and battalion; when double agents "traveled" through a part of southeastern England, they knew which units they'd run into. Garbo's Agent 7 (7), the treasurer of the Brothers in the Aryan World Order, "spotted" tank officers in

Ipswich, hundreds of miles from their home base, and reported it; the Germans duly moved the flag for their unit on their big map: "The 6th American Armored Division, hitherto believed to be in the county of Worcester, is . . . said to be in the East of England in the Ipswich area." Every sighting pushed the German gaze east, away from the real embarkation points in the west. "The main enemy concentration," a May 15 intelligence report stated, "is showing itself ever more clearly to be in the South and South-East of England." The real invasion force hadn't moved an inch. The fake one was now facing Calais.

Garbo flashed sightings from his subagents, who spotted FUSAG insignias — the black Roman numeral I on the blue pentagon he'd planted in the Germans' minds weeks before — in towns near the coastline. Plotting the reports onto a map, the Germans saw the forces were heading toward the ports around Dover. On May 29, a massive convoy of actual fighter aircraft, composed of 66 airborne squadrons, took off from airfields in Hampshire, in the south of England. One of Garbo's invented subagents watched them go, but reported they were really leaving from fields around Kent and Sussex, which pointed the finger away from Normandy. The planes dropped their bombs on Calais, and the Luftwaffe confirmed the raid.

As D-Day drew closer, Garbo's 80-watt radio glowed hot. May 25: "Through an American contact in the 28th Division I have learnt that Churchill, Smuts, Eisenhower and Patton were on the 12th May at the demonstration of a secret weapon . . ." (It was a device for blowing up concrete fortifications like the ones dotting Omaha Beach.) May 31: "Sutton Common North east Sutton Shottisham Road has been churned by tanks and is obviously tank exercising and testing ground." Garbo's network was now so large that he could feed the Abwehr production information from the United States: "Present aircraft production 300 per month. Military transport vehicles about 15000 per month. Priority now given to aircraft and signals equipment. Canada sending to England 1 million tons flour, ½ million tons bacon and pork, 43000 tons canned fish, 64000 tons cheese, 480 million eggs."

The spy even tried a classic reversal technique. On May 22, Garbo told Madrid that J (3), his Ministry of Information contact, had invited him to work for the Political War Executive (PWE), the masters of black propaganda. Madrid leapt at the chance, giving its approval the next day. The purpose of Garbo's scheme was to supply the Germans with propaganda leaflets that they would read in reverse: if the PWE said Normandy was the target, then the Germans could be certain that the Allies were headed for Calais. "What I was clearly able to get out of it," wrote Garbo after studying the PWE's work, "and what I consider to be of the maximum importance is the intention to hide the facts in order to trick us."

This was the flowering of Garbo's longest game, begun back in the wild old days of Lisbon. He was playing analyst again, doing what no other spy did. Garbo wasn't just aiming to outwit people like Roenne. He wanted to, in a sense, replace them.

As the days counted down, conflicts arose. The XX Committee ordered Harris and Pujol to pass traffic about a proposed invasion of Bordeaux, a feint called Operation Ironside, which would be launched with two divisions on "D plus 10"—that is, ten days after D-Day. The two men didn't think much of the plan: Bordeaux wasn't on the Germans' radar as a target, and just how many feints were the Nazis expected to believe anyway? Two second-tier agents—Tate and a young Peruvian beauty code-named Bronx—did as ordered and hinted about a coming invasion. Bronx had been given special codes by the Germans, each of which indicated a different target. A telegram reading, "I need 175 pounds for dental work," meant the attack was coming in the Balkans, and a request for 200 pounds meant Greece. Bronx now sent a message to the Abwehr that her dental work would cost 125 pounds. It was the signal for Bordeaux.

But Garbo held out. He would eventually send a message on June 5, but then he qualified the report by saying he doubted its accuracy. Pujol and Harris weren't about to sacrifice their hard-won reputation over a trifle like Ironside.

Even between agents, tempers flared. When Garbo and Agent Brutus passed almost identical messages relating to Patton, Brutus's case officer blew up: "It seems to me preposterous," he wrote to his

MI5 superiors, "that two agents should have obtained such exactly similar material on so important and secret a matter." Identical messages pointed to a script — which could indicate to the Germans that the two agents were under Allied control. Luckily, the Abwehr saw Garbo's report not as exposing Brutus's information, but as confirming it. The Allies' luck was holding.

As Garbo moved his army group east toward its imaginary jumping-off point, Allied Bomber Command joined the effort. Their planes dropped high explosives on forty-nine enemy airfields, hitting twice as many in Calais as in Normandy. Nineteen railroad junctions were bombed in Calais, none in Normandy. Pilots flew sorties and blew out the bridges over the rivers Seine, Oise and Meuse and the Albert Canal, snapping the telephone and telegraph wires that led out of Calais. But they had done the same for Cockade, and everyone knew what the result had been. Were the Germans watching? Were they putting the pieces together correctly?

In May, the German general Hans von Cramer, a veteran of Rommel's Afrika Korps, was released from an Allied POW camp because of ill health. As a high-ranking officer, before leaving he'd been treated to a dinner with the legendary General Patton, who was described throughout the meal as the commander of FUSAG. Patton charmed General von Cramer, and no expense was spared on the food and wine. The conversation drifted now and then to the delights of the French regions, in particular Calais.

Von Cramer left the dinner and was taken to a Red Cross ship that sailed across the English Channel to occupied France. After arriving, von Cramer rushed to the High Command in Berlin and told them about the amazing things he'd seen and heard: on the way to the ship, he'd managed to sneak several peeks out of the transport window. The roads were packed with American and British troops, thousands upon thousands of them, clearly getting ready to embark for an invasion. The harbor he was taken to was thick with assault craft of every description. And the two officers who'd escorted him to the ship had let slip where they were: near Dover, straight across the Channel from Calais.

The members of the High Command listened with growing astonishment. Von Cramer was the only German eyewitness to the D-Day preparations. The veil had slipped. They packed von Cramer into a car and sent him to Hitler's headquarters, where he repeated his story to the Führer.

Of course, von Cramer's route to the Red Cross ship had been carefully planned to show him as many troops as possible. From the car he'd had a clear view of the regiments marching along the road. The two British officers who'd gossiped about their whereabouts were actually intelligence officers. The roads von Cramer had been traveling on were in southwestern England, not the southeast. And the harbor where the ship was waiting had been Portsmouth, the natural launching point for an attack on Normandy.

Hitler remained suspicious about Normandy, yet Garbo and the XX Committee were making progress. Churchill was reading reports of Garbo's successes. Heinrich Himmler sent a personal note of congratulations to Kühlenthal in Madrid on his finding such a valuable gem — and asked Garbo to keep a sharp eye out. "The object of further reconnaissance [that is, Garbo's espionage] must be to ascertain in good time when embarkation began and the destination of the groups of forces in south east England." Colonel Roenne even quoted Garbo in a report on enemy intentions, pasting a snippet of conversation between Garbo and his friend at the Ministry of Information into his own evaluation. Tommy Harris marveled: "It is a unique case of an agent's report being quoted verbatim in an official report of so high a level."

MI5 also noticed a subtle change in the incoming questionnaires: not only was the Abwehr asking about Garbo's phantom divisions, indicating that the fake FUSAG had turned real in the German mind, but the questionnaires were no longer originating in Madrid. They were coming directly from Berlin.

With twenty-three days left until D-Day, Garbo began the overture for the last part of the caper. He met with his phony paramour at the Ministry of War and "learned" that the invasion would open with a diversion, to draw Hitler's reserves away from the still unknown target area. True to Strangeways's maxim, Garbo never mentioned Calais or Normandy, but the implication was clear. The first attack would be a feint, and the Germans must hold their forces back until the real invasion began. Eight days later, it was the Ministry of Information's turn: Garbo was asked to help write pamphlets on the second front, based on actual military reports, which would be sent to Latin America. It was through a Ministry of Information leak that Garbo had predicted the invasion of North Africa, the news of which had tragically reached the Germans one day too late to be of any use. This time, he would send the warning by wireless, so there would be no delay. He would reveal the truth about D-Day as it happened.

It was impossible to keep Normandy completely off Hitler's radar. It held too many advantages for an invading force. So as the clock ticked closer to the final hour, the trick was to make Hitler believe that what he would soon witness wasn't entirely real. Though you are seeing troops at Normandy, Garbo was saying, you are not *really* seeing troops at Normandy. They are fakes, imposters, bugaboos. Ignore them.

On May 28, only nine days before D-Day, there was a sign that Garbo and Brutus were getting through to Hitler: the Allies had intercepted a message from the Japanese ambassador to his superiors in Tokyo that contained the record of a long conversation with the Fürher:

> Speaking of the Second Front, Hitler . . . thought that about eighty divisions had already been assembled in England . . . I accordingly asked the Führer if he thought that these British and American troops had completed their preparations for landing operations and he replied in the affirmative. I then asked him in what form he thought the Second Front would materialize, and he told me that at the moment what he himself thought was most probable was that after having carried out diversionary operations in Norway, Denmark and the southern part of the western coast of France and the French Mediterranean coast, they would establish a bridgehead in Normandy or Brittany, and after seeing how things went would then embark upon the establishment of a real Second Front in the Channel. Germany would like nothing better, he said, than to be given a chance of coming to blows with large forces of the enemy as soon as possible.

So Normandy would be followed by the "real Second Front." The information, Hitler said, came from "relatively clear portents." The portents were Garbo, Brutus and a few other trusted sources. They'd penetrated to the core of the German leadership.

It was excellent news. But a thousand miles away, in Lisbon, events were reaching a climax in a drama that would throw Garbo's entire mission into doubt just as it seemed to be paying off. A month before, on April 29, a mysterious and conflicted man, a friend of P. G. Wodehouse's, a spy-runner close to Hitler's personal interpreter, described in his MI6 file as "a blond, monocle, very bad black teeth, very clever," had vanished from the spy capital of Europe. The Gestapo was suspected in his disappearance. And the missing man knew everything there was to know about Garbo.

19

The Prisoner

IS REAL NAME WAS Johann "Johnny" Jebsen, and like the clichés of an old-school German villain, he clamped a monocle over his right eye, but with a slight air of irony. The son of a wealthy Hamburg shipping mogul, he'd studied at the medieval German university at Freiburg. Jebsen played the part of a young shipping scion impeccably: fine suits, dazzlingly beautiful girlfriends, a supercharged Mercedes-Benz 540K convertible to roar through the shady depths of the Black Forest. In the early 1930s, the university was swarming with brownshirts (the Sturmabteilung, or storm troopers) and blackshirts (the SS), but Jebsen disdained them. He was a free spirit who hated Hitler and the book burners who patrolled the campus.

It was at Freiburg that Jebsen met the suave Dusko Popov, the future Allied double agent Tricycle, who was also studying at the university and casting a mocking eye at the local SS boys. The two became fast friends. In fact, Jebsen served as Popov's second in a duel over a woman, in which the Serb had shocked the Freiburg student body by choosing pistols over the traditional sabers. The other duelist protested the choice, and Jebsen handled the complex negotiations, claiming that obscure Serbian cavalry honor codes obligated his friend to fight only with firearms. It was a white lie. Popov had chosen guns because he was a deadly shot; he'd won marksmanship contests back in Dubrovnik. The duel was soon called off.

Popov's almost reckless daring showed in other ways. He railed against Hitler in student debates and was soon visited by four members of the Gestapo, interrogated for eight days and thrown into prison, where fellow inmates told him he was fated for the concentration camps. Many of Popov's university friends turned on him, but Jebsen did the opposite, and worked to get him out. The Germans expelled the young Serb from the country with a passel of veiled threats and warnings not to return. When Popov got off the train in Basel, he found his German friend Jebsen waiting for him at the station, having driven the convertible at top speed across the Swiss border. This swirl of intimate connections — women, fast cars, mockery of the *lumpen* brownshirts and a certain taste for danger — bound the two young men together.

When the war came, the pair reunited in Belgrade. Popov found the dapper young man changed: disheveled, drinking heavily, smoking cigarette after cigarette, his teeth stained with tobacco — and working for the Abwehr. Why, Popov wondered, would a virulent anti-Nazi like Jebsen join the German intelligence service? But Popov owed his life to his old college friend, and he agreed to help him in his new career. He soon realized that Jebsen was no friend of his supposed bosses.

Months later, Popov found himself in Belgrade at a dinner with a "friend" of Jebsen's named Müntzinger, who touted the inevitable German triumph and asked the Serb, none too subtly, if he'd like to join the side of the victors. Jebsen fidgeted and avoided Popov's eyes as the pitch was made. "I can't say I was shocked, or that I was surprised — subconsciously I must have been prepared for the offer — but I did feel a burst of adrenaline running through me." Jebsen later admitted that the German was his boss at the Abwehr and that he himself had put Popov's name forward as a possible spy.

Popov pretended to take up the Abwehr's offer. He was given a phial of secret ink and told that the enigmatic Jebsen would be his controller and contact. The Serb promptly went to the British embassy and volunteered to work for the Allies as a double agent.

Days later, Jebsen burst into Popov's bedroom with upsetting news: the family's chauffeur, who'd been driving Popov around town, had betrayed him. He'd recorded every place the new spy had visited, including six stops at British passport control, which was commonly known as the working address for MI6 in Belgrade. If the list made its way to others in the Belgrade Abwehr, Popov was a dead man.

The chauffeur was found in a train yard in Belgrade two days later, shot multiple times. Popov paid for the funeral and sent a beautiful bouquet of flowers. Who killed the duplicitous chauffeur remains a mystery. Who ordered him shot is not. Popov had done what he'd needed to do to survive.

Popov returned the favor by repeatedly trying to get MI5 to bring Jebsen into the fold: he was brave, smart, connected and anti-Nazi. The British demurred; they already had the star of the network, Popov. Jebsen was a playboy and an Abwehr operative — who knew if he could be trusted? And if MI5 brought Jebsen in and he turned out to be loyal to the Third Reich, Popov would be irretrievably compromised.

By the summer of 1943, the situation was changing. Jebsen was in serious danger from his own side. He was involved in a currency-smuggling scheme that allowed Gestapo officers to stash money in Switzerland, against strict German regulations. All was going well until one day Jebsen took a closer look at the notes that Himmler's men had been passing to him: they were counterfeit. Furious, he exposed the scheme and accused the Gestapo of cheating him. Jebsen believed his own agency, the Abwehr, would back him up in his war against the Gestapo, but when he was called to headquarters in Berlin to discuss the controversy, he received a mysterious telegram telling him not to go.

Frantic, Jebsen went to the British embassy in Madrid and revealed everything. By now, he trusted no one. "He wanted to find out if the Abwehr were after him, as well as the Gestapo," the embassy wrote London. "If they were, then Tricycle was blown, in which case Jebsen would fake his suicide" and disappear. He wrote a note addressed to the Madrid Abwehr, saying that he'd been driven to kill himself because of his friendship with Popov, who he knew was a secret agent for the British. "I know that a Court Martial would sentence me to death for what I have done . . . Do not be afraid that there will be a scandal. I shall send my things to Father Confessor for the poor. Then I shall take poison and swim far out into the sea."

MI5, with the advantage of the Ultra intercepts, knew that Jebsen wasn't in mortal danger. The meeting in Berlin was routine; there was no witch-hunt. But MI5 couldn't tell Jebsen that without revealing the existence of Ultra. Instead, they allowed the drama to run its course, and when the Gestapo didn't knock on Jebsen's door, the spy began to calm down. But Jebsen soon realized what an enormous risk he'd taken by going to the British. If anyone had seen him slip into the enemy's headquarters, he'd end up in a concentration camp. He tried to withdraw his offer to spy for the British. MI5, however, had other ideas. "We have pointed out to him . . . that he has already taken an irrevocable step." It was too late to turn back.

A meeting between Jebsen and the British was scheduled for Lisbon in December 1943. It was to be Jebsen's coming-out party as a double agent, code-named Artist. Two British intelligence officers, Major Frank Foley of MI6 and Ian Wilson of MI5, flew to Lisbon to debrief him. The stylishly dressed Popov was on the same flight, though the Brits pretended not to notice him. At the Lisbon airport, the secret service agents jumped in a car headed for the embassy, while Popov directed his driver to the Estoril Casino, the scene of Garbo's first great triumph with the stolen diplomatic passes. In Popov's shoulder holster was a new Luger pistol, and in his briefcase was a diplomatic bag brimming with secret documents and rolls of undeveloped film — much of it shot by an MI5 officer that morning. The XX Committee had given the Serbian agent a treasure trove of Fortitude material to pass to the Abwehr.

As Jebsen prepared to speak with the British agents, Popov waited on a Lisbon street to meet his German controller, a Major von Karsthoff, who knew him as "Ivan." A car pulled up and Popov got in the rear, ducked down and adjusted his back against the leather seat so the Luger didn't pinch. When he got to Karsthoff's new villa, however, alarm bells began to go off in his mind. The girl who greeted him was new, not the usual secretary he'd been accustomed to. She walked him back to the drawing room and went to get the German officer. He waited, nerves taut.

Always the dandy, Popov was studying himself in a pair of glass-windowed doors when he heard Karsthoff's voice behind him.

"Turn around slowly, Ivan," the voice said. "And don't make any sudden moves."

Popov stiffened. He was certain that he was blown and that Karsthoff had a pistol trained at the base of his spine. If he was going to die, Popov wanted one last chance to display his old Dubrovnik skills with a gun. His hand slipped under his suit coat toward the Luger. He began to pivot. But just before he turned fully and whipped the gun around toward his Nazi controller, he caught a reflection in the glass doors. Karsthoff wasn't poised with his own Luger, ready to kill him. He was standing rather awkwardly, unarmed, with an apprehensive monkey perched on his shoulder.

Popov let go of the Luger's butt, turned and laughed. "What's the matter?" Karsthoff barked in mock anger. "Do I look ridiculous?" The monkey had been a gift from an Abwehr agent who'd just returned from Africa. The spy-runner had been afraid his agent would startle it. That was the reason for the warning about sudden moves. Popov had nearly shot Karsthoff and blown his cover and that of Jebsen and God knows who else.

An even more shocking moment was waiting for the British agents Foley and Wilson as they sat down to debrief Jebsen. Their new recruit, it turned out, knew there was a British-controlled double agent feeding information to the Abwehr. In fact, Jebsen gave the two officers enough information about Garbo to identify him beyond a doubt. By bringing Jebsen into MI5, the agency had unintentionally put its star agent at enormous risk. If Jebsen told his MI5 handlers about the Spanish spy and saw that they did nothing to arrest him, Jebsen would realize that the agent was already under their control.

The revelation was chilling. When Foley and Wilson returned to London and gave a full report on their meeting, it dawned on the top brass at MI5 that this sordid little drama in the back streets of Lisbon could change the course of World War II.

MI5 was worried enough that they considered terminating Popov as a double agent *and* smuggling Jebsen out of Portugal. Better to lose Tricycle than Garbo. The agency even considered killing Jebsen. The risk of exposure was just too great.

But in the end, the idea was rejected. The deception planners could only hope Jebsen would stay loyal and, most importantly, free. Tricycle was taken off Fortitude because of fears that he could jinx the scheme. "The whole Tricycle set-up might collapse at any moment . . . ," Guy Liddell wrote in his diary on December 8, 1943. "Artist has also heard about Plan Dream" — the 1942 currency-smuggling operation that was one of Juan Pujol's first operations in London — "which brings him perilously close to Garbo." But over the next few months, Jebsen stayed free and the worries over his fate slowly dissipated.

The optimism lasted exactly four and a half months. Then, in late April 1944, word reached London: Jebsen had vanished. Intercepts from Ultra told the grim story: he'd been kidnapped by his own side.

Jebsen's position had begun to unravel in February. A good friend and fellow Abwehr officer had defected to the Allies; Jebsen was a regular visitor to the defector's mother's home. The Abwehr began to watch Jebsen to see if he would lead them to the fleeing man. More bad news for Jebsen came in April: his supporter Canaris had been dismissed from the Abwehr after suspicions about his loyalties deepened; he was soon under house arrest. Canaris's power would now flow to the hard-line SD, which had no loyalties to Jebsen. He'd lost his staunchest protector.

But the spy-runner remained jaunty with confidence. When a friend, a baroness he'd known for years, informed Jebsen that a special team of agents from the RHSA (the agency that directed the SD) had flown to Lisbon to get to the bottom of the currency scam, Jebsen told her not to worry. In fact, a trap was being set. One of his business colleagues was informing on him, feeding the SD a record of his every connection to the Allies and every incriminating remark he made. The net was growing tighter.

Jebsen was ordered to an April 21 meeting in Biarritz to talk about Popov's exorbitant demands for money (he'd asked for $150,000, a king's ransom even to free-spending German intelligence). Jebsen finally began to worry: Biarritz was just across the border in France; if the SD wanted to spirit him out of the country, there was no better place to kidnap him. He refused to attend the meeting. His superiors warned him that not attending was tantamount to desertion.

And then the skies seemed to clear. The SD agreed to give Jebsen $75,000, to be handed on to Popov. In addition, they had decided to award Jebsen a prestigious medal, the Kriegsverdienstkreuz first class, which no other German operative in Lisbon had received. Jebsen breathed a sigh of relief, writing to Popov on the day of the meeting in Biarritz, "I congratulate you on being my Beloved Führer's best agent, who is genuine without any doubt." He even met with an MI6 agent before his departure. The British operative reported back to London that their mole appeared happy and at ease. It was the last time the Brits talked to Jebsen.

On April 29, the spy and a friend were called to a meeting with an SD officer. When Jebsen arrived, the SD man told him the truth: he was going to be taken to Berlin that very moment. Jebsen dashed for the door, but the officer overpowered him, forcibly drugged him and stuffed him into the false bottom of an enormous metal trunk. His friend received the same treatment. The two trunks were loaded into a Studebaker and driven to Biarritz, where the two prisoners, now fully conscious and surely aware of their fate, were transferred to an airplane and flown to Berlin and handed over to the Gestapo.

With D-Day just two months away, Jebsen was installed at the Sachsenhausen concentration camp, twenty miles north of the capital. The Allies assumed he was being tortured. The Gestapo's methods in the camps included beating prisoners with a stick wrapped in barbed wire, crushing their fingers with thumbscrews, burning them with cigarettes, applying electrical shocks to the testicles, and wrapping a man in chains and then tightening them with a tourniquet until the flesh burst apart. "Under interrogation," wrote J. C. Masterman, head of the XX Committee, "it was to be presumed that much, if not all, of the history of his activities would come to light, and in that case many of our best cases were doomed." If Jebsen talked, not only Popov but the whole slate of double agents, Garbo included, would be blown.

Should they shut Garbo down? On May 10, with D-Day less than a month away, Tommy Harris met with Masterman, MI5 counterespionage chief Guy Liddell and Tar Robertson, who was in charge of the double agents, to decide. The meeting was tense; Harris's nerves were wearing down. "Tommy is still extremely apprehensive," Liddell reported. Masterman began by arguing that no change should be made this late in the game; they didn't know for sure what Artist was confessing or how badly Tricycle was compromised. If information came through that the situation was deteriorating, "the agents should be used to fill the German mind with confusion instead of passing over a complete cover plan." Otherwise, stay the course.

Tommy Harris vehemently disagreed. He was clearly suffering a crisis of faith, and his worst nightmare was now coming true. He couldn't get the image of Jebsen in the concentration camp out of his mind; he imagined the spy blurting out the details of Garbo's secret life. Harris knew what would happen next. A sharp-minded analyst like Roenne would listen to the tortured man, then go into the archives and carefully reread Garbo's messages about FUSAG, not through the lens that Kühlenthal had placed in front of Garbo from the beginning — that of Garbo as super-Nazi — but as a hard-nosed skeptic hot on the trail of a mole. Conceivably, he could go all the way back to 1941. For God's sake, they still had the messages in which Pujol talked about Glasgow stevedores craving liters of wine! It was a disaster. Harris knew it took only the tiniest shift in perspective, a sudden soul-chilling loss of confidence, to unmask an agent for what he really was.

That wasn't all. The analyst would then take Tricycle's traffic, read the two side by side, then Brutus's, and then Tate's, and the Abwehr would realize that what they were looking at were not simultaneous reports of the same phenomena — an actual invasion originating in southeastern England aimed at the Pas de Calais — but a plot of unimagined proportions to disguise the real target, which could only be Normandy.

MI5 drew up a table comparing the traffic passed by Garbo and by Tricycle, with dates and regiments and divisions written in small boxes, along with the information sent over to the enemy. The two sets of phantom messages matched up almost exactly, of course. Then MI5 gave copies of Garbo's traffic to one of its officers who knew nothing about Fortitude. Could he detect a targeting of one part of the French shoreline? The officer said that there was a bias toward the Pas de Calais, but only a slight one. The test was inconclusive.

Harris was feeling exposed, the old worry — *how the hell do you hide the largest invasion in history?* — needling him. Smoking black cigarette after black cigarette, he pushed his colleagues to take what they'd gotten and walk away. Garbo's controller was the sensitive con artist who has lost his nerve the night before the out-of-town rube is to be taken for everything he's worth.

Everyone in that room at MI5 headquarters was under enormous pressure. But Harris had his own hidden burdens. The half-Jewish MI5 officer was secretly privy to information about the pogroms and the mass murders happening inside Germany and elsewhere. He had many Jewish friends in London who'd escaped the horrors of Germany before the borders were closed, and they openly discussed with him their reasons for fleeing. He'd even hired a refugee to work in his art gallery. "They told him about what had happened in Germany," says his biographer, Andreu Jaume.

Harris's drinking was getting worse, and the nervous, vaguely Van Gogh–like line of the few paintings he worked on during the war were becoming more hectic — *atormentado,* tormented, is the word Harris's nephew uses. It couldn't have helped that the character he was helping to create, Garbo, was more than a casual anti-Semite: at one point Garbo, in a letter to Kühlenthal, signed off by writing that he was giving him the Nazi salute. The rhetoric provided excellent cover for Garbo, made him appear to be what Guy Liddell once called "a hot Nazi." But Harris knew that the Third Reich was acting on its hatreds and murdering his fellow Jews. When Garbo wrote of the Allies that "I am not certain whether I am being carried away by my impulse and desires to see these people exterminated," it must have pained Harris.

Ironically, Pujol was unaware that the man he sat next to every day for three years was half-Jewish. "His mother was Spanish and Gypsy," Pujol later said, "and his father was British, a man of strong social position in London." As close as the two men had become, Harris had kept his secret from his partner.

Now, because of Jebsen, Harris saw the Garbo operation falling apart. And he was terrified.

Liddell and the others heard Tommy Harris out, then argued for pushing forward. If the XX Committee shut down its star agent, the Germans might ask why Garbo had disappeared. And if they closed down Tricycle completely, that might tip off the enemy. As the four men examined the tangled case, studied every permutation from every possible angle, at the center of each equation sat a number of variables whose value couldn't be determined on that particular May evening: why the Germans had arrested Jebsen, what he was telling them, what the Abwehr's level of confidence in Garbo and Tricycle was. "Whichever way you look at this case," Liddell sighed, "it is full of imponderables."

The four men finally agreed they should hold the course. Churchill was told about the Jebsen case three days before D-Day. The Garbo operation was still alive.

20

The Hours

TOMMY HARRIS WANTED his agent to be the one to carry the game to its final hour. He lobbied for Garbo to be given the honor of announcing D-Day to the Germans, and the XX Committee agreed. The coup would boost Garbo's star even higher, and he could use his influence to stop the Germans from committing their reserves. Keeping the panzers away from Normandy meant both fooling the Germans about Calais and, a much tougher trick, persuading them to ignore Normandy even *after* the landings, on D-Day plus one, D-Day plus two — and as many additional days as possible.

But first, Garbo had to maneuver the enemy into position.

Agent No. 4, the waiter from Gibraltar, was pushing the Norway theme, watching destroyers and assault craft practicing maneuvers in Loch Fyne in Scotland; he could "see" the sailors on deck wearing arctic gear. Garbo sent the news on May 14. Madrid radioed back: "I am particularly interested to know urgently whether the 52nd Division is still in the camps in the Glasgow area." Garbo called another Scotland-based agent — "a Greek seaman" — down to London to get the latest. "He says that the 52nd Division is at present in camps in the areas Saltcoats-Kilmarnock-Preswick and Ayr." Garbo gave the Greek a code word to send when the ships on the river Clyde departed.

On June 3, a startling development from his "agent" in Harwich: "Sign, not previously seen, of a yellow shield with three blue mountain peaks outlined in white. This newly arrived division from USA." New assault forces were now arriving from America, which indicated the invasion was close. The information was true, except the Americans weren't in Harwich, they were farther south. A day later, the illusory Greek seaman reported the "landing in Scotland of a large contingent of troops coming from Ireland . . . Insignia is the red rose on a white ground. He believes it to be the 55th English Division." When the Greek supposedly returned to Glasgow, the streets were choked with "vehicles and men in full equipment in large numbers."

As the days counted down, as the camps in southern England — not eastern — filled to the bursting point with GIs, and as the harbors turned gray with navy convoys, all of Garbo's work was very nearly undone by a series of blunders. London parties, in particular, turned out to be highly dangerous affairs. The combination of alcohol and the desire to impress was fatal to more than one officer. One U.S. Army Air Force general — a West Point classmate of General Eisenhower's — listened to a group of women complain how bad the dessert was. The general informed the guests that the supply ships were all carrying war materiel and they could expect the pastries to improve dramatically after June 15. He was stripped of his rank and sent packing back to the States. In May, an American naval officer got plastered and stood in the middle of a party and gave a sozzled lecture on the real D-Day, down to the embarkation areas and the all-important date. "I could cheerfully shoot the offender myself," Eisenhower wrote. A young British officer told his parents when the invasion would happen, and they promptly turned him in to Allied counterintelligence.

A gust of wind on a blustery London day caused another scare. The breeze blew open a window at the War Office and twelve copies of the invasion plan went fluttering out onto the wet pavement below. Staff members raced down to the street and swiftly scooped up eleven of the documents. After a frantic search for the last copy, it was finally found at a sentry station on the other side of Whitehall. A man wearing thick glasses had handed it over, saying the print was so small that it was very hard to read. The War Office tried to track down the man, but he was never found.

Another copy of the D-Day plan was found in a briefcase left on a British train. A quick-thinking conductor found it and locked it away until security officials could pick it up. And when the planners opened the *Daily Telegraph* on May 2, they nearly fainted: the cross-word clue for 17 across was "one of the US." The correct answer was "Utah," one of the target beaches. The next day, the clue for 3 down was "Red Indian on the Missouri," and the answer was "Omaha." From then on, MI5 kept a careful eye on the *Telegraph*. On May 22, a seemingly innocent crossword clue turned up: "But some big-wig like this has stolen some of it at times." On May 30 and June 1, two more appeared: "This bush is a center of nursery revolutions" and "Britannia and he hold to the same thing." The answers all came on June 2: "Overlord," the code name for the invasion, "Mulberry," the secret name of the man-made harbors to be used during the assault, and "Neptune," the code word for the Normandy landings themselves. MI5 had had enough. Two of its officers knocked on the puzzle creator's door and demanded to know if he was sending messages to the Abwehr. The man answered that the puzzles had been composed months before. It had been a simple — and incredible — coincidence.

On June 4, a bored teletype operator for the Associated Press in London was practicing her technique. As part of her drill, she typed out the sample text: URGENT AP NYK FLASH EISENHOWER'S HW ANNOUNCED ALLIED LANDINGS IN FRANCE. When her supervisor handed her a Russian communiqué to be sent to America, the operator accidentally sent out the invasion message along with it. The AP rushed to retract it and got a correction out twenty-three minutes later, but Radio Berlin and Radio Moscow had already flashed the message to their listeners.

Garbo was rushed in to calm the waters. "Surprised by the news in the papers about the girl who communicated the false alarm of the opening of an offensive," he radioed Madrid at 2027 hours. "I went this morning to the Ministry hoping to be able to learn there exactly what had taken place. The impression I obtained, though it seems very strange, is that what was published in the papers is the truth . . . There may be a target deception . . . in case of what might happen I shall give priority to the reply which I receive from Agent 3 (3)." He'd turned the mistake into a preview of his coming announcement about Normandy.

The "appalling slip-up" of the telegram set everyone's nerves further on edge. "I hope to God I know what I'm doing," Eisenhower said as June 6 approached. If Overlord failed, he wanted to be ready. The general wrote his famous message announcing that the mission had misfired, stating plainly that "if any blame or fault attaches to the attempt it is mine alone." He then put it in his wallet, to have it ready at a moment's notice.

When the stress of the approaching invasion became too much, Pujol would sneak off for a solitary walk in one of London's still glorious parks. He recalled, "From the moment I set foot in England . . . I gained great pleasure from the beauty of the countryside, from the lush greenness of London's gardens." But the happiness was mixed with darker emotions. There were dozens of soldiers on the same paths, either alone or with their sweethearts, enjoying one last stroll together before the troops headed for their embarkation points. And Pujol knew he had a secret connection to them that they had no idea existed. He was their deeply worried guardian angel.

Pujol wasn't inclined to abstract thought; Harris and the others perhaps saw the war's political and ideological big picture more clearly. But on his walks, Pujol was presented with the thing that mattered most to him in the Garbo project: the lives of these anonymous soldiers. They were the potential victims or benefactors of his work, and they were all around him on the warm nights of early June.

As the hours counted down to June 5, Garbo sent messages that ticked to a staccato drumbeat: "The Division is destined for an attack on the south Atlantic French coast in cooperation with a large army which will come direct from America to the French coast . . . In addition to the defense troops seen in the town I saw the following troops: Large numbers First Army and SOS [services of supply] . . ." At 2000 hours, the German propaganda broadcaster known as Axis Sally came on the air and told the Allied troops: "Good evening 82nd Airborne Division. Tomorrow morning the blood from your guts will grease the bogey wheels of our tanks." That night, General George Patton addressed the men of the real Third Army: "We want this war over with. The quickest way to get it over with is to go get the bastards who started it. The quicker they get whipped, the quicker we can go home . . . And when we get to Berlin, I am personally going to shoot that paper-hanging son-of-a-bitch Hitler." A "very depressed" Eisenhower headed to Wiltshire to talk to the men of the 101st Airborne Division. When the last of their planes left the ground, he turned, tears in his eyes, and walked slowly back to his jeep. At the Berghof, his retreat high in the Bavarian Alps, Hitler went to sleep.

Hours before the armada launched, Garbo flashed a message to Madrid: "I have just received a telegram from Agent 3 (3)"—the Greek seaman—"to say that he will be arriving in London tonight at eleven. Something must have happened which cannot be explained in the code which had been agreed between us for announcing the sailing of the Clyde Fleet. Therefore you should be listening tonight at 0300 GMT." The Abwehr usually signed off at 11:30 p.m., so Garbo wanted to make sure an operator was available when he broadcast his invasion announcement, which Eisenhower had personally approved for 3 a.m., three and a half hours before the first soldiers hit the beaches. Agent No. 4, Garbo's trusty Gibraltarian waiter, was also on the way from Hampshire with two American deserters, promising big news, Garbo claimed.

That night, Pujol, Tommy Harris and Tar Robertson gathered at Harris's magnificent home for a "modest but beautifully prepared meal." They eyed their watches as they ate. When the time came, the men jumped into a British-made Humber owned by the War Office and drove to 35 Crespigny Road. Charles Haines, the radio operator, was already working the transmitter, the vacuum tubes glowing beneath the radio's black metal vents. Harris and Pujol finalized the text of the announcement and Pujol himself translated it into Spanish and enciphered it.

At that moment, 6,483 ships were cutting through chop in the English Channel on the way to the silvery beaches of Normandy: ocean liners, battleships, destroyers and thousands of landing craft. Thirteen thousand fighter planes and bombers were being fueled and loaded with bombs destined for German pillboxes and panzers, and 20,000 vehicles were strapped onto transports. But the number that most concerned Garbo were the 120,000 men—first in the wave of 2 million that would join in the invasion—that were peering ahead into the inky darkness or vomiting their guts out in the landing craft as the swells grew in the English Channel. Pujol, as a student of history, would probably summarize his fears in one word: Verdun, the

World War I battle that, as he said, "lasted so long and caused so many deaths." If his message wasn't believed in Berlin — if he failed to convince Roenne and Hitler that he was the one true oracle of the invasion — then thousands of men would die.

Along with the real destroyers, two different and much smaller armadas were under way that night. Each contained a handful of launches equipped with a device called a Moonshine, which could absorb the electronic signals from German radar stations, magnify them, then bounce them back. The tiny launches would then appear on the enemy's screens as 10,000-ton destroyers. The craft also carried amplifiers that could blare out the sounds — recorded at the invasion of Salerno the year before — of shouted commands, bosuns' pipes, bugle calls, the rattling of anchor chains and other nautical noises. These few boats were impersonating two convoys: one approaching Calais, the other Boulogne. Above them were RAF bombers shoving bundles of aluminum foil — which would appear on radar screens as airplanes — into the night sky. These false "echoes" would give the terrified radar operators the impression that thousands of planes were heading their way. They were the final representatives of the Allies' huge gamble on a phantom army.

At 7:29 p.m., an incoming message began tapping out in Charles Haines's black headphones. It was routine traffic from Madrid. On the eve of the invasion, it was clear the Abwehr's low-level men had no idea what was happening. It was just another night in the long war.

At 1 a.m., Haines adjusted his headset and listened to the scratchy sound of the ether, ringing with electricity and static, flood into the earpieces. He tapped out Garbo's call sign. The men around him tensed. Would the Germans take the bait? Would they hold their forces away from the beaches and towns where thousands of Allied soldiers would soon be exposed?

The men listened anxiously, waiting for the moment when Haines would start sending Garbo's message. But again and again they heard the operator tap out the call sign. His finger lay still on the button.

The unthinkable had happened. The Germans weren't listening.

The men huddled around the wireless were gutted. All that work, only to have a radio operator let them down. Finally, at 8 a.m. the

Abwehr operator tapped back and Garbo blasted a response. "I am very disgusted as, in this struggle for life and death, I cannot accept excuses or negligence," he snarled before sending a slightly altered text saying that Agent No. 4 had made contact:

> He arrived after a difficult journey created by the steps he took to slip through the local vigilance. He told me that three days ago cold rations and vomit bags had again been distributed to troops of the 3rd Canadian Division and that the division had now left the camp, its place now taken by the Americans. The American troops which are now in the camp belong to the First US Army.

The only conclusion that the Germans could draw was that the invasion was under way — yet if FUSAG was still in camp, Normandy had to be a feint. The radar indications of thousands of "airplanes" approaching Calais must be part of a complex deception.

Now the deceivers waited.

At the same time that Haines's Morse key was sounding in the ether, an American GI named William Funkhouser was crawling up Omaha Beach with a 60-mm mortar strapped to his back. He was with the 1st Infantry Division, the Big Red One. Moments before he'd stepped off a landing barge and struggled ashore, ripping off his life preserver as he went. A German machine gun was sending tracers inches above his head. "I was so scared that if I never moved again from that place, that would be all right." As his fingers dug into the wet sand and he willed himself down into the earth, Funkhouser saw a "white explosion" go off to his left in the murky light. Oddly, he felt no concussion wave travel through his body, just the flash of white. Ahead of him when Funkhouser looked up, spread in a radius from the center of the explosion, was a collection of randomly distributed pieces of flesh — not limbs but chunks of flesh, the largest the size of a man's fist, all of them "just as white as snow." A soldier named Speckler had been carrying a load of TNT to blow up German pillboxes, and it had exploded too soon. Funkhouser stared at a single piece of flesh that had come to rest in his path. In the midst of the noise and concussions, it held his attention as if it were some kind of talisman. "I can't crawl through that," he said to himself. He tried to stand but his legs gave out. He felt for the 60-mm mortar on his back and threw it aside. The lost weight seemed to give his body strength. He stood and began to run, armed only with a .45.

Before D-Day, Funkhouser had believed, or been led to believe, that the Germans would surrender as soon as the American troops came trudging up the beach. Instead, every officer in his company was either dead or wounded, or would soon be dead or wounded. Now bodies were rolling in the surf, back and forth, three and four deep. "My company was just more or less eliminated as a fighting unit."

It was men like Funkhouser whom Garbo had been assigned to protect in the next seventy-two hours. Sitting in the house on Crespigny Road, Pujol could only imagine the scene at Omaha Beach. "I remember thinking that the American beaches were in danger of being turned into a bloody fiasco. They were suffering terrible casualties and it was up to us to prevent a massacre."

Harris had other things to worry about. Was Jebsen talking? Was Garbo's last message being read in reverse and the panzer divisions already rolling toward the Normandy beaches?

As the Americans shot their way ashore at Omaha, the phone rang in Rommel's headquarters at the château in La Roche-Guyon, forty miles west of Paris. Rommel himself was home, in Herrlingen, Germany; he'd spent part of the previous day picking a bouquet of wildflowers for his wife's birthday. On the other end of the phone was Colonel Roenne, in his bunker at Zossen, just outside Berlin. The invasion was under way, the slim aristocrat told Rommel's second-in-command, but Roenne's analysis indicated that a second, much more powerful blow was being readied for Calais. "Not a single unit of the 1st US Army Group, which comprises around 25 large formations north and south of the Thames, has so far been committed . . . This suggests that the enemy is planning a further large-scale operation in the Channel area, which one would expect to be aimed at a coastal sector in the Pas de Calais area." He emphasized that no forces were to be withdrawn from Calais to reinforce Normandy. It was a victory for Garbo and the XX Committee, but the higher-ups still had to decide on a final strategy.

Rommel's chief of staff nodded. He'd already been informed that some of the paratroopers who had landed near St. Valéry behind the German lines had turned out to be fakes. In fact, they were another of Operation Bodyguard's stratagems: four live paratroopers from the SAS had jumped in with two hundred dummies, a number of gramophones to play battle sounds and cries for help, along with chemical bombs that gave off the odor of cordite. The diversion helped convince the chief of staff that the whole invasion was a ploy.

At General Rundstedt's headquarters, a clerk remembers, "D-Day . . . was marked by a 'let's not get excited' attitude . . . This was regarded as just another feint." But Rundstedt's chief of staff was worried. He called Berlin and requested the release of the strategic reserve of panzers to smash into the divisions that were rolling up from Omaha and Utah beaches.

Now the decision lay with General Jodl in Berlin. He pondered the request and declined to send in the tanks. The invasion was a sham, he believed, and the real blow was coming at Calais. He refused to wake Hitler. The German Seventh Army, positioned in Normandy but being held away from the action, slumbered through the darkness and failed to emerge from their barracks when the American troops poured ashore. Jodl's deputy chief of staff would later admit, "On 5 June 1944 . . . German Supreme Headquarters had not the slightest idea that the decisive event of the war was upon them." It wasn't until Hitler awoke and ordered the Panzer Lehr and 12th SS divisions to the battle — at 4 p.m., hours after the invasion had begun — that the High Command reacted. The order was too late to affect the first day's action.

The foothold had been established — but the Allied generals had planned on that. The question was, would the illusion last? And would the German divisions guarding Calais break out of their camps and head toward Normandy? "We feared a massive counter-attack every minute," Pujol said. D-Day plus one and D-Day plus two passed without any more significant German reinforcements. How much longer would the illusion last?

On June 9 beginning at 1:44 a.m., Garbo sent his most important message of the war. He announced that he'd met with his four key operatives — Agent No. 7 (2), the Welsh seaman from London; 7 (4), the Indian poet from Brighton; 7 (7), the Aryan fascist from Harwich;

and No. 4, the Gibraltarian waiter from Scotland. It was a gathering of Garbo's supposed brain trust, and he confirmed their conclusions with a visit to his "source" at the Ministry of Information. Garbo no longer fed the Germans bits and pieces of the Calais plot; that time had passed. He now presented them with the whole conspiracy, gathered from his dazzling array of sources.

> I today lunched with 4 (3) and obtained from him an interesting bit of information. He told me that FUSAG had not entered into the present operation . . . being carried out in the greater part by troops who have come from the Med, reinforced mainly by Canadian and American troops. From the reports mentioned it is perfectly clear that the present attack is a large scale operation but diversionary in character for the purpose of establishing a strong bridgehead in order to draw the maximum of our reserves to the area of operation to retain them there so as to be able to strike a blow somewhere else with ensured success . . . The constant bombings that the area of the Pas de Calais is suffering and the strategic situation of these forces make me suspect an attack on that French region, which is also the shortest route to their prized final objective, that is, Berlin.

For nearly two hours and two minutes, Haines's right index finger tapped out the encrypted message, the climax of Garbo's role as the great soothsayer of Allied war plans, the role he'd been crafting for three long years. He wasn't just feeding the Germans information, he was drawing conclusions and trying to convince Hitler that he, above all others, knew what the Allies were planning to do.

As the message was being sent, General Rundstedt in Berlin was urgently requesting Hitler to give him the armored reserve in order to attack the invaders at their most vulnerable point, the Normandy coast. His Seventh Army had emerged from its barracks and was embroiled in a ferocious battle with the invading forces in the town squares and hedgerows. But was this the real invasion? "It is clear that Hitler and his entourage were in a highly undecided frame of mind."

Finally, Hitler gave in. He agreed to send Rundstedt the 1st Panzer Corps, along with the 2nd Panzer and 21st Panzer divisions. The commanders on the ground received the order to move south to attack the American and British forces at Normandy. What Eisenhower had feared most was beginning to unfold. It was D-Day plus three.

At that moment, a condensed version of Garbo's message was being flashed from Madrid to Berlin, arriving at 10:20 p.m. Hitler's personal intelligence officer, Friedrich Adolf Krummacher, read the report and drew a pen stroke under the phrase "diversionary maneuver," then added his own note: "Underlines the opinion already formed by us that a further attack is to be expected in another place. (Belgium?)" He rushed the message to Jodl, who drew his own line under the words "south-east and eastern England," initialed it and put it on the Führer's desk. Roenne wrote to Jodl to confirm Garbo's analysis: "The main thrust must be expected momentarily in the Pas de Calais."

When Hitler spotted Garbo's report sitting on his gleaming desk, he read it carefully and contemplated its message. Then he reached for his pen, dipped it in ink and signed it "erl," for *erledigt* ("done," or in this context, "seen"). Soon afterward, a message flashed out from the High Command: "As a consequence of certain information, C in C West has declared a 'state of alarm II' for Fifteenth Army in Belgium and Northern France . . . The move of the 1st SS Panzer Division will therefore be halted." The long lines of German panzers gunned their 300-horsepower Maybach engines and turned back toward Calais.

Ten armored divisions in France and Belgium had been ready to reinforce Normandy, including the 85th Infantry and the 116th Panzer, the latter stationed just west of Paris. Now all but one returned to Calais or broke camp to head there, to prepare for Garbo's spectral army. Only a single armored division, the 2nd Panzer, crossed the Seine and headed south toward Normandy.

Garbo had not only stopped the German army in its tracks, he'd forced it to reverse course.

The person who nearly undid all this good work was none other than Winston Churchill. On the morning of the invasion, he gave a speech in the House of Commons. The entire British government — its ministers and diplomats — had been ordered not to mention a second landing at Calais or anywhere else on the French coast, or even to imply one was on the way. If the attack really was coming, as Garbo was telling the Germans, then no one would dare talk about it. Except the prime minister did, in front of microphones broadcasting his speech to the world. "I have also to announce to the House that during the night and the early hours of this morning, the first of a series of landings in force upon the European continent has taken place." The deception planners gasped.

Garbo rushed to his radio to explain the gaffe to the Germans: "In spite of recommendations made to Churchill," he told Madrid, "that his speech should contain every possible reserve, he based it on the consideration that he was obliged, on account of his political position, to avoid distorting the facts and would not permit that his speeches should be discredited by coming events." The Germans, amazingly, accepted the explanation. They wanted to believe their agent, even if it meant believing that Churchill had made a terrible blunder.

Pujol and Harris celebrated their world-altering coup with a dinner at a tiny black-market restaurant in Soho owned by a Basque expatriate. Harris had asked the man to prepare an authentic Basque meal: *huevos escalfados bilbaína,* cold poached eggs served on a layer of chopped onions and tomatoes, substituted for impossible-to-get pimientos. The owner poured glass after glass of Basque wine, from a glass pitcher known as a *porrón,* as the two men moved on to *pollo de Pamplona,* laughing and telling stories as they ate, until the proprietor was holding the *porrón* high above their heads and, cheered on by the other diners, pouring ropes of vino directly into their mouths as the Spanish and Basques do when celebrating a great event. Four *porrones* later, the two men stumbled giddily out into the London night.

It was the American GIs, British troops and Canadian aviators now moving toward Paris who would save Europe and the Western world. But it was these two mysterious and half-soused men who'd saved those soldiers.

Two weeks after the Normandy invasion, there were actually more Axis forces in the Pas de Calais than there had been before the attack. A month after, a total of twenty-two Calais divisions stood on alert, ready to repel the invaders that would never come. In a top-secret interview conducted the following year in Nuremberg, an interrogator asked Field Marshal Wilhelm Keitel, Germany's equivalent of a war minister, why the panzers ordered to Normandy had turned around at the last moment. He pointed to Garbo's June 9 report. "You can accept it as 99 percent certain that this message was the immediate cause of the counter order." General Eisenhower was just as certain:

> Lack of infantry was the most important cause of the enemy's defeat in Normandy, and his failure to remedy this weakness was due primarily to the success of the Allied threats leveled against the Pas de Calais . . . I cannot over-emphasize the decisive value of this most successful threat, which paid enormous dividends, both at the time of the assault and during the operations of the two succeeding months. The German Fifteenth Army, which, if committed to battle in June or July, might possibly have defeated us by sheer weight of numbers, remained inoperative throughout the critical period of the campaign.

Before he committed suicide by cyanide on October 14, 1944, Field Marshal Rommel made a curious confession to his son. It had been "a decisive mistake," he said, "to leave the German troops in the Pas de Calais."

As Pujol and Harris walked unsteadily through the streets of London, Operation Fortitude's mastermind, the irrepressible David Strangeways, was battling his way through France. Strangeways was at the head of R Force, a unique unit composed of both deception technicians and infantry soldiers. The unit was tricking the Germans into sending their panzers and troops into what were called "notional areas" — that is, empty fields or deserted farms — by using the full battery of physical deception: fake wireless traffic, "night lighting exercises" that could simulate everything from airstrips to large convoys, false division HQs, flash simulators to mimic artillery guns, battle noise simulators to suggest the landing of paratroopers, misleading signposts, phony tanks, fake bomb craters and a host of operations cooked up on the march. The unit's technicians even mocked up some very convincing "dummy sniper heads," which were so successful in drawing out enemy sharpshooters that one officer went to the studio of a local artist, Monsieur Deleroulk, and asked if he could mass-produce 500 of them. (He could, for 200 francs each.) They churned out rumor after rumor and spread them across the French countryside. R Force, with David Strangeways at its head, was like a traveling carnival, drawing rabbits out of their hats.

By late summer of 1944, his R Force was pushing toward the Rhine. On August 31, Strangeways led his soldiers toward the French city of Rouen from the south. As usual, his daring surprised and infuriated his superiors. The brigadier of one infantry group was "horrified to learn that R Force is lying so far forward and recommends that it is withdrawn at once." Strangeways and his men eventually took the city, after which he departed to give a lecture on the elegant art of deception at the Palais des Beaux Arts. "It is fair to say," concluded one report on R Force's work in this period, "that no major attack has taken place which has not to some degree gained surprise."

Strangeways passed wide of Le Postel, the town far to the south of Rouen that had been obliterated as part of the failed Operation Cockade. One late afternoon in September, as R Force was heading north toward Germany, a small milestone was marked in the coastal town. The last German garrison in the area around Le Postel had surrendered. But there was no one around to celebrate; no townspeople rushed into the streets and waved the tricolor or offered wine to advancing troops. Le Postel was empty. It had never recovered from the bombing that was intended to cover Cockade.

The man who could have destroyed Garbo, Johann Jebsen, spent D-Day in Sachsenhausen, one of the oldest concentration camps in the Third Reich, earmarked for political prisoners and enemies of the state. Sachsenhausen was a model camp, surrounded by electric wire and a high stone wall, as well as a "death strip" of pale gravel that the inmates were forbidden to step on. Anyone who did was shot by the guards. A man who'd occupied the cell next to Jebsen's later reported that, after the spymaster had been dragged back to his cell following a brutal beating, he called out to the guards, "I trust I shall be provided with a clean shirt." Another prisoner met Jebsen in September

1944 and found him lying on his bed, his ribs broken. It was the last sighting of the tragic spy.

His friend Dusko Popov, Agent Tricycle, feeling both guilty and enraged about Jebsen's fate, drove through the ruins of postwar Germany searching for the man he held responsible for his colleague's death. His name was Walter Selzer, and he was a minor functionary who'd carried out Jebsen's execution. After weeks of detective work, Popov found Selzer in the German city of Minden. Popov abducted him and drove him to a lonely forest to kill him. But Selzer proved so meek and pathetic that Popov found himself unable to pull the trigger. He left Selzer cowering in the trees and consoled himself by rescuing Jebsen's wife; Popov even knocked on the doors of theater directors in Berlin's British zone, trying to get her work as an actress. It was an act of atonement for the man he felt he'd failed.

Jebsen apparently never told his interrogators what he knew about Garbo.

As summer turned into fall, the planners and the generals finally had time to look back on the deception operation and Garbo's part in it. The praise began to roll in. "Connoisseurs of the double cross," J. C. Masterman would later say, "have always regarded the Garbo case as the most highly developed example of their art." Anthony Blount called Garbo's coup "the greatest double cross operation of the war." The deception planner and historian Roger Fleetwood-Hesketh put it most succinctly: "His contribution to D-day was indeed stranger than any fiction . . . It could not have been done without him . . . It was Garbo's message . . . which changed the course of the battle in Normandy." When Eisenhower had the chance to meet Tommy Harris (he never spoke to Pujol himself), at the ceremony honoring the spy-runner's OBE, or Order of the British Empire, the American general stood up and reached out his hand. "Your work with Mr. Pujol most probably amounts to the equivalent of a whole army division," he said as the two men shook hands. "You have saved a lot of lives, Mr. Harris."

Though German reinforcements had begun moving toward Normandy in late August, by then it was too late to crush the second front. When the Allies captured German intelligence maps, they showed Garbo's phantom divisions in the exact spots the spy had said they were. On Roenne's big map of the Western Front, the flag of the imaginary FUSAG remained pinned in place until October.

When the war diarist for the German High Command, Professor Percy Schramm, was being interrogated by the Allies after V-E Day, an odd and telling moment occurred. Schramm was a historian of medieval ritual; his specialty was the study of how the rulers of the Holy Roman Empire projected their power through images and symbols. During the war, he'd had unfettered access to the leaders of the German military.

In the middle of the interrogation, a question suddenly popped into the historian's mind. He interrupted the conversation and asked it.

"All this Patton business wasn't a trick, was it?" he asked the Allied officer suspiciously.

"What do you mean by that?"

"What I mean is this," Schramm said. "Were all those divisions sent to south-east England simply to hold our forces in the Pas de Calais?"

The interrogator paused, then gave a rather nuanced reply. The forces were there to reinforce Monty in Normandy, he claimed, and would have only invaded Calais if the Germans had abandoned it.

"Ah," Schramm said, relieved. "That is what we always thought."

The war had been over for months, but the German expert on imagery still believed that FUSAG had been real. Garbo's fiction lived on.

21

The Weapon

GARBO HAD TRIUMPHED, but two lingering threats — to England and to his marriage — required immediate attention. The national crisis came first.

In the summer of 1943, rumors had swept London that Hitler was developing a superweapon. MI6's sources had heard that it was to be some kind of enormous rocket, weighing between ten and fifteen tons, which would travel through the stratosphere loaded with high explosives, a weapon that couldn't be shot out of the sky or defended against with existing technologies. MI5 wanted Garbo to see if he could find out what this dream weapon was. On June 10, he wrote Madrid: "I must now discuss another matter connected with the report of a Swedish journalist called Gunnar T. Pihl who . . . spoke of an enormous rocket gun which is installed on the French coast to bombard London as a reprisal . . . The result of this was that my wife became panicky and wants at all costs to leave England . . . [I] promised her that if it were true I would send her to the country out of the range of this weapon." So, was it true? Madrid brushed him off, saying only that "there is no cause to alarm yourself."

But months later, out of the blue, came this bulletin from the Abwehr: "Circumstances dictate that you should carry out your proposition with regard to setting up your home outside the capital." Not only that, a second radio transmitter was to be built "without regard to price" in case the first was destroyed. What was the "threatened action" Madrid referred to later in the message, this wondrous weapon that was so frightening it would drive Garbo out of London? He asked for a few days' notice before the reprisals began, which would give the British Ministry of Home Security time to prepare for the mysterious attack. But Madrid steadfastly refused to give any more information. Meanwhile, Garbo moved Araceli and the children out to the country.

The Ultra intercepts showed that the project was so secret even Madrid didn't know what was happening; the directives were coming directly from Berlin. The Abwehr headquarters told Madrid to expect a series of highly sensitive questionnaires for Garbo about the secret weapon, prefixed by the code name Stichling. The answers were to be forwarded immediately to Berlin with the same prefix. Madrid would not be allowed to decipher the messages before sending them.

Londoners watched the skies and waited for Hitler's last chance to arrive. And Garbo waited for the Stichling messages. The weapon came first. On June 13, 1944, seven days after the Normandy invasion, a buzzing whine was heard in the sky over London and the first V-1 rocket dropped onto a railway bridge in the East End, killing six. Looking like a sleek unmanned plane, the V-1 was a remote-controlled flying bomb that carried a 2,200-pound warhead. The British called the V-1s "flying robots" and "doodlebugs." Germans cheered them as the "omnipotent miracle weapon" that would save the country. "Day and night [the V-1] thunders down with fiery blows on the city on the Thames," crowed the German newspaper *Das Reich*. "There is a new wheel in the machinery of war."

On June 16, Berlin sent the long-awaited message to Madrid: "Arras reports Stichling is beginning." The Germans requested that Garbo mark the impact zones of the V-1s on a special London map. The reason was clear: the German engineers wanted to fine-tune the rockets' guidance system to ensure strikes in central London, to kill as many people as possible.

Garbo stalled. If he and the other double agents who'd been given the Stichling message, Brutus and Tate, acted as scouts for the V-1 program, they'd be assisting in mass murder. Garbo passed along information only on a recent strike in the West End, believing that diplomats from neutral countries still living in London would report the attacks anyway. "8 dead and 13 wounded . . . Square 10, grey section. Many houses damaged. Square 82 . . . Many victims in the street." Hoping to dampen the enthusiasm for the V-1, Garbo then wrote Kühlenthal a long personal letter. Its theme was simple: "We are wasting our time." The flying bomb was ineffective as an offensive weapon, he argued, and a disappointment as a psychological one. Londoners simply weren't terrified enough.

But Garbo could delay only so long. If he didn't send the coordinates and the impact times, he would lose standing with the Abwehr. A solution had to be found. Harris and Pujol came up with an idea: Why not run the same gambit on the Abwehr that they had on Araceli? It was a natural way out. One day when he was out looking at bomb damage, Garbo failed to return home. His "deputy," No. 3, reported by wireless to Madrid that their chief was missing and that Araceli was frantic. All indications pointed to the likelihood that Garbo had been arrested.

In time the "details" came out. While looking at a bomb site in Bethnal Green, Garbo had attracted the notice of a plainclothes policeman. Garbo, to use a term from a later era, had been profiled. "[The policeman] started to insult me," Garbo claimed to Madrid, "saying that Spaniards were a lot of dogs and followed the footsteps of the greatest butcher ever recorded in history and that we should be treated as enemies." Taken to the local station house, Garbo swallowed a piece of paper with suspicious writing on it before the bobbies could stop him. Luckily, his powerful friends in the Ministry of Information intervened on his behalf, and in a few days he was released, worried but still defiant. MI5 forged a letter of apology from the home secretary, which Garbo passed on to Madrid. His Abwehr handlers were shaken, and it was decided in Berlin that Garbo was far too valuable an asset to risk on the V-1 program. He was released from his bomb assessment duties — exactly what MI5 had wanted.

On July 29 came news from Kühlenthal that "with great happiness and satisfaction" they could announce that Garbo had been awarded the Iron Cross. The medal was usually given only to front-line combatants, but the High Command had made an exception for its star spy. Garbo wrote back effusively: "I cannot at this moment, when emotion overcomes me, express in words my thanks for the decoration conceded by our Führer ... I must state that this prize has been won, not only by me, but also by Carlos [Agent No. 3] and the other comrades ... My desire is to fight with greater ardor to be worthy of this medal which has only been conceded to those heroes, my companions in honor, who fight on the battlefield."

By August 1944, the end of Garbo's career was in sight. Scores of former Abwehr agents were turning themselves over to the Allies, and in their debriefs a few of them referred to the miraculous Garbo, who'd managed to report from London throughout the war. It was only a matter of time before the Germans realized that, with this new information, Garbo should have been shut down. The British failure to catch him would reveal that Garbo was a double agent. A Spanish informer named Roberto Buénaga even called the Madrid office of MI6 and volunteered to give up the most powerful German spy in London if the British paid him a large amount of money. The MI6 officers questioned the Spaniard, and it soon became clear that the man knew enough about Pujol to blow his cover. MI6 considered sending an agent to kill Buénaga, but that might have drawn yet more suspicion to the Garbo operation.

There was only one solution: Garbo had to disappear, permanently. The spy's deputy, No. 3, would wrap up the remaining business of the network. Garbo would "leave" London (in reality, he didn't go anywhere). He told the Germans he'd fled to a hideout in southern Wales, a farm miles from any town, which he shared with "an old Welsh couple, a Belgian deserter and a half-witted relative of the owners."

Back in London, MI5 pretended to conduct a search for him. As the details of his nefarious work emerged, the police closely interviewed a supposedly terrified Araceli, and the British embassy in Madrid filed a protest, shocked to discover that a German spy ring had been operating in London for the whole course of the war.

Months passed, with Garbo sending occasional messages to Madrid and supposedly hiding in the countryside. But as World War II ground to a close in the spring of 1945, MI5 was faced with a dilemma: whether or not to deactivate once and for all one of the most effective spies in their history. The specter of Nazism was fading, but Stalin loomed in the East. MI5 began to explore the idea of running Garbo against the Russians. Guy Liddell recorded the details in his diary: "[Tommy Harris's] plan is to get [Garbo] to write to the Soviet military attaché in London anonymously before he leaves for Spain. He would tell the latter the whole of his story and give them his code. He would tell them that he had been working for the English against Franco and that if they liked they could monitor communications between ourselves and the Germans to get what information they liked and incidentally to satisfy themselves as to his bona fides."

The plan seemed like a natural, but it was quickly nixed by Pujol's old pursuer Kim Philby. Years later it would become clear why. Philby, of course, was spying for the Russians and had been ever since his days as a newspaper correspondent in the Spanish Civil War. He knew Garbo's skills well enough; he didn't want the Spaniard playing in his garden.

Back in December 1944, in recognition of his services, Pujol had been awarded the MBE (Member of the Most Excellent Order of the British Empire), the first British agent to be so honored. A formal investiture at Buckingham Palace was impossible because of the need for secrecy, but the key players — Harris, Guy Liddell, Masterman, Tar Robertson and a few others — celebrated with Pujol. The director general of MI5, Sir David Petrie, gave a "nice little speech" at agency headquarters, and afterward his friends took Pujol for lunch at the Savoy, where he stood up and thanked them in halting English. "I think he was extremely pleased," wrote Liddell in his diary. The men banged on the table and cheered as Pujol finished his short monologue. "It was a very moving moment," he remembered.

To the Germans, Garbo predicted that a "world civil war" was coming and it would result in the "disintegration of our enemies." Five days after he wrote that message, on May 8, 1945, Germany surrendered to what Garbo called (to the Abwehr) the "Anglo-American-Bolshevik onslaught." The moment Pujol had worked toward for so long had arrived. "London exploded with joy," Pujol recalled. "People invaded Piccadilly Circus and Regent Square, and traffic came to a standstill; everyone was drinking beer, singing and dancing."

His personal war with Hitler was over. All that he'd worked for and all that he'd sacrificed was reflected in the faces of those delirious Londoners.

Still, he kept up the charade. "I am certain that the day will arrive in the not too distant future when the noble struggle will be revived," he wrote Madrid, "which was started by [Hitler] to save us from a period of chaotic barbarism, which is now approaching." Madrid responded in a final message, setting up a meeting between Garbo and Federico in the Spanish capital: "We ask you to frequent the Cafe Bar la Moderna, 141, Calle Alcala, every Monday between 20 hours and 20:30 hours, starting on June 4th. You should be seated at the end of the cafe and be carrying the newspaper *London News*."

MI5 decided that Pujol should make the rendezvous. Before he disappeared forever, the Spaniard had one last mission to complete.

The British wanted Garbo to meet with Federico and Kühlenthal to see if the Nazis were "proposing to carry on any form of underground organization in the post war." But to get to Madrid, Garbo first had to "escape" from England clandestinely. It was too dangerous to allow him to travel on his own passport, especially since the Brits were supposed to be checking every airplane and merchant ship for him.

In June 1945, Pujol left his adopted homeland and flew on a Sunderland seaplane to Baltimore, Tommy Harris sitting beside him. By then, though unknown to the public at large, Garbo was a private legend among the initiated on both sides of the Atlantic. One captain in Luftwaffe intelligence, bitter about the way the spy had hornswoggled the entire German intelligence community, put forth the theory that Garbo had been so successful . . . because there was no Garbo. "He . . . had been invented by the Abwehr so that they could pretend they were doing important work, justifying their comfortable jobs . . . far from the fighting fronts and the bombs and hardship of war." It was perhaps better to believe that he was a German fantasy than a British double agent.

But the Americans were in awe of him. Mickey Ladd, an assistant to the FBI director, sent a message to one of the agency's operatives in London "instructing him to give every assistance with regard to Garbo." J. Edgar Hoover himself demanded to shake the hand of the man who'd fooled Hitler, and arranged for Harris and Pujol to be brought to Washington as soon as they arrived in the United States. "[He] wanted to meet me personally," Garbo wrote. "He invited both Tommy and me to his house, where we had dinner in an underground room." Though Hoover was "most affable throughout," he didn't ask Pujol to work for the FBI, which seemed to surprise him. The Americans gave him some much-needed travel documents, and he flew to Cuba alone to establish the alibi that he'd been smuggled out of London to Havana.

Getting the right entry and exit stamps on his papers took longer than expected, and Garbo didn't reach Madrid until September 8, well after the date specified in the letter. He reunited with Harris and Desmond Bristow, the two men who'd debriefed him at the house on Crespigny Road more than four years earlier, and together they worked out how he'd approach Kühlenthal and Federico.

Garbo went to La Moderna and sat at a table, holding a copy of the *London News,* as the Abwehr had instructed. The contact never showed, so using his local contacts, Garbo tracked Federico down to a house in a small village near the Guadarrama Mountains, which ring Madrid to the north. "Very overcome" by the sight of the master spy standing in his doorway, Federico nervously told Pujol to follow him to a nearby woods where it would be safe to talk. They hiked up to the treeline, and Federico explained that he was now living in fear of being deported back to Germany, or even kidnapped and shot by the Allies. "Speaking of the future, he prophesied utter misfortune for himself and his family." Federico had lost contact with Kühlenthal, the whole Abwehr apparatus was in disarray, and he feared everyone around him.

Federico, who'd once been for Pujol the very image of the tough, cosmopolitan spy, was close to being a broken man. As the wind sighed through the trees, Federico rather pathetically asked if Garbo could use his skills in deception to get him out of Spain. Garbo told him he would do what he could. As he left, the double agent told Federico that the German cause was not yet finished. They would work together in the future, when Nazism rose again.

"He fell for it completely," Garbo later said.

Next the Spaniard went to Ávila, where Kühlenthal was living with his wife in reduced circumstances. When Garbo knocked on the door, Kühlenthal was "overcome with emotion" and told him that he'd always visualized this reunion. Kühlenthal sat in his humble living room and told Garbo his life story, including the difficulty of being half-Jewish in Hitler's Germany and his dedication to the cause — if he could bring about the Fourth Reich, he told the spy, he wouldn't hesitate, though "he did not believe that it would be possible to rebuild Germany again." The pair talked about possibly going into business together, selling information and splitting the profits fifty-fifty, but the German spy-runner was, at present, deactivated: "I was able to deduce that he was at present out of touch with all Service matters." Garbo asked his Abwehr control if the wild letters he'd sent from London had made him sound crazy. Kühlenthal confirmed what MI5 had always suspected, that "on the contrary those letters had in themselves been evidence of Garbo's good faith and honesty." But above all, Kühlenthal marveled at the superagent who had represented the pinnacle of his career in the Abwehr. "He thought me almost a God, saying that he still did not know what advice to give me."

The second great post-D-Day crisis concerned the state of Pujol's marriage. And that would prove harder to fix than the locations of bombs falling on London or the possibility of a Fourth Reich.

Pretending to be writing from his hideout in southern Wales, but actually still in London, Garbo asked the Germans to forward a few letters to Araceli and to help him convince her that he was now in Spain. They were cover messages but, as always, Garbo's spycraft seemed to contain little hints of his real life. He wrote:

> At present I am a man unaware of life and its pleasure. I am disillusioned because I see the misfortune which has dogged my footsteps. My only desire is to behave as well as possible in the future in order that all the bad memories which you have of the past are wiped out.
>
> Again and again I ask you to forgive me for what I have made you suffer. I know that you held no spite and this relieved me.
>
> Goodbye my dear with many kisses from your, José.

And a month later, supposedly from Granada, in southern Spain:

> It is only a few days since I arrived here. This city which I always thought of with pleasure now appears sad and bitter. I remember

the many times we came to visit it together and the happy days we spent.

How much I think of you, my dear. At every moment and every instant you are in my mind.

. . . When I think of our sorrowful position I am truly repentant of the steps which brought about your perdition and mine. I feel I shall never enjoy peace of mind again and that calm will never reign over me. Only you with your tenderness and feeling could cure the trouble, which is known as "remorse" for all I have made you suffer.

Was Juan feeling guilty over the fake arrest that had caused her so much pain? Even though they were meant to deceive the Germans, the letters seem rooted in strong emotions of remorse and foreboding about the future of his marriage.

Evidence that the marriage was in trouble can be found in a report in the MI5 files. Later in 1945, with her husband still "in hiding" (actually he was by then in Venezuela), Araceli, who had returned to Spain earlier that year, went to see Kühlenthal. She hoped to collect the last of the money due her husband, though Pujol had warned her not to make contact with the Germans. The spymaster paid her what he called the "debt of honor," then asked if he could hide out in her family home in Lugo. When Pujol found out that she'd gone to see Kühlenthal against his instructions, he exploded. The MI6 representative in Madrid then met with her, and reported on her state: "I interviewed Mrs Garbo myself and found her in a most difficult mood. Swearing that Garbo had said the most unpardonable things to her over the telephone and that she would not stand for that, that she would sever all connection with him and with us and would in future go her own way. She further added that it was a pity there was no divorce in this country."

Despite their battles in the past, Tommy Harris defended Araceli — at least partially. "I do not feel that Mrs. Garbo had any ill intentions towards us," he wrote on November 1, "though I think it highly probable that should she start to mix with Kühlenthal and his friends she will, either inadvertently or in a spirit of adventure, come to harm and thus compromise us."

Telegrams flew between Madrid and London. One draft, which bears the marks of Pujol's now vitriolic attitude toward his wife, called her "an adventuress" who was "likely to attempt to renew adventures with Germans, possibly influenced by the idea that she may extract more money from them if she breaks with Garbo." Clearly, Pujol suspected his wife of going behind his back to blackmail the Abwehr, a very dangerous game for both of them.

Eventually the matter was smoothed over and the pair reunited. Araceli had only been seeking what was owed her family, and there is no evidence she was trying to extort more or cut a separate deal. But the suspicion between two people who had once trusted each other with their lives was now palpable.

IV

BREAKOFF

22

The End

ONCE HE HAD TYPED UP his notes on his meetings with
the Abwehr men, Pujol ceased to be Garbo. And having
shed the character he'd inhabited for the past four years,
he wanted to shed his surroundings as well. He was determined to
leave Europe. "I was afraid the Germans would take revenge. They
must have thought I was one of their biggest traitors."

MI5 gave Pujol half of the money that the Abwehr had paid him
to spy on England, a total of 17,554 pounds (about $1 million today)
and offered him more from its own funds; he refused the latter. Pujol also turned down a job with the Eagle Star insurance company
that MI5 had arranged. He and Araceli — their marriage hanging by
a thread — would fly to Venezuela with their two young boys. Harris
and Anthony Blunt formulated a cover story for their friend: Pujol
would move to Caracas and advertise himself as an art expert ped-
dling works of the Spanish masters: Goya, Velázquez and El Greco.
Pujol and his family made the trip and settled in a luxurious house
on the Avenida de Bolivia. Harris supplied his coconspirator with a
number of paintings from his own collection to sell, perhaps to the
Venezuelan government as the basis for a national art museum.

The venture began badly. The chargé d'affaires of the Spanish embassy in Caracas noticed a newspaper announcement of Pujol's arrival in the capital — along with his valuable artworks — and alerted
the Spanish government that objects of the "public artistic treasure
taken out of Spain during the Civil War" were possibly going to be
sold. An investigation was launched. One investigator reported on
Araceli's presence in Caracas: "This lady is attracting extraordinary

attention due to her eccentric ways and the kind of life she leads. She frequents leisure societies, trying her best to move in the most select circles; she dresses elegantly and adopts gestures in order to attract the looks of the people around her." Araceli had a "splendid automobile" and apparently plenty of money, but as to her husband, he "was nowhere to be seen."

Desmond Bristow would later claim that Pujol and Harris had cooked up a scheme to sell forged masters in Caracas, the fakes to be dumped on unsuspecting Latin American collectors. But there's no proof to back up the claim. The Spanish government found nothing suspect in Pujol and Harris's business and closed the investigation.

After two years in Caracas, Pujol had had enough. He moved the family to Valencia, three hours from the capital, and bought a large farm. The erstwhile chicken farmer poured 100,000 bolívares into the estate, proceeds from his work with MI5, buying farm equipment and modernizing the facilities around the stately home. "No one in Venezuela had seen anything like it," his son says. "It had the latest technology, the latest irrigation systems." But in 1948, protests swept the country as a group led by Carlos Delgado Chalbaud, Venezuela's minister of defense, overthrew the elected government and installed a military junta. Rich landowners became a target; Pujol's Valencia estate was attacked and destroyed. Forced to sell the property, he earned back only 25,000 bolívares, a quarter of his investment.

Pujol was devastated. First Franco, then Hitler, now Chalbaud. "It was as if the dictators were following me."

That same year, Araceli left him, taking the children, including their infant daughter, Maria, and returned to Spain.

There are two stories to the end of every marriage. Some say that Pujol sent Araceli home for a visit and callously "abandoned" her there. The MI6 officer Desmond Bristow certainly saw it this way. But Araceli's family strongly believes the decision was hers. Sophisticated and ambitious, Araceli hated farm life and the Venezuelan boondocks. She saw no future for herself in Valencia, and having sacrificed her relationship with her family for World War II, she was in no mood to do it again. The trust between her and Juan had broken down long ago. So it is likely that she left of her own free will, taking her two boys and her baby daughter, Maria, with her to Spain.

The break was bitter and deep. After Araceli arrived in Madrid, Pujol wrote to his children on occasion, but the correspondence faded away over time.

Pujol made his way alone. Araceli struggled to make a new life in Madrid, working as a tourist guide and translator. She rented a boarding house and let out rooms to diplomats from the nearby British embassy; MI5 had not completely forgotten her, and the British government sent lodgers her way so that she could survive. Money was scarce, and the balls and parties and evening dresses of Caracas were now distant memories. "When the world war was over, the personal war against hunger and poverty began," she wrote, decades later, in a remarkable letter to her grandchildren. "My husband left me, money left me, my social position was difficult. I carried on with the dignity of a lady who would rather die than ask for help."

In 1949, a year after Araceli left Venezuela, the British ambassador to Spain came calling with official news: Juan Pujol had died of malaria in Mozambique, in East Africa. What he'd been doing there nobody could say for certain: perhaps seeking his way in a new land, perhaps chasing another fortune like the one he'd lost in Venezuela.

Araceli was now a widow. Pujol, whom she had once called her "destiny," was dead.

Araceli's feelings at the news of her first love's passing aren't recorded. Did she regret their ugly separation? Was she relieved, perhaps, that she hadn't followed him on his last, fatal quest? Whatever she was feeling, Araceli kept it to herself. She wouldn't speak of Pujol for many years to come.

Through hard work and sheer force of her remarkable personality, Araceli pulled through. She began to work in a souvenir shop owned by a Jewish-American expat, Edward Kreisler, a handsome former stunt double for the silent-screen star Rudolph Valentino. Soon she was acting as his translator and secretary. Love bloomed, and the two married in Gibraltar in 1958. Araceli helped Kreisler run the shop in Madrid, which was a fabulous success, and they later expanded into Spanish art. The Kreisler gallery became one of the premier art dealers in the country, and Araceli was finally at the center of Spanish high society. She entertained Charlton Heston, Sophia Loren, Frank Sinatra and Roger Moore at her home at 8 Calle de Pedro de Valdivia, and she helped recruit the most exciting young painters to the gallery. Kreisler, closely allied with the American embassy, became a player in Spanish politics; after an attempted coup on February 23, 1981, he was the mediator who brought two right-wing factions together in a posh Madrid hotel, in a failed attempt to guide Spain down the road to full democracy. Araceli's dream — love, family, wealth, parties, glamour — had at last come true.

When asked about Pujol and that phase of her life, Araceli would grow silent, then say, "If I could only tell you." Instead, she began writing a memoir of her adventures with a fellow gambler, the Spanish writer Raúl del Pozo — who confesses that he was half in love with her, though she was in her seventies — but their relationship never progressed very far. Araceli did have a few fabulous stories of life in wartime London. She talked about meeting with Churchill in his Whitehall office, and how, when the ashes of his cigar fell to his lapel as they chatted, she reached out and brushed them away. And how the Duchess of Kent came calling one day at her home to pick up a package.

They were wonderful stories, but they represented Araceli's wishful life more than her actual one. Churchill's secretary kept a record of all his visitors during the war, and Araceli's name doesn't appear in it. Churchill's official biographer and other experts doubt the meeting ever happened. "The Pujols were kept very, very, very isolated," says the son of a Spanish journalist active in the expat scene in London. The idea that the Duchess of Kent would come out to the home of an obscure Spanish couple is simply not credible.

But when Araceli told her stories, people say, you could almost see the gray ashes on Churchill's dark wool suit.

After the war, Tommy Harris retreated to his villa, Camp de Mar, on the island of Mallorca, off the coast of Spain. Though he'd been awarded an OBE for his service to the crown, he wanted to forget all about MI5 and the war and espionage in general. "Mallorca was a perfect place for him to disappear," his nephew says. Harris wanted to think about art, to make art and to live well. Whether he was able to is another story.

Harris's home life was often tense. His wife, Hilda, hated the solitude and boredom of Mallorca, and the pair engaged in epic, drunken fights that terrified their friends. After one plate-throwing blowout, his friend Desmond Bristow recalled the scene: "Hilda began crying hysterically . . . Tommy was sitting on a stool, running his hands through his hair. 'Oh Christ, Desmond, I'm sorry about this.'" They asked Hilda what the fight had been about, and she replied enigmatically, "Philby."

Art was his solace, his refuge. He wrote penetrating essays on Spanish masters; his "Goya, Engravings and Lithographs" is still considered one of the finest studies of the artist's graphic works. And he painted, often from seven in the morning until eleven at night. The work was often stark: dead bodies, Jesus on the cross, landscapes in sickly greens, beautiful but almost nauseating in their effects. At a 1954 show of his work, the critic for the *Scotsman* found the paintings' bleakness to be a challenge. "If the works had been painted in crushed glass, they could scarcely have suggested a greater degree of brittleness."

But something else besides a failing marriage was bothering Tommy Harris. He'd gone to Mallorca for the light and the solitude, but the war had followed him. When his villa needed to be rewired, the electrician who arrived turned out to be the Abwehr radio operator who'd received Garbo's messages in Madrid. The Spanish secret service had reportedly been keeping a close eye on the Brit, suspecting he was spying for the Russians and had chosen his seaside home not for the ocean breezes but for the views it afforded of the American Sixth Fleet steaming along the coast.

Was Harris the notorious "fifth man" of the Cambridge spy circle, along with his friends Anthony Blunt and Kim Philby and the other two traitors? He'd paid the school fees for Philby's son, and even returned a 3,000-pound advance to a British publisher when Philby was unwilling to complete a memoir. He'd also had contact with Melinda Maclean, the wife of the Soviet spy Donald Maclean, before she defected to the USSR. London gossip fingered Harris as the paymaster for the Cambridge group. "As an art dealer he had the perfect cover," said one art expert. "He could be seen to be handling a lot of money and it would not look strange." Harris's exhibitions were thronged with journalists, not because of the paintings but because of his notoriety.

The rumors were untrue; Harris wasn't the fifth man. But the suspicion hounded him. He consulted a psychiatrist, and as payment gave him Goya lithographs. "He was restless, altered," says Harris's nephew. "What Hitler did affected him deeply." Andreu Jaume, a family friend, says, "I think the war destroyed him."

It was an art-related errand that led to his death. Harris and Hilda left a drink-soaked lunch at a Mallorca restaurant with the poet and novelist Robert Graves and drove their brand-new Citroën to get a piece of his pottery fired. The couple began to argue, as they often did. Harris lost control of the car, veered off the twisting road and smashed into a tree, a favorite almond that he'd often used as a subject in his paintings. The elegant ex-spy was thrown from the car. Hilda found him, his shoes knocked off, bleeding from the mouth and ear, near death. "I just cannot say how it happened," she said.

The mysterious death only fed the anti-Red hysteria surrounding Harris. He died still enmeshed in the world that he and Garbo had created. Some in the intelligence community suggested that someone who was so good at espionage could never really give it up.

One of the things left behind in his papers was a review of a painting in white and green. One critic testified that the work "astonishes with its electric and dazzling precision." It was called *Portrait of Juan.* Harris had probably painted Pujol in South America, where he visited him at least twice.

The painting is now lost.

23

The Return

I N 1984, AN AGING MAN strolled through the La Trinidad neighborhood of Caracas. He was a balding seventy-two-year-old retiree with warm eyes, often accompanied by his much younger wife, mild and a little chubby. Together they would walk in the middle-class neighborhood of unpretentious, low-rise houses. The man was well known among the locals, a doting father who regularly filmed the family's excursions to the Venezuelan coast, waving at the camera and skipping with his young children, a smile on his face. In the evenings, he sometimes watched sports on TV — he loved soccer and the Olympics especially, but would follow anything, as long as it was competitive — or met with other Spanish exiles in Caracas. There, because of the wild and unorthodox nature of his politics, he was known as "the Anarchist." Cheerful and almost courtly, he liked to meet friends on sultry evenings and, after dinner and a glass of anisette, to play canasta, a game he'd learned from his father.

Buried nearly forty years before by MI5, Juan Pujol was actually alive and well and living in Venezuela.

The death of Pujol had been a fake, Garbo's last operation. It was meant to throw off the trail any Nazi loyalists who might want to take revenge on him, something that worried Pujol throughout his postwar life. Federico, his former handler in the Abwehr, had caused his pseudo-death. In May 1948, Pujol's brother-in-law had received a letter from the spy-runner, asking to get in touch with Pujol, giving no explanation. Araceli's brother passed on the message.

Pujol wrote Federico back but never received an answer. This worried him, and he got in touch with Tommy Harris to see what he could do. (Pujol had never believed the Harris-as-Russian-spy rumors, by the way: "If he'd worked for the USSR, I would have known it.") "I begged him to tell anyone who asked after me that I had died," Pujol recalled, "leaving no trace, as I still wished to be protected from the Nazis." So Harris killed off Garbo with a bout of malaria in Angola (not Mozambique, as the English ambassador to Spain had told Araceli); later rumors attributed his demise to a bite from a poisonous snake. He'd spread the word through the ranks of MI5 and the British diplomatic service.

As for Araceli, she had seen through the scheme. Perhaps she'd wised up after Pujol's performance in Camp 020, but she never bought the malaria story. In 1957, she even wrote her ex-husband and asked him for a divorce so she could marry Edward Kreisler.

After Araceli left for Spain in 1948, Pujol had rebuilt his life from scratch at the age of thirty-six. He met and married a woman twenty years younger than himself, Carmen Cilia Álvarez, a mixed-race descendant of Canary Islanders, well known in Spain for the beauty of their women. They married in Mexico in 1959 and had two sons, Carlos Miguel and Juan Carlos, and a daughter, Maria Elena. Pujol ran a newsstand to support his family but eventually went to work for Shell Oil in Maracaibo, teaching English to the Venezuelan workers and Spanish to the imported foreign staff. In the small resort town of Lagunillas, he also opened a small souvenir shop in a luxury hotel — ironically, the same business that Araceli had found herself in briefly. He kept the Iron Cross in its fading silk-covered box, and when a friend came across it, Pujol said, "Oh, I won a medal during the war," and nothing more.

His last attempt at being an independent businessman — operating a hotel called Marisel ("Sea and Sky"), in the former plantation town of Choroní, where there were hardly any roads to deliver the tourists — failed spectacularly, as all his ventures had. Children in the village remembered the movies Pujol showed at the little cinema in the hotel, one of the last remnants of his old life in Spain, but that business, too, went nowhere. He'd chosen a town that today boasts dozens of hotels and has become a well-known tourist destination, but he was too early for the boom. Through it all, Pujol never grew bitter. He delivered food regularly to the poor and was a devout Christian, until Maria Elena after giving birth to her son. Then Pujol gave up the faith in anguish.

So the greatest spy of World War II lived in obscurity, telling stories about his escapades to his family but nobody else. "I wanted to forget all about the war," he said. He'd never found a role in life to equal his work as Garbo; his fertile and riotously colorful mind had never proved useful for another occupation. He worked, raised a family and traveled occasionally to see his sister and brother in Barcelona. Araceli had never spoken about him to their children, however, and his sons and daughter by her grew up believing he'd died years before. Pujol also mourned his friend Tommy Harris: "[He'd] endeared himself to me right from the start, not just from the firm way he had shaken my hand but also from the way he had also put his arm around my shoulders in a gesture of protection."

As with Harris, the war had never left Pujol; it had turned him into a kind of permanent double agent. "He had the mania for safety that all spies have," one journalist remembered. In cafés, he would sit with his back to the wall, facing the entrance, so he could observe everyone who came in. He would never leave a phone number or tell his contacts where he was calling from. When visiting Spain, he stayed in a hotel close to the airport, "just in case he had to make a fast getaway." When he visited his family in Barcelona, he was always heading to the consulate on mysterious business he wouldn't talk about, and he refused to give his own family his address in Venezuela. Making up an excuse about its being a "very difficult address to write to," he handed them a slip of paper with a post office box written on it. When he wanted to post a letter, he'd walk by ten mailboxes on the way to the central post office. He just didn't trust the boxes.

Pujol's family in Barcelona loved him deeply, but there was no question that Uncle Juan was different. "We thought it strange," his nephew admitted. "A normal person doesn't do these things." He would realize later that in fact his uncle was two people: "There was Juan Pujol and there was Garbo. With Juan Pujol we had a close, loving relationship." But Garbo they didn't know at all.

• • •

In 1973, Pujol's youngest son in Venezuela, Juan, received a call from his father. Two strange men with British accents had called Juan Sr. out of the blue and asked to meet him in a Caracas hotel. Juan knew the stories of his father's World War II adventures; they'd become a small part of his childhood. It was hard to think of this gentle man playing spy in London and pitting his wit against the Nazis; Pujol just didn't seem like a man who'd mastered the art of deception. "He was a very simple man, an honorable man. If he said he was going to do something, he did it."

The secret had flashed out only a few times. Once, when Juan Jr. was a college student in Mississippi, he began dating a local girl. Her stepfather didn't like Latinos, or anyone dark-skinned, in fact. "He was very old and very racist." When his father came to visit him, Juan mentioned the problems he was having with the man. It stung the ex-spy. Soon after, at lunch with the girlfriend's family, Pujol leaned across the table and talked directly to the stepfather. "He told him what he'd done during the war, how he'd tricked the Germans and saved thousands of American lives." The stepfather listened silently to the story, "amazed" that the Spaniard with the strange accent sitting across from him was the man who'd helped save D-Day.

Now the past had emerged in the form of these British agents. Over the phone, Pujol asked his son to come to the hotel as backup, in case something happened. Exactly what that might be, Pujol couldn't say. As he thought about it, the young man grew worried. South America was honeycombed with old Nazis who'd fled Germany after the war. What if this was a setup? What if his father was at long last going to be assassinated for the murky things he did in the forties? Juan decided to be ready: he went to a friend and borrowed a gun.

He arrived at the hotel with his father, and Pujol went up to meet the two agents. Downstairs, Juan felt the weight of the pistol in his pocket as he counted the minutes on the lobby clock. "Thirty minutes and you come up," his father had said. Five minutes passed with no sign of his father. Then ten. At about twenty-five, Juan realized that he was so frazzled he'd completely forgotten the number of the room where the rendezvous was taking place. He hurried to the front desk and got the number. The gun slapping against his thigh, he ran to the elevator and pressed the button for the right floor, but the car began sinking toward the basement and stopped. Panicking a little, Juan got the elevator car moving upward, found the room, pushed open the door and rushed inside. It was empty.

He found his father in the lobby downstairs, smiling. The two men were officials from the British embassy in Caracas who'd wanted to discuss some MI5 matters. There were no Nazi assassins on his trail. And the agency's files, thankfully, didn't reveal Pujol's real name.

The identity of Garbo had been the holy grail for espionage historians of World War II for many years. One book, *The Counterfeit Spy* — written by the agent Sefton Delmer, who'd taught the Germans how to say "I burn" after the rumors of a flammable English Channel had spread across the Continent — had laid out some details of the operation, with Pujol given the code name Cato. But most people believed the real man was long dead. Even those who'd worked closely with him at MI5 — Cyril Mills, Desmond Bristow, Tar Robertson — believed he'd succumbed to disease in the jungles of Angola. The number of people who knew the truth could probably be counted on one hand.

The British intelligence historian Nigel West, however, had made finding Garbo a personal cause. He'd begun searching for the legendary double agent in 1972, after reading Sir John Masterman's account of the double-cross operations in World War II. Twice West thought he'd found the real Garbo, only to have his candidates turn out to have nothing to do with the case. Then, in 1981, West interviewed Anthony Blunt, a friend of Tommy Harris's and member of the Cambridge spy circle. Blunt had mentioned Garbo in a book he'd published, and West asked for more details. Blunt recalled only one: Garbo had used the name Juan or José García.

West included the name and the story of Garbo in his book on MI5. A former member of the agency picked up the book in Málaga, the southern Spanish coastal city dotted with pubs and fish-and-chips restaurants that was a favorite of British retirees. Desmond Bristow, the man who'd first debriefed Juan Pujol, read the book and wrote West a letter, describing the young Spaniard he'd met forty-odd years before in the house at 35 Crespigny Road. When West flew to Spain, the two Brits met and Bristow revealed the man's name: Juan Pujol García.

West felt the prize within his reach. He hired a Spanish researcher to call every Juan Pujol García in the Barcelona phone book. The researcher asked the men and women who picked up the phone three questions: Did they know a Juan Pujol García, was he in his sixties or seventies, and was he in London during the war? For weeks, the investigator worked his way through the names. But each call gave the same result: there was no elderly Juan Pujol García who had spent time in England during the forties. For West, years into his quest, it was another dead end in a case full of them.

In reviewing the calls, however, the researcher did remember one that didn't go like all the rest: "I spoke to one person, who I could tell was too young to be our target, who kept on asking me questions. After so many abortive conversations, this one stands out in my mind as being quite different." The young man demanded to know who was looking for Juan Pujol García, and why.

West urged the investigator to try again, and after a series of guarded conversations, the man on the other end of the phone made a startling admission: he was Juan Pujol's nephew, and he'd received a postcard from his uncle several years before, postmarked Venezuela, though he hadn't seen him for twenty years.

In 1984, as the fortieth anniversary of D-Day approached, West invited Tar Robertson, Cyril Mills and Desmond Bristow — all of whom knew the spy's real identity, and all of whom believed him to have died decades before in the jungles of Angola — to the Special Forces Club in London to meet "the real Garbo." The former intelligence officers agreed, believing West was going to make an ass of himself once again. "I'd been wrong twice before. They probably thought they were going to get a free drink off me. They assumed the character that I was going to produce from South America was almost certainly the wrong person."

At the appointed time, Juan Pujol walked into the room. In silence the men studied the features of the old man standing in front of them. Finally, Cyril Mills shouted, "I don't believe it. It *can't* be you.

You're dead." Tar Robertson burst into tears, and the men rushed to embrace the diminutive Spaniard as his wife, Carmen Cilia, looked on. The former spies, separated for forty years, "hugged each other like footballers after a goal." Watching, West thought it was "one of the most remarkable things I'd ever seen in my life."

The man who'd been there at the beginning, the tough-minded Desmond Bristow, embraced Pujol, but still couldn't figure out who he really was. Was Pujol a hero or a con man? "Some very strange things happened around Pujol . . . I'm still not sure of his reasons [for spying] today." Bristow's friendship with Araceli after the war had soured him on the man. "My father respected him in a certain way," says his son, Bill, "but didn't like him as a human being. He thought Pujol was cold, calculating and totally self-motivated."

The rest of the world disagreed. Pujol was revealed to the British and the world as the last great hero of World War II. "The Spy Who Came Back from the Dead" announced the *Mail on Sunday.* A newspaper ran television ads saying, "You've heard of General Eisenhower. You've heard of General Montgomery. On Sunday we reveal the name of the third person who made the success of D-day possible." Pujol was invited to Buckingham Palace to formally receive his MBE, and there he met the Duke of Edinburgh, the husband of Queen Elizabeth II, who asked him why he'd felt compelled to volunteer to save England and the free world. "I knew the Nazis had to be destroyed," Pujol told him. "And I knew they could only be destroyed from within." In the whirlwind of interviews and personal meetings, Pujol reinforced one point over and over again: his greatest satisfaction hadn't been about ideology or nationalism. It came from knowing that he'd saved thousands of lives, including those of the German soldiers who would have died had D-Day failed and the war dragged on for months or even years longer than it did.

Omaha Beach, then, came as a shock to the ex-spy. West took Pujol there as part of the D-Day remembrances; the sands swarmed with 100,000 visitors, many of them American and British veterans of the invasion. When Pujol visited the cemetery that housed the remains of thousands of servicemen who'd died yards away on the beaches, he began to weep. He knelt on the sand, made the sign of the cross and bowed his head. West remembered thinking that they'd come to Normandy to celebrate, but here was Pujol, inconsolable. When he finally rose from his knees and approached West, all Pujol could say was "I didn't do enough."

But soon word spread along Omaha Beach just who the diminutive Spaniard was. One American colonel was being interviewed on the beach and the journalist asked him if he'd heard of the spy code-named Garbo. "Yes, I've heard of that gentleman," the colonel replied. "Well," said the reporter, "he's standing right next to you." The man turned to embrace Pujol. Another soldier took him by the hand to a group of veterans and said, "I have the pleasure of introducing Garbo, the man who saved our lives." Old men jostled to shake his hand, and the wives and daughters of the soldiers hugged and kissed him. Tears were shed. "It was very, very exciting," Pujol remembered. The happiness of seeing that these men had gone on to live full lives, to raise children and see their grandchildren born, because of what he and Tommy Harris had done, was written on Pujol's face with a certain sly joy. These were the soldiers he'd walked among on those strolls in London's parks, their guardian angel who prayed for their deliverance.

Pujol's reemergence into a brilliant and welcoming light, however, also exposed the dark ending of the London story: How could this warm-hearted man, who adored his father and his second family, have cut himself off from his own Spanish children for decades? It was the final mystery of the secret agent's life.

When he saw the headlines in the British newspapers, Pujol asked West if the news would reach Spain. Of course, West told him, you're the greatest World War II hero Spain has. You'll be everywhere.

Pujol grew nervous. Even after all these years, he was fearful of old Nazis and neo-Nazis learning his name. In fact, when he returned home to Venezuela after the D-Day celebrations, five American skinheads, "blond and Teutonic-looking," showed up searching for the man who'd betrayed Hitler. "My telephone rang and rang with threats and intimidation and malicious words of every kind." He had to go to the mayor to get the thugs run off.

But Pujol had a deeper fear. "He told me that some of his Spanish family were unaware that he was still alive," West remembered. And now his children would know his secret.

In Madrid in June 1984, Juan, Pujol's eldest son by Araceli (he'd given the same name to his youngest son by Carmen Cilia), was in the bathroom getting ready for the day when the radio announced that a long-lost Spanish war hero had resurfaced. When the announcer said the man's name, Juan froze in astonishment. He began calling his brother and sister and everyone in the family he could reach. At around the same time, Pujol's sister Elena was riding the Barcelona subway when a work friend spotted the article about the Catalan spy who'd saved D-Day. Elena glanced over and saw her brother's photograph; she stared at the picture in shock. Araceli, too, saw a Spanish newspaper with Pujol's face on the front page. "She went to bed for three days," her granddaughter remembers. The reappearance of her first true love shook her to the core.

A reunion between Pujol and his Spanish children was arranged at Barcelona's Hotel Majestic. Before the meeting, Araceli gave her children — Juan, Jorge and Maria — one piece of advice: "Don't open old wounds," she told them, adding, "Just listen to whatever he says." When they saw each other, the children and their father burst into tears and ran to embrace. Pujol apologized profusely for missing out on their lives, and they spent a wonderful few hours together. But he never really explained the lost decades.

In the absence of that explanation, his children could only speculate. His eldest son, who was a boy in London during the bombings and the Garbo adventure, spreads his hands. "Perhaps he felt he couldn't do anything for us." Juan Pujol's own father had provided for his son's education, but Pujol himself had no money to contribute to his Spanish family; perhaps the thought of showing up in Madrid empty-handed cut him too deeply. Pujol came from a time and a stratum of Spanish society when fathers were expected to provide for their families. But his budget was stretched too tightly to see to his children's education. Nazi retribution was another possible factor; Pujol genuinely feared it. Keeping in touch with his family, to him, perhaps meant putting them in danger too.

In the years that followed their reunion, Pujol wrote his children and grandchildren long letters full of love and regret. "Destiny intervened in a very painful way," he wrote his son Jorge about the moment Araceli took him and his brother and sister to Spain. "I wanted to die." But the full explanation never quite came. "I was always a good father, but I don't want to talk more about this because it's the past and it makes me very sad." In another letter, more hints: "I don't talk much about my personal relationships. My life has been very full of events, patience, illusions, sufferings and deceptions."

For his children by Araceli, those decades without their father still burn. Even today, his eldest son cannot talk about Pujol without weeping openly, though he swears he feels no bitterness. The letters, however, did help repair the deep wounds of abandonment. They were beautiful and sad, filled with a longing to recapture lost time. "Today, as yesterday, as always, your letters are fountains of happiness and love for the health of this old man. Reading your letters is like receiving fresh energy and a love that makes me come back to life. I'm very happy to believe that you remember me . . . I love you very much and I'm very sad that I was not able to enjoy more years with you."

But in reading them, his family must have known that, in some way, the old fabulist was at it again. Wasn't this the method — long, passionate messages written from a distant exile — that had bewitched the Abwehr? Weren't the missives written by, as one Spanish journalist who met him said, "the great pretender, the comedian nonpareil"? And weren't the details a bit sketchy here and there? He wrote that after the neo-Nazis came looking for him, he "had to disappear for a long time" and so couldn't write. Yet his Venezuelan children don't remember any such disappearance. Isn't it possible that even with the most painful episode of his life, Pujol couldn't resist inventing a dramatic detail or two?

It didn't matter to his children and grandchildren. They accepted Pujol and welcomed him back into their lives. The letters matched the person they met: compassionate, funny, gentle and wounded. Even the evasions were filled with tenderness. His children embraced

Pujol as he was, and he loved them back. "He seduced us with the writing," admits his granddaughter, without regrets.

Pujol never stopped being Pujol. When, in Spain after his public coming-out, a woman saw the old spy being interviewed, she came over and asked who he was. "I'm a famous writer," he said nonchalantly, and his interviewer stared at him in horrified amusement. Pujol posed for a photograph for the Spanish newspaper *El País* wearing an army hat and holding a grenade in each hand, re-creating his death-defying escape from the Republican lines during the Civil War. And at the German embassy in Madrid, he climbed up the stairs and posed with a smile on his face, the light dancing mischievously in his eyes. As much as he'd risked his life for humanism and for those innocent boys in uniform, it was clear that making utter asses out of the Nazis gave Pujol a wicked, unending pleasure.

Araceli, too, wasn't safe from his mischief. When he saw how well his Spanish children had turned out, he turned to her and asked, "Why don't we get married again?" (Never mind that they were both happily married to other people.) Araceli, for once, was speechless. She relayed the story to the children later, saying only, "Your father is crazy."

Forty years before, Pujol told a story to his debriefers in that house on Crespigny Road, a story about his brother Joaquín and terrible Gestapo massacres, as Tommy Harris watched every twitch of the Spaniard's handsome face. That white lie allowed Pujol to connect his fantasies to the real world of war and espionage, enabled him to walk out of the realm of boyhood dreams and into the great drama of his time. But his imagination remained stubbornly his own; he reserved all rights to employ it as he saw fit. One senses Pujol believed that, no matter how much he let his secrets into the world, they belonged to him and to him alone.

On October 10, 1988, Juan Pujol died after suffering a stroke. He was buried in Choroní, next to his daughter, in Venezuela's Henri Pittier National Park, filled with cloud forests and swept by warm rains from the Caribbean Sea. The graveyard is poorly maintained and overgrown with weeds. Many of the graves are missing their markers. Pujol's tombstone, however, remains untouched. It has a simple inscription — "Remembered by his wife, children and grandchildren" — along with his name and dates of birth and death.

What else could one write, really, about Pujol's life other than the usual clichés about "loving father" and "dutiful husband"? The blank stone is true to his achievement. The best spies dwell in silence.

APPENDIX A: ORGANIZATIONS

Abwehr: The German intelligence-gathering organization responsible for human espionage, established in 1921.

BiA: Section within MI5 that "ran" all the controlled agents in England.

German High Command: The military staff that coordinated the activities of the Luftwaffe, the German navy and the Wehrmacht, the German army.

London Controlling Section: Founded in June 1942, the LCS was an arm of the Joint Planning Staff responsible for the creation of strategic deception policy and planning.

MI5: The British internal counterintelligence and security agency.

MI6: The British Secret Intelligence Service, responsible for foreign intelligence operations.

SD: the Sicherheitsdienst ("Secret Service"), the intelligence organization of the SS and the Nazi Party.

War Office: The British government office responsible for the administration of the British army.

XX Committee: The organization that supplied information to the double agents in Britain, chaired by J. C. Masterman.

APPENDIX B: THE GARBO NETWORK
(ENTIRELY FICTITIOUS)

J (1): Pilot on regular flights between England and Portugal. Garbo's courier.

J (2): RAF officer and "unconscious collaborator" who passed information on rocket batteries in Hyde Park.

J (3): Top official in the Spanish Department of the Ministry of Information. Another "unconscious collaborator" who was assumed by the Germans to be the real W. B. McCann, head of the Spanish section of the ministry. Perhaps Garbo's most essential agent.

J (4): Censor at the Ministry of Information.

J (5): Secretary at the Secretariat of the Ministry of War and Garbo's mistress.

No. 1: Portuguese commercial traveler named Carvalho who reported on Devon and Cornwall. "A rather colorless individual," somewhat lazy and haphazard in his reports.

No. 2: William Maximilian Gerbers. An Englishman of Swiss-German ancestry who was the source for the "Malta convoy" report that first revealed Pujol's operation to the British.

No. 2 (1): William Gerbers's widow, recruited into the network, used as a radio operator and "cutout" between Garbo and his agents.

No. 3: University-educated Venezuelan, nicknamed Carlos, and chief deputy of the Garbo network.

No. 3 (1): Noncommissioned officer in the RAF, stationed in Glasgow. The agent who purchased the aircraft recognition handbook, later baked into a cake by No. 2 (1).

No. 3 (2): Lieutenant in the 49th British Infantry Division, used mainly in Operation Torch.

No. 3 (3): Greek merchant seaman and fervent communist based in Glasgow, used in Operation Fortitude.

No. 4: "Fred," a waiter from Gibraltar, essential to the Chislehurst Caves scheme and later used in Fortitude South.

No. 4 (1): Left-leaning technician who helped Garbo obtain a wireless set.

No. 4 (2): Guard in the failed Chislehurst Caves plot and source for No. 4.

No. 4 (3): American NCO, befriended by No. 4 and the source for much of the information on FUSAG.

No. 5: Brother of the Venezuelan student, No. 3, and a "restless character" who roamed the southern coast of England and Wales before relocating to Canada.

No. 5 (1): Commercial traveler and cousin of No. 5 who passed information on American subjects from his home base in Buffalo.

No. 6: Nicknamed Dick, a South African linguist with strongly anticommunist views. Had to be killed off when his real-world scribe died in a plane crash while traveling from Scotland.

No. 7: Welsh sailor known as Stanley who became head of one of Garbo's subnetworks.

No. 7 (1): British soldier in the 9th Armored ("Panda") Division who was used during Operation Starkey.

No. 7 (2): Retired Welsh seaman and founder of the Brothers in the Aryan World Order, used extensively in Fortitude South.

No. 7 (3): English secretary of the Brothers in the Aryan World Order who was the lover of No. 7 (4). Later moved to India.

No. 7 (4): Indian poet and Aryan fanatic known as Rags who reported from Brighton during the run-up to D-Day.

No. 7 (5): Welsh employee of a commercial firm who monitored the areas around Taunton and Exeter.

No. 7 (6): Low-grade operative and member of the Welsh fascists who reported from Swansea.

No. 7 (7): Treasurer of the Brothers in the Aryan World Order who sent in military updates from the Harwich area.

NOTES

The references to KV, AIR, PRO WO, PRO AIR, HW and WO all refer to files kept at the National Archives at Kew, England.

Introduction

page

xi   "This damned secrecy thing": George S. Patton, letter to Beatrice Patton, March 6, 1944. Quoted in Patton, p. 421.

xii   "a living dynamo": Quoted in Ambrose, *Eisenhower*, p. 88.
He was smoking four packs: D'Este, p. 326.
"bowed down with worry": McManus, p. 116.
Waiting for him in France: Hesketh, p. 101.

xiii   "thought to be held as a centrally controlled mobile reserve": Ibid.
"slim, elegant little man": Holt, p. 216.
"Just keep the Fifteenth Army": Quoted in Holt, p. 579.

xiv   "the best actor in the world": Pujol and West, p. 120.

xv   "power-drunk egocentric": Quoted in Ambrose, *Eisenhower*, p. 52.
"I had the idea": Juan Pujol, interview with Josep Espinas, *Identities*, Catalan TV documentary, date unknown.
the man they called Jesus: Bristow, p. 271.
"I wanted to start a personal war": Author interview with Rafael Fraguas.

1. Tom Mix in Barcelona

4   "complicit expression in his ironic gaze": Juárez, p. 39.
"In my house": Juan Pujol, letter to Tamara Kreisler, May 6, 1988.
"I really believed": Ibid.
"I was constantly covered": Ibid.

5   "That cowboy was doing": Ibid.
"The contents of my fevered fantasies": Ibid.

"I wanted to be the beloved hero": Ibid.

his nickname was Bullet: Ibid.

"I didn't hurt anybody": Juan Pujol, letter to Tamara Kreisler, May 8, 1988.

"Punishments and retribution": Ibid.

"sturdy and straightforward": Pujol and West, p. 22.

"He taught me to respect": Pujol and West, p. 24.

four "interminable" years: Ibid., p. 23.

6 "My imagination would travel with them": Ibid., p. 20.

the leftists' idea of a joke: Carr, p. 60.

"One day a right-wing faction": Pujol and West, p. 31.

"Every morning my father went": Ibid., p. 19.

7 they settled into a magnificent home: Juárez, p. 44.

"a hefty fellow of fifteen": Pujol and West, p. 28.

"endless and dull": Ibid.

"I've always adored romanticism": Juan Pujol, letter to Tamara Kreisler, May 25, 1988.

8 "I was destroyed": Juan Pujol, letter to Tamara Kreisler, August 16, 1988.

he would awaken: Pujol and West, p. 23.

"I felt my stubbornness": Ibid.

"prudent, very religious": Ibid.

Pujol had learned to ride: Juárez, pp. 46–47.

9 "Everybody was crying and shouting": Juan Pujol, letter to Tamara Kreisler, August 24, 1988.

"The flight of his soul": Pujol and West, p. 29.

10 "He was a *terrible* businessman": Author interview with Juan Kreisler.

"I don't know": Juan Pujol, letter to Tamara Kreisler, August 24, 1988.

2. The Training Ground

11 "in such a fratricidal fight": Pujol and West, p. 37.

"I loved liberty": Juan Pujol, letter to Tamara Kreisler, August 24, 1988.

"nothing great has ever been achieved without violence": Carr, p. 13.

12 "Every shop and café had an inscription": Orwell, p. 4.

"snatched from certain death": Pujol and West, p. 37.

"a brutish appetite": Ibid., p. 94.

"A horrible atmosphere of suspicion": Orwell, p. 140.

"Trotskyist treachery": Ibid, p. 173.

13 one of many young Spaniards: Thomas, p. 481.

"I was petrified": Pujol and West, p. 38.

"I kept assuring [them]": Ibid.

14 "I had . . . become a criminal": Ibid., p. 39.

16 "I began to look like a decrepit old man of forty": Ibid., p. 40.
In order to plan an escape: The details of Pujol's life after his confinement are found in Pujol and West, pp. 40–53.
20 The hotel had one other guest: Juárez, p. 78.
"Years of hiding and persecution": Pujol and West, p. 43.
21 "I am only his shadow": Juan Pujol, letter to Tamara Kreisler's mother, October 29, 1987.

3. Araceli

22 her mother nicknamed her Antoñita la Fantástica: Author interview with Maria Kreisler.
"There is a part of the family": Araceli Kreisler, letter to her grandchildren, undated.
23 "She was the most seductive woman": Author interview with Tamara Kreisler.
"Lugo was the kind of place": From the documentary *Hitler, Araceli y Garbo,* directed by José de Cora. A Lugopress/Cora Production for Galician television.
"It was the best way to leave us": Araceli Kreisler, letter to her grandchildren, undated.
"We lived in a fantasy world": Ibid.
She took with her an enormous wooden chest: Ibid.
"All my friends would say": Ibid.
A friend and fellow nursing student: Interview with Cachita Nuñez, from *Hitler, Araceli y Garbo.*
24 "I went to Burgos": Quoted in *Hitler, Araceli y Garbo.*
"Where he was weak, she was strong": Author interview with Maria Kreisler, September 2011.
In Navarre, men in short-sleeve shirts: The details of life under Franco are from Carr, pp. 211–13.
Those suspected of speaking against the Führer: This and the anecdotes about Hans Lazar are from "Los espías nazis que salvó Franco," *El País,* January 26, 2003.
25 what London could reasonably expect: Carr, p. 187.
"The countryside . . . was pockmarked": Bristow, p. 10.
"It didn't even deserve one star": Pujol and West, p. 54.
26 "Francoist Madrid was too small for him": Author interview with Rafael Fraguas.
"a maniac, an inhuman brute": Pujol and West, p. 26.
"My humanist convictions": Ibid., p. 61.
"I would be tormented": Ibid., p. 60.
27 "If a Pythian oracle": Ibid., p. 57.
"Aryan race," "superior being": Ibid.
"I must do something, something practical": Ibid., pp. 60–61.

28 "They considered such a drink essential": Ibid., p. 55.

"We were just fighting for the right to survive": Ibid., p. 61.

"Your services of *what?*" The phrase is from the author's interview with Rafael Fraguas, who spoke to Pujol about the incident after his reemergence in 1984.

"I must confess that my plans were fairly confused": Pujol and West, p. 62.

29 The future Il Duce: The details of Hoare's caper are from "Recruited by MI5: The Name's Mussolini. Benito Mussolini," *Guardian*, October 13, 2009.

30 "Out of *amour-propre*": Pujol and West, p. 62.

"In order to offer myself to the Nazis": Ibid., p. 63.

31 "My contact with the Germans": Ibid.

it employed 391 people: Macintyre, p. 156.

"All classes were represented": Ibid.

Knappe-Ratey had grown up in luxury: Juárez, p. 114.

"slight but rather athletic": KV 2/101.

32 a "hot Nazi": Liddell, p. 23, referring to Richard Sorge.

"extraordinarily magnificent": Pujol and West, p. 64.

"It dawned on me": Ibid., p. 63.

"a thousand foolish things": Ibid.

"It's something you have to know": Juan Pujol, interview with Josep Espinas, *Identities*.

33 "dreaming up new rigamaroles": Pujol and West, p. 64.

When Pujol showed up: For an account of the meeting, see Harris, pp. 44–47.

4. The White City

35 still maintained flights: Kahn, p. 79.

MI6 and American OSS officers: Pujol and West, p. 74.

36 whose bartender reportedly made: Lochery, pp. 125–26.

One American visitor: Ibid., p. 126.

Graham Greene, then working the Lisbon desk: The information about Greene, Fleming and Casino Estoril comes from Miller, p. 50, and James Milton, "Discovering Lisbon, the 'Capital of Espionage,'" *Daily Mail*, March 24, 2010, www.dailymail.co.uk/travel/article-1260276/Portugal-holidays-Discovering-Lisbon-capital-espionage.html.

Our Man in Havana, which was inspired: Denis Smyth, "Our Man in Havana, Their Man in Madrid: Literary Invention in Espionage Fact and Fiction," in Wesley Ward, ed., *Spy Fiction, Spy Films and Real Intelligence* (London: Frank Cass, 1991).

"She . . . would play three times": Quoted in Kahn, p. 289.

"It was an expensive code": Ibid.

37   "I was getting desperate": Pujol and West, p. 69.
"I resolved to become better acquainted": Ibid., p. 68.

39   "I was fully aware of the risks": Ibid., p. 70.
the Zueleta brothers: Juárez, pp. 102–3.
"He was becoming increasingly interested": Pujol and West, p. 72.

40   "He did not wish . . . to be caught a second time": Harris, p. 47.
"You must return urgently": Ibid.

41   "Alarmed and furious": Ibid., p. 48.
"Greatly impressed": Ibid., p. 49.

42   "[He'd] swallowed the story": Ibid., p. 73.
"In a few days I'll depart": Ibid., p. 49.
"No conquest conquered me": Juan Pujol, letter to Tamara Kreisler,
March 3, 1988.

5. The Game

43   "In what stage of construction": KV 2/63, summary of letters and
questionnaires.
"Why he had such blind faith": Pujol and West, p. 73.

44   "With the British he was British": Author interview with Xavier Vinader.
Federico was so taken with his new agent: The Calvo anecdote is recounted in Harris, p. 50.
"Oval face . . . fleshy": KV 2/102.

45   "my own bizarre form of espionage": Pujol and West, p. 74.
"[He] had no idea": Harris, p. 51.
"What follows may seem unbelievable": Pujol and West, p. 74.

46   This would later amaze Pujol's handlers: Ibid., p. 121.
"The method of communication is good": KV 2/63, message of July
29, 1941.
"I had become a real German spy": Pujol and West, p. 90.

47   "Why, I kept on asking myself": Ibid., p. 74.

48   "verbal equivalent": Holt, p. 211.
"I do not wish to end": Quoted in Harris, p. 95.
"I tried hard to introduce new information gradually": Pujol and
West, p. 90.
"in detail how I had grappled": Ibid.
His subagent William Gerbers: KV 2/63 and Harris, p. 41.

49   "Try to find out the details": KV 2/63.
An advertisement in a Portuguese paper: KV 2/63, "Translation of
notes to letters 1 through 39."
"very secret apparatus": KV 2/63, appendix 2, letter no. 20.

50   "R.A.F. Pilot School situated near Sandwitch": KV 2/63.

Pujol went to a local detective agency: Harris, p. 60.
When Tommy Harris later revealed: Ibid., p. 58.
"You refer by number": KV 2/63, incoming letter no. 15.
"I am surprised at your announcement": KV 2/63.
51 "It is unnecessary for you to send us proof": Ibid.
"It can be said that from this point onwards": Harris, p. 86.
"There are men here": KV 2/63.
"She became highly excited": Harris, p. 55.
52 "Talk to me about the baby": KV 2/63, message of October 7, 1941.
"[Pujol's] existence was precarious": Masterman, p. 116.
"The farce was coming to an end": Pujol and West, p. 92.
53 "[She] mystified the American": Liddell, p. 253.
She also demanded $200,000: Harris, p. 64.
"LeClerc Fils of Paris reports": Ibid., p. 65.
"Agent 172 of Chicago": Ibid., p. 64.
54 "Here you are": Ibid., p. 65.
"She *never* stepped back": Author interview with Maria Kreisler.
"There is no doubt": Harris, p. 65.

6. The Snakepit

56 Desmond Bristow was a tough-minded young man: For the intelligence officer's early life, see Bristow, pp. 1–8.
"I watched in horror": Ibid., p. 13.
In late October 1941: The account of Subsection V (d) is drawn from Bristow, pp. 16–44, and from an author interview with Bill Bristow.
57 Tim Milne, a former copywriter: Timothy Milne's obituary, *Sunday Times*, April 8, 2010.
"This sounds very odd": Bristow, p. 19.
58 "the British were going crazy": Pujol and West, p. 91.
saying that the Caernarvon convoy: Bristow, p. 21.
"We know there is no bloody convoy": Ibid.
"The Abwehr's trust": Ibid., p. 25.
59 The Germans planned to ambush: Pujol and West, p. 104.
MI5 chimed in with a theory: Bristow, p. 22.
it was even believed: Delmer, p. 39.
60 a Spanish national named Juan Pujol: Bristow, p. 33.
"If it was within Pujol's power": Author interview with Nigel West.
61 "discreet interview": Bristow, p. 35.
Gene Risso-Gill, a well-bred Portuguese: Pujol and West, p. 94.
On an unseasonably hot February evening: The rendezvous is described in Bristow, pp. 36–37.
"My legs were shaking": Pujol and West, p. 94.
"a wad of sterling notes": Ibid., p. 96.

62 "I was suddenly acutely aware": Ibid., p. 97.
"It seemed a miracle": Harris, p. 66.
"It was crazy": Juan Pujol, interview with Josep Espinas, *Identities*, Catalan TV documentary, date unknown.

7. A Fresh Riot of Ideas

65 On the morning of May 1, 1942: The details of Pujol's debriefing are from Bristow, pp. 41–42.
66 "mischievous glint": Ibid., p. 38.
whose nickname inside the agency: Ibid., p. 271.
67 "He is such a dreamer": Ibid., p. 42.
One officer recalled a story: Recounted in Andrew, *Secret Service*, p. 443.
68 "in a gesture of resignation": Ibid.
The sounds had actually been doors slamming: Ibid., p. 432.
"We are bred up": Brown, p. 9.
"Don't go near them": Andrew, p. 217.
69 The cell — now office — doors: Ibid.
some of which were read: Holt, p. 170.
"newfangled business": Wheatley, p. 39.
"a racket": All the reactions are from Wheatley, pp. 39, 84.
"The very fact that the Allies": Holt, p. 62.
Down the hall: Wheatley, p. 25.
Close to Wheatley's office: The description is from the author's visit to the war rooms.
70 "the lost section": Wheatley, p. 54.
"smoked salmon or potted shrimps": Ibid., p. 30.
"The day has brought forth nothing": Ibid., p. 49.
Wheatley submitted a memo: The information on the Bote plot is from Wheatley, p. 50.
71 When they were desperately trying: The "burning sea" plot comes from Crowdy, p. 55.
72 In April 1942, the British secret service: Wheatley, p. 56.
73 "Obviously, [they] missed the whole point": Ibid.
"reference books": Crowdy, p. 75.
case officers sometimes hired prostitutes: Ibid., p. 71.
"appointed scribes": Harris, p. 105.
74 "The running of double-cross agents": Masterman, p. 70.
"to work out the crime": Quoted in Macintyre, p. 62.
At more than 226 weekly meetings: Crowdy, p. 72.
75 Plan Machiavelli: Masterman, p. 83.
Plan Guy Fawkes: Ibid., p. 88.
In Plan Brock: Ibid., p. 126.

nearly causing the planners: Churchill, p. 293.

"How should we feel": Masterman, p. 127.

76 At one point: Ibid., p. 102.

a dozen double agents: The relevant agents are listed in Holt, p. 150.

one branch, the Naval Intelligence Division: Andrew, *Secret Service,* p. 455.

"I can't tell you what sort of job it would be": Ibid., p. 472.

"playing casually with detonators": Ibid., p. 473.

A Force, the Middle East deception unit: Delmer, p. 26.

"We were complete amateurs": Levine, Kindle location 368.

77 When Winston Churchill toured: Andrew, *Secret Service,* p. 454.

"bubbled and frothed": Philby, p. 68.

78 "whizzing up and down the corridors": Ibid., p. 77.

"He smoked like a chimney": Pujol and West, p. 224.

"a fresh riot of ideas": Philby, p. 47.

"a casting director's ideal choice": Delmer, p. 76.

"There are many questions about him": Bristow, p. 271.

"He's like a runaway figure for me": Author interview with Andreu Jaume.

79 they kept horses in stables: *Oxford Mail,* December 1, 1954.

"During my occasional visits": Philby, p. 73.

The house next door: Author interview with Bill Bristow.

the basement served as a bomb shelter: Author interview with José Antonio Buces, nephew of Tommy Harris.

"These paintings do have an intriguing, disturbing vibrancy": Review in the *Scotsman,* December 4, 1954.

80 "Pujol's genius was Latin": Author interview with Rafael Fraguas.

8. The System

81 "our best batsmen": Masterman, p. 90.

"production teams": Holt, p. 541.

82 "Lighting, Scenery, Costumes": Ibid., p. 80.

Over his career: For a discussion of Pujol's earning power, see Harris, "Appendix III: Financial Arrangements," p. 335.

breaking for meals: Holt, p. 212.

entering into a new logbook: Pujol and West, p. 119.

83 "realistic enough to create a clear picture": Harris, p. 78.

To flesh out the lives: Hesketh, p. 45.

their KLM pilot-courier: Harris, p. 87.

all of Pujol's outgoing messages: The Pujol MI5 files at the National Archives at Kew retain the color codings.

84 "an extremely indiscreet": Liddell, p. 40.

"and knew how to use it": Holt, p. 232.
The code name might also confuse the Germans: Harris, p. 87.
"The beach here is mined": KV 2/64, letter of October 24, 1942.
"Several large hangars": KV 2/64, letter of October 18, 1942.
"The small port of Irvine": KV 2/63, letter of September 4, 1943.
85 "You moisten a sheet of paper": KV 2/65.
"Obviously, as an affectionate brother": KV 2/64, letter of July 11, 1942.
"I have been asked": KV 2/64, letter of November 30, 1942.
86 "the greatest burden of the work": Harris, p. 77.
"It is . . . true to say": Ibid., p. 79.
"according to him": KV 2/63, letter of February 16, 1942.
"suited for the passing": Hesketh, p. 51.
87 "If these two conditions exist": Quoted in Holt, p. 58.
88 "Exact details and sketch": Quoted in Masterman, p. 80.
"Can you get hold of a gas mask?": KV 2/63, letter no. 14.
clearly the Germans wanted: KV 2/64, message of August 13, 1942.
"3¾ oz of Plain Nut Charcoal": KV 2/64, message of August 28, 1942.
"I have been passing through a long period": KV 2/64, page 13 of undated letter, allocated on August 28, 1942.
89 "pass from the notional": Harris, p. 98.
Dream was a currency scheme: Plan Dream is outlined in Harris, pp. 98–100, and in the MI5 file K 2/64, especially the outgoing letter (no. 99) of September 29, 1942.
"I have a message": KV 2/64, letter of September 9, 1942.

9. The Debut

91 "ten-hour second front": Kahn, p. 471.
"The job I am going on": Letter to Frederick Ayer, Patton, p. 92.
92 "If the assault failed": Wheatley, p. 100.
"For him to remain there": Harris, p. 105.
Tommy Harris had consulted a physician: Delmer, p. 100.
93 "Although I cannot confirm the rumor": KV 2/64, message of November 10, 1942.
"There were also about the town": KV 2/64, message of November 23, 1942.
"All radiators to be drained": KV 2/64, message of September 23, 1942.
"Second front! Very important!!": KV 2/64, message of October 14, 1942.
"No. 6 tells me that rumors are circulating": KV 2/64, message of October 11, 1942.

94   "None of the troops with Arctic uniforms": KV 2/64, message of October 29, 1942.
     "It was impossible for me": KV 2/64, message of November 1, 1942.
     "Your last reports are all magnificent": KV 2/64, message of November 26, 1942.
     "We didn't even dream of it": Brown, p. 232.

95   "GERBERS. November 19 at Bootle": Harris, p. 107.
     "the poor girl is very broken up": KV 2/66, message of July 15, 1943.
     "Think about me a lot": KV 2/63, message of May 25, 1942.
     "She was alone with a new baby": Author interview with Maria Kreisler.

96   "'liquidate' some of our agents": Quoted in Macintyre, p. 83.
     Harris obtained an 80-watt: Harris, p. 341. Harris indicates the radio was a 100-watt set, but the Abwehr suitcase sets given to its South American agents were typically 80 watts.

97   Madrid sent the cipher plan and codes: Pujol and West, p. 121.
     By August 1942, all reports: Ibid., pp. 128–29.
     Garbo and the operator: For ciphering, see Harris, Appendix XXXIII, "Cyphers and Transmitting Plans," p. 343.

10. The Blacks and the Santa Clauses

98   formed the biggest: Farago, p. 205.
     working under the auspices: Kahn, p. 278.
     the Fakir of Ipi: Farago, p. 205.
     They hired deaf-mutes: Brown, p. 205.
     "What is that?": Kahn, p. 277.

99   the staples in a typical Russian passport: Ibid., p. 283.
     "very brilliant and lively": Perrault, p. 55.
     "In many ways": Ibid., p. 57.

100 Worked into the beautiful mahogany desk: Ibid., p. 66.
     To divine the whereabouts: Ibid., p. 127.
     There was a running joke: Breuer, p. 20.
     "must found itself upon a race": Quoted in Kahn, p. 270.

101 "The Germans consider espionage": Perrault, p. 153.
     "ostracized officers who dealt with spies": Kahn, p. 532.
     He claimed he would never shake the hand: Farago, p. 17.
     "In the future, you will use Jews": Perrault, p. 136.
     "No one among the staff": Ibid., p. 167.

102 It was the Führer: Ibid.
     "dumb as a carp": Cameron and Stevens, p. 293.
     "Everything you've written is pure nonsense": Perrault, p. 166.
     "He closed his mind against the truth": Speer, p. 261.

"I don't want any wretched spies": Farago, p. 94.

103 "Send them into England as quickly as possible": Ibid., p. 297.
"Arrived safely, document destroyed": Ibid., p. 303.

104 "he looked like the man": Ibid., p. 651.

105 "It is known that [he] is trembling": KV 2/102, "Extract from Camp 020 interim report on the case of Ledebur."
"His characteristic German lack of sense of humor": Harris, p. 70.
"We are separated from England": Cameron and Stevens, p. 101.
Roenne was the descendant of an old family: Breuer, p. 39.

106 "impossible to make friends with": Holt, p. 100.
"the Western allies would protest": Macintyre, p. 240.

107 Listening stations would write "Z reports": Kahn, p. 181.
"worthless," "swindle": Ibid., p. 366.
"The fact," Canaris boasted: Farago, p. 772.

11. The Rehearsal

109 "We should never resort to it": Quoted in Holt, p. 72.

110 In a message marked "Urgent": Harris, pp. 106–12.

111 the RAF had initiated: Ibid., p. 122.
"I saw my cannon shells": *Evening News* (London), March 15, 1943.
others, veering away: *Daily Sketch* (London), February 8, 1943.
"The Germans' tactics are apparently to shoot up": Liddell, p. 47.

112 "my experience when traveling": KV 2/65, message of February 23, 1943.
"It displeases me very much": KV 2/65, message of February 27, 1943.
"I have been able to estimate": KV 2/66, message of August 2, 1943.
"We beg you not to be impatient": Quoted in Harris, p. 108.
His dispatches began showing up: Harris, p. 75.
from methylene blue to "tetra base": Liddell, p. 110.

113 the spy had to cut his finger: Kahn, p. 290.
"the most important development in the case": Harris, p. 132.
"Denys Page tells me that the information": Liddell, p. 71.
No. 3 drove a hard bargain: KV 2/65, message of March 14, 1943.
"left [the] last days of January": Harris, p. 130.
The dog was a toy: Liddell, p. 167.

114 the two *t*'s in Odette: KV 2/65, message of March 4, 1943.
"Inside the cake you will find": KV 2/66, message of June 9, 1943.
"We have received the cake": KV 2/66.
"he had an agent in England": Ibid.
"I would never have had the nerve": Levine, Kindle location 470.
"[The] activity of Arabel": Quoted in Harris, p. 75.

115 LESLIE HOWARD IS LOST: Quoted in the documentary *Garbo the Spy*.

116 Plan Bodega was a "most complex and elaborate" scheme: Bodega is described in detail in Harris, pp. 115–20.

117 From that, the Germans could deduce: In the MI5 files, Bodega is covered in KV 2/65, message of May 3, 1943, and many other reports of the period.

118 "He would . . . have been allowed": Harris, p. 118.
"It was explained that by blowing up one of the trains": Ibid., p. 117.

12. The Dry Run

124 "an elaborate camouflage and deception scheme": Quoted in Holt, p. 477.
"a major amphibious feint": Pujol and West, p. 137.
There was also a provision: PRO WO 106/4223, Encl. 29A COSSAC 43, dated May 24, 1943.
squadrons of seaborne commandos: Cumming, p. 6.
an "Armageddon-of-the-Air": Ibid., p. 9.

125 These unfortunates were to be executed: Helm, p. 81.
condemned to have their necks placed on the block: Perrault, p. 78.
"I have now completed arrangements": Andrew, *Defend the Realm*, p. 257.
"If there is any danger": Ibid.

126 Back in Le Portel: Cumming, p. 48.

127 Some of them had been shanghaied: Ibid., p. 50.
"The effects of these operations": AIR 20/4557 Annex, Final Draft, July 8, 1943.

128 "All the northern part of Southampton Common": KV 2/66, message of August 12, 1943.
"where the enemy was known to be operating": Harris, p. 150.

129 "This makes her all the more accessible": KV 2/67, message of September 25, 1943.
"You must let me know": Ibid.
"It appears that the situation has become worse": KV 2/66, message of August 26, 1943.
"Agent 1b in Portsmouth reported": KV 2/66, message of August 12, 1943.

130 Forty thousand tents were erected: Cumming, p. 27.
Notices were slapped on the walls: Ibid.

131 The French Committee of National Liberation told its members: Brown, p. 323.
"I had the power to advance": Juan Pujol, letter to Tamara Kreisler, undated.

13. An Intimate Deception

132 "distinctive Slav beauty": Holt, p. 13.
"the huge red glow of the distant flames": "WW2 People's War," BBC online oral history, memories of Mrs. S. Gaylor, www.bbc.co.uk/ww2peopleswar/stories/30/a3545930.shtml.

133 "found lodged on top of a telephone box": Ibid., memories of Bill Clavey.
the charred sap of trees with their bark blown off: Ibid., memories of Ken Long.
"dust, dirty water, the cabbagey smell of gas": Ibid., memories of Bill Clavey.
"One by one": *News Chronicle* story, exhibit at the Imperial War Museum, London.
"sweetheart badge": "WW2 People's War," memories of Ken Long.

134 "There has been a crisis": Liddell, p. 79.
The Spanish embassy was a well-known nest: Harris, p. 328.
"I am telling you for the last time": Ibid.

135 "She ought really to be locked up": Liddell, p. 79.
"anxious to assassinate the ambassador": Ibid.
"highly emotional and neurotic": Harris, p. 327.

136 "In contrast to her husband": Ibid.
"It is now proposed": Liddell, p. 79.

137 "stubborn, immoral and immutable": Levine, Kindle location 935.
The scheme was quickly put into action: The incident is recounted in Harris, pp. 328–31.

138 "Was she capable of pretending": Author interview with Tamara Kreisler.
"This was clearly a bit of play-acting": Liddell, p. 80.

139 "had only avoided being arrested": Ibid.
"rather like Lenin": Ibid., p. 252.
"that the conclusion which Garbo had drawn": Harris, p. 331.

140 "I gather that [Pujol] is somewhat shaken": Liddell, p. 80.
"for whom some considerable time ago": Ibid., p. 284.

14. Haywire

141 "gnawing anxiety": Masterman, p. 127.
From then on, it would be a pure deception exercise: PRO WO 106/4223, Encl. 34b, July 16, 1943.
The planners went looking: Howard, p. 81.

142 "Will someone kindly tell me what I am to say": Brown, p. 322.
Rain and storms meant canceled sorties: Cumming, p. 82.
"I cannot feel," he wrote: PRO AIR 8/1202, September 5, 1943.

143   they were quickly formed into a second prong: Cumming, p. 26.
"A mounting wave of desperation rose": Howard, p. 81.

144   "If I do just one thing": Juan Pujol, interview with Josep Espinas, *Identities*, Catalan TV documentary, date unknown.
"45 torpedo boats in Dover": Quoted in Harris, p. 142.

145   "England and the United States will assume the offensive": Brown, p. 323.
A grenade detonated in Lille: "Paris Frenchmen Battle Germans," AP report, *Palm Beach Post*, March 9, 1943.
Danes trampled a German soldier: The last three incidents are from Brown, p. 323.
The Reich's divisions in France: Harris, p. 144.
"Good luck to Starkey": PRO AIR 8/1202, September 5, 1943.
flooded with bright moonlight: WO 205 449, "Immediate Interpretation Report No. K. 1715," September 10, 1943.

146   dropping one bomb every eight seconds: Cumming, p. 73.
the lone survivor was found amid: Ibid., p. 84.

147   "We [were] waiting to die because this is inevitable": Ibid., p. 87.
"It was an inspiring sight to see everybody": Howard, p. 488.

148   "I can definitely prove the lie": KV 2/67.
"I do not think that the British High Command": KV 2/67, message of September 13, 1943.
"Their confidence in me": Juan Pujol, interview with Josep Espinas, *Identities*.

149   "Your activity and that of your informants": Quoted in Holt, p. 493.
"Both reports are first class": Quoted in Harris, pp. 145–46.

150   "The movements made were rather too obvious": Quoted in Howard, p. 30.
"The multiplicity of the at-times utterly fantastic reports": Quoted in Brown, p. 494.
"[He] watched and shook his head": Quoted in Holt, p. 501.

151   "Violence is contrary to all my ideas": Juan Pujol, interview with Josep Espinas, *Identities*.
The Allied planners produced an in-depth report: HW 13/215, "German reaction to Starkey," 1/8/43–9/9/43, page 1, in file "Western Europe Situation Reports," nos. 1–20.

15. The Interloper

153   On December 20, 1943: See Kahn, pp. 479–81.
"The danger in the east remains": Quoted in Delmer, p. 148.

154   Finally, the Führer announced: Ibid., p. 149.
"the location of the defenses better": Ambrose, *D-Day*, p. 37.
"It would be good": Quoted in Kahn, p. 479.

southeastern England is closer: Ambrose, *D-Day,* p. 29.

bolstered by 16-inch guns: Farago, p. 760.

155   There was only one panzer division: Ambrose, *D-Day,* p. 73.

"This cannot be": Quoted in Kahn, p. 187.

green scrambler telephones: Perrault, p. 101.

156   When the Allies attacked the heavily defended coast: Ambrose, *D-Day,* p. 41.

Casualty rates were predicted to be 90 percent: Perrault, p. 5.

the Germans had fifty infantry: Ambrose, *D-Day,* p. 41.

"Well, there it is": Quoted in D'Este, p. 32.

"I see the tides running red with their blood": Quoted in Ambrose, *D-Day,* p. 129.

157   "it had become a hopelessly depressing document": Quoted in Holt, p. 505.

"The plan has to be just close enough": Quoted in Breuer, p. 13.

158   "no large scale cross-Channel operations": Harris, p. 174.

"were proving themselves to be by far": Hesketh, p. xvi.

"I have read in the English press": KV 2/67, message of January 5, 1944.

"Conversation with a friend": KV 2/67, message of January 21, 1944.

159   The Abwehr's sources reported that artesian wells: Hesketh, p. 60.

"News from various sources": KV 2/67, message of January 5, 1944.

"For tactical reasons one must assume": KV 2/67, message of January 14, 1944.

"Numerous reports of the alleged postponement": Quoted in Hesketh, p. 157.

people joked that you could walk: Perrault, p. 114.

"They came by land, by train, bus, truck": Ambrose, *D-Day,* p. 151.

160   campfires were forbidden: Ibid., p. 152.

"The work Tommy Harris and I did": Pujol and West, p. 226.

161   "What evidence there is": Masterman, p. 187.

"hated the British like death": KV 2/65, message of April 24, 1943.

the minister believed that Germany: KV 2/67, message of January 21, 1944.

"She emphasized one point above all": KV 2/67, message of January 24, 1944.

162   "an impossible and insufferable *enfant terrible*": Quoted in Levine, Kindle location 2867.

"'I was not a much loved person'": Unpublished transcript, Thaddeus Holt interview with David Strangeways, August 26, 1992.

Although a wonderful speaker: From Strangeways's obituary, *Independent,* August 17, 1998.

Strangeways spied an abandoned Thames barge: Ibid.

163   MI6 knew that Gibraltar hotel employees: Wheatley, p. 86.

"the most all-containing brain": Quoted in Holt, p. 14.

where he'd placed his office below a brothel: Levine, Kindle location 255.

"He was certainly the most unusual Intelligence officer": Quoted in Holt, p. 14.

It could even dye a man brown: Ibid., p. 29.

164   The battle for Tunis: From Strangeways's obituary, *Independent*.

165   "He was . . . so beautifully turned out": Quoted in Holt, p. 334.

"Put it this way": Thaddeus Holt interview with David Strangeways.

166   "It gave maximum offense": Quoted in Levine, Kindle position 2902.

"Everybody was furious": Quoted in Holt, p. 537.

"the beau ideal of an English country squire": Roger Hesketh's obituary, *Telegraph*, December 27, 2004.

"one of the best claret cellars in England": Quoted in Holt, p. 478.

"a few new ideas" thrown in: Unpublished transcript, Thaddeus Holt interview with Christopher Harmer.

One day soon after his pronouncement: The account of Harmer's conversation with Hesketh is from Thaddeus Holt's interview with Harmer.

16. The Ghost Army

167   "putting a hooped skirt": Quoted in Holt, p. 504.

"flatly refused to believe that it would be possible": Howard, p. 506.

"But we are not *going* to land": Quoted in Holt, p. 524.

168   "After the initial shock": Quoted in Levine, Kindle location 2934.

"true to the tradition of English eccentricity": Brown, p. 2.

"awful, ghastly staff procedures": Quoted in Holt, p. 69.

"We got away with murder": Unpublished transcript, Thaddeus Holt interview with David Strangeways, August 26, 1992.

Tate was a Danish spy: Hesketh, p. 55.

170   "The enemy will probably succeed": Quoted in D'Este, p. 116.

171   "I'm not Jewish or Polish": Juan Pujol, interview with Josep Espinas, *Identities*, Catalan TV documentary, date unknown.

"It would be of the greatest interest": KV 2/68.

so much traffic was flowing: Harris, p. 179.

The Abwehr in Madrid: Macintyre, p. 164.

"By the main road between Leatherhead and Dorking": KV 2/68, message of March 6, 1944.

172   "There are two or three American camps": KV 2/69, message of March 19, 1944.

"You don't take a great big silver salver": Holt, p. 75.

"[German commanders] know we do not wish to see": KV 2/67, message of February 23, 1944.

173 "German troops are now evacuating French territory": KV 2/67, included with message of February 23, 1944.

It ordered them to find out: Perrault, p. 31.

17. The Backdrop

174 "goddamned natural-born ham": Quoted in Macdonald, p. 101.

"See you in the Pas de Calais!": Quoted in Levine, Kindle location 3226.

the barge's captain and crew were arrested: Ibid., location 3284.

175 The deception planners hoped that Luftwaffe night raiders: Breuer, p. 161.

All his staff officers got fake promotions: Holt, pp. 85–86.

The Allies requisitioned a wind machine from a British movie studio: Breuer, p. 115.

176 "Here is your bird": Ibid.

Map 51, of course, covered the Pas de Calais: Ibid., p. 117.

Entire books and technical journals were written: Ibid., p. 163.

In March, Churchill visited a sham armored division: Ibid., p. 114.

177 received checks that were five times the pay: Holt, p. 136.

The result of the last invention: Ibid., p. 84.

Battle sounds were recorded: Ibid., p. 86.

178 Coastal areas from Land's End: Levine, Kindle location 3541.

There were the "Bunsen burners": Holt, p. 87.

179 Prisoners of war in German concentration camps: Hesketh, p. 40.

Insignia were invented for Garbo's phantom armies: Holt, p. 897.

A single wireless truck impersonated: Hesketh, p. 36.

In January 1944, Roenne estimated: Ibid., p. 169.

180 The Americans contributed: Holt, p. 504.

the Royal Air Force flew dummy aircraft: Hesketh, p. 70.

"80 Div. request 1,800 pairs of crampons": Ambrose, *D-Day*, p. 81.

"Reliably reported soundings": Hesketh, p. 166.

181 Hitler decided to keep 250,000 badly needed troops: Pujol and West, p. 166.

"Standing with his stiff fat neck": Quoted in Phillips, p. 46.

"on the theory that the Second Front": Quoted in Levine, Kindle location 3676.

182 "Eagerly he turned to the Colonial Secretary": Ibid., Kindle location 3690.

When they had wanted the Germans: Holt, p. 78.

"Then, having allowed the person to look": Wheatley, p. 146.

183 the deception planners also looked into: Holt, p. 500.
"The world of make-believe": Quoted in Levine, Kindle location 3119.
"I created them. They were my children": Juan Pujol, interview with Josep Espinas, *Identities*.
184 By May, Roenne counted: Hesketh, p. 179.
"From now on we have to exaggerate": Kahn, p. 496.
"Tangle within tangle": Quoted in David Jablonsky, *Churchill, the Great Game and Total War* (New York: Routledge, 1991), p. 55.
Every single message: Harris, p. 190.
185 "The movement and regrouping": Ibid.

18. The Buildup

186 "I am for bringing all our strength": Holt, p. 574.
On May 2, the deputy of General Jodl: Kahn, p. 487.
"A partial success by the enemy": Holt, p. 573.
187 "The situation as explained to me": KV 2/67, message of April 9, 1944.
188 The blunder reinforced his growing belief: Ambrose, *D-Day*, p. 86.
189 "4 has displayed the ability of a simpleton": KV 2/68.
"We here, in the very small circle": KV 2/70, message of December 12, 1944.
"You should give him more encouragement": KV 2/68.
In May, the French resistance reported: Perrault, p. 146.
There were rumors that other panzer divisions: D'Este, p. 108.
190 A squad of writers eavesdropped: Levine, Kindle location 3327.
until IBM invented a machine: Holt, p. 91.
The Third Army's wireless network in the west: Hesketh, p. 91.
A card catalog was even kept: Levine, Kindle location 3409.
191 "The 6th American Armored Division": Quoted in Hesketh, p. 176.
"The main enemy concentration": Delmer, p. 160.
Garbo flashed sightings from his subagents: Pujol and West, p. 156.
"Present aircraft production 300 per month": KV 2/68, message of February 18, 1944.
192 "What I was clearly able to get out of it": Hesketh, p. 133.
"It seems to me preposterous": Quoted in Levine, Kindle location 4074.
193 Pilots flew sorties and blew out the bridges: Hesketh, p. 118.
After arriving, von Cramer rushed: Levine, Kindle location 3574.
194 Churchill was reading reports of Garbo's successes: Liddell, p. 93.
Heinrich Himmler sent a personal note: Harris, p. 74.
"It is a unique case of an agent's report": Ibid., p. 190.
195 "Speaking of the Second Front": Quoted in Hesketh, p. 193.
196 "a blond, monocle, very bad black teeth": KV 2/854.

19. The Prisoner

197 His real name was Johann "Johnny" Jebsen: Jebsen's story is drawn from Popov's memoir *Spy, Counterspy* and from Miller.
201 The agency even considered: Andrew, *Defend the Realm*, p. 297.
"The whole Tricycle set-up might collapse": Liddell, p. 151.
202 Jebsen was ordered: Pujol and West, p. 154.
if the SD wanted to spirit him out of the country: Harris, p. 155.
203 "Under interrogation," wrote J. C. Masterman: Masterman, p. 154.
"Tommy is still extremely apprehensive": Liddell, p. 192.
"the agents should be used": Ibid.
205 "They told him about what had happened": Author interview with Andreu Jaume.
atormentado, tormented: Author interview with José Antonio Buces.
he was giving him the Nazi salute: Harris, p. 136.
"I am not certain whether I am being carried away": KV 2/67, message of February 23, 1944.
"His mother was Spanish and Gypsy": Juan Pujol, interview with Josep Espinas, *Identities.*
206 "Whichever way you look at this case": Liddell, p. 193.

20. The Hours

207 "I am particularly interested to know": KV 2/67.
"He says that the 52nd Division is at present in camps": KV 2/67.
208 He was stripped of his rank: Perrault, p. 147.
"I could cheerfully shoot the offender myself": Ambrose, *D-Day*, p. 84.
A young British officer told his parents: Perrault, p. 131.
And when the planners opened: Ibid., p. 148.
209 URGENT AP NYK FLASH: Ibid., p. 220.
"Surprised by the news in the papers": KV 2/69, message of June 4, 1944.
"appalling slip-up": Liddell, p. 205.
"I hope to God": Quoted in D'Este, p. 527.
210 "From the moment I set foot in England": Pujol and West, p. 223.
"The Division is destined for an attack": KV 2/69, message of June 5, 1944.
At 2000 hours, the German propaganda broadcaster: Ambrose, *D-Day*, p. 192.
"very depressed": The words of Eisenhower's driver, Kay Summersby, quoted in D'Este, p. 519.
211 "modest but beautifully prepared meal": Delmer, p. 178.
212 These false "echoes": Breuer, p. 176.

213 "I am very disgusted": KV 2/69, message of June 7, 1944.

an American GI named William Funkhouser: Funkhouser interview, Virginia Military Institute, John A. Adams '71 Center for Military History and Strategic Analysis, Military Oral History Project, www.vmi.edu/uploadedFiles/Archives/Adams_Center/FunkhouserW/FunkhouserW_interview.pdf.

214 "I remember thinking that the American beaches": "The Spy Who Saved Europe," *Mail on Sunday*, June 3, 1984.

"Not a single unit": Delmer, p. 514.

215 The diversion helped convince the chief of staff: Levine, Kindle location 3792.

"On 5 June 1944": Ambrose, *D-Day*, p. 91.

"We feared a massive counter-attack": "The Spy Who Saved Europe."

216 "I today lunched": KV 2/69, message of June 9, 1944.

"It is clear that Hitler and his entourage": Hesketh, p. 204.

He agreed to send Rundstedt: Ibid., p. 202.

217 "The main thrust must be expected": Farago, p. 801.

"As a consequence of certain information": Delmer, p. 189.

Ten armored divisions: Hesketh, p. 101.

218 Pujol and Harris celebrated: Delmer, p. 190.

A month after, a total of twenty-two: Juárez, p. 338.

219 "You can accept it as 99 percent certain": Quoted in Hesketh, p. xix.

"Lack of infantry was the most important cause": Ibid., p. xxi.

It had been "a decisive mistake": Quoted in Holt, p. 589.

"night lighting exercises": WO 171/3832, War Diary, May 18, 1944, 2230 hours.

battle noise simulators: WO 171/3868, "Report on Operation Transcend, Part II," March 11, 1945.

misleading signposts: WO 171/3869, January 1945.

fake bomb craters: WO 171/3868, January 12, 1944, 1830 hours.

"dummy sniper heads": WO 171/3868, "Camouflage: Lessons from June 1944 to February 1945," March 14, 1945.

220 He could, for 200 francs each: WO 171/3868, War Diary, March 1945.

"It is fair to say": WO 171/3868, report on "Insignia, Symbols, Marks and Signs," February 1945.

It had never recovered: Cumming, p. 3.

"I trust I shall be provided": Miller, Kindle location 5349.

221 Popov even knocked on the doors: Ibid., location 5445.

"Connoisseurs of the double cross": Pujol and West, p. 11.

"the greatest double cross operation": Ibid., p. 13.

"His contribution to D-day was indeed stranger": Hesketh, p. xix.

"Your work with Mr. Pujol": Bristow, p. 274.

222 When the Allies captured German intelligence maps: Unpublished transcript, Thaddeus Holt interview with David Strangeways.

On Roenne's big map of the Western Front: Kahn, p. 520.

When the war diarist: The Schramm anecdote is drawn from Levine, Kindle location 4122.

21. The Weapon

223   In the summer of 1943: Harris, p. 242.

"I must now discuss another matter": KV 2/69, message of June 10, 1944.

"Circumstances dictate that you should carry out": Quoted in Hesketh, p. 254.

224   "Day and night [the V-1] thunders down": *Das Reich*, July 2, 1944.

"8 dead and 13 wounded": KV 2/69, message of July 3, 1944.

225   "[The policeman] started to insult me": KV 2/69, message of July 14, 1944.

"I cannot at this moment": Quoted in Hesketh, p. 274.

226   He told the Germans he'd fled to a hideout: Harris, p. 264.

the police closely interviewed a supposedly terrified Araceli: Ibid., p. 268.

"[Tommy Harris's] plan is to get [Garbo] to write": Liddell, p. 287.

227   "I think he was extremely pleased": Ibid., p. 251.

"It was a very moving moment": Pujol and West, p. 226.

"world civil war": KV 2/69, message of May 3, 1945.

"London exploded with joy": Pujol and West, pp. 226–27.

228   "We ask you to frequent the Cafe Bar la Moderna": KV 2/69, message of May 8, 1945.

"He . . . had been invented by the Abwehr": Delmer, p. 21.

"instructing him to give every assistance": Liddell, p. 295.

"[He] wanted to meet me personally": Pujol and West, p. 227.

229   They hiked up to the treeline: Harris, p. 230.

"Speaking of the future": KV 2/102, "Summary of meeting with Federico," undated.

"He fell for it completely": Pujol and West, p. 230.

"overcome with emotion": KV 2/102, "Summary of the conversation with Carlos, November 11, 1945."

230   "He thought me almost a God": Ibid.

"At present I am a man unaware": KV 2/69, message of January 14, 1945.

"It is only a few days": KV 2/69, message of February 2, 1945.

231   "I interviewed Mrs Garbo myself": KV 2/102, "SIS Report No. 5108," November 14, 1945.

"I do not feel that Mrs. Garbo": KV 2/102, message of November 1, 1945.

232   "an adventuress" who was "likely to attempt": KV 2/102, extract from an undated draft telegram.

22. The End

235   "I was afraid the Germans would take revenge": "The Spy Who Saved Europe," *Mail on Sunday,* June 3, 1984.
a total of 17,554 pounds: Juárez, p. 380.
Harris supplied his coconspirator: Details of Pujol's business are from Juárez and from the correspondence of Thomas Harris in the collection of José Antonio Buces.
"public artistic treasure taken out of Spain": Juárez, p. 384.

236   The erstwhile chicken farmer: Ibid., p. 393.
"No one in Venezuela had seen anything like it": Author interview with Juan Kreisler.
Forced to sell the property: Juárez, p. 393.
"It was as if the dictators were following me": Juan Pujol, letter to Tamara Kreisler, undated.
Some say that Pujol sent Araceli home: Author interview with Bill Bristow.

237   "When the world war was over": Araceli Pujol, letter to her grandchildren, undated.
In 1949, a year after Araceli left Venezuela: Author interview with Nigel West.
Through hard work and sheer force: The details of Araceli's post-Venezuela life are drawn from author interviews with Juan, Maria and Tamara Kreisler.

238   "If I could only tell you": Author interview with Raúl del Pozo.
She talked about meeting with Churchill: Author interviews with Maria and Tamara Kreisler.
"The Pujols were kept very, very, very isolated": Author interview with Felipe Fernández-Armesto, son of a noted Spanish journalist who resided in London during the war.
"Mallorca was a perfect place": Author interview with José Antonio Buces.

239   "Hilda began crying hysterically": Bristow, p. 277.
"If the works had been painted in crushed glass": *Scotsman,* December 4, 1954.
When his villa needed to be rewired: *Daily Express,* October 22, 1971.
had chosen his seaside home: *Arts & Antiques Weekly,* February 1980.
He'd paid the school fees for Philby's son: Bristow, p. 276.
"As an art dealer he had the perfect cover": *Daily Telegraph,* November 17, 1979.

240   "He was restless, altered": Author interview with José Antonio Buces.
"I think the war destroyed him": Author interview with Andreu Jaume.

"I just cannot say how it happened": *Majorca News,* undated article, from the collection of José Antonio Buces.

"astonishes with its electric and dazzling precision": Author interview with José Antonio Buces.

23. The Return

241   he loved soccer and the Olympics especially: Juan Pujol, letter to Tamara Kreisler, August 24, 1988.

he was known as "the Anarchist": Author interview with Javier Juárez.

242   "If he'd worked for the USSR": Juárez, p. 235.

"I begged him to tell anyone": Pujol and West, p. 232.

After Araceli left for Spain in 1948: The account of Pujol's life in Venezuela after Araceli's departure is drawn from Juárez, Pujol and West, and an interview with Juan Pujol, the spy's son with Carmen Cilia.

"Oh, I won a medal during the war": Juan Pujol, interview with Josep Espinas, *Identities,* Catalan TV documentary, date unknown.

243   "He had the mania for safety": Author interview with Xavier Vinader.

He would never leave a phone number: Ibid.

When he wanted to post a letter: Interview with Joan Miguel Pujol Maimo, Pujol's nephew, in the documentary *Garbo the Spy,* directed by Edmon Roch, 2009.

"We thought it strange": Ibid.

244   In 1973, Pujol's youngest son: The story of the men with British accents is from an author interview with Juan Pujol (Jr.).

Once, when Juan Jr. was a college student: Ibid.

245   He'd begun searching: Author interview with Nigel West.

246   "I spoke to one person": Ibid.

247   "hugged each other like footballers after a goal": "The Spy Who Saved Europe," *Mail on Sunday,* June 3, 1984.

"Some very strange things happened": Bristow, p. 222.

"My father respected him in a certain way": Author interview with Bill Bristow.

"You've heard of General Eisenhower": Author interview with Nigel West.

"I knew the Nazis had to be destroyed": "The Spy Who Saved Europe."

248   "I didn't do enough": From *Garbo the Spy.*

One American colonel was being interviewed: Juan Pujol, interview with Josep Espinas, *Identities.*

"blond and Teutonic-looking": Juan Pujol, letter to Tamara Kreisler, Easter 1987.

249 "He told me that some of his Spanish family": Author interview with Nigel West.

In Madrid in June 1984: Author interview with Juan Kreisler.

"She went to bed for three days": Author interview with Tamara Kreisler.

A reunion between Pujol and his Spanish children: Author interviews with Juan and Maria Kreisler.

"Perhaps he felt he couldn't do anything for us": Author interview with Juan Kreisler.

250 "Destiny intervened in a very painful way": Juan Pujol, letter to Jorge Kreisler, October 29, 1987.

"I don't talk much about my personal relationships": Juan Pujol, letter to Tamara Kreisler, May 25, 1988.

"Today, as yesterday, as always": Juan Pujol, letter to Jorge Kreisler, October 29, 1987.

"the great pretender, the comedian nonpareil": Author interview with Rafael Fraguas.

"had to disappear for a long time": Juan Pujol, letter to Tamara Kreisler, Easter 1987.

251 "He seduced us with the writing": Author interview with Tamara Kreisler.

"I'm a famous writer": Author interview with Rafael Fraguas.

And at the German embassy in Madrid: Author interview with Xavier Vinader.

"Why don't we get married again?": Author interview with Juan Kreisler.

BIBLIOGRAPHY

Ambrose, Stephen E. *D-Day*. New York: Pocket, 2002.

———. *Eisenhower: Soldier and President*. New York: Touchstone, 1990.

Andrew, Christopher. *Defend the Realm: The Authorized History of MI5*. New York: Knopf, 2009.

———. *The Secret Service: The Making of the British Intelligence Community*. London: Heinemann, 1985.

Breuer, William B. *Hoodwinking Hitler: The Normandy Deception*. New York: Praeger, 1993.

Bristow, Desmond, with Bill Bristow. *A Game of Moles*. London: Little, Brown, 1993.

Brown, Anthony Cave. *Bodyguard of Lies*. Guilford, CT: Lyons Press, 2002.

Burns, Jimmy. *Papa Spy: Love, Faith and Betrayal in Wartime Spain*. New York: Walker and Co., 2009.

Cameron, Norman, and R. H. Stevens, trans. *Hitler's Table Talk, 1941–1944: His Private Conversations*. New York: Enigma Books, 2000.

Carr, Raymond. *The Spanish Tragedy*. London: Weidenfeld, 1993.

Carter, Miranda. *Anthony Blunt: His Many Lives*. London: Pan Macmillan, 2002.

Churchill, Winston. *The World in Crisis, 1911–18*. New York: Simon and Schuster, 2005.

Crowdy, Terry. *Deceiving Hitler: Double-Cross and Deception in World War II*. London: Osprey, 2008.

Cumming, Michael. *The Starkey Sacrifice*. Phoenix Mill, UK: Sutton, 1996.

Delmer, Sefton. *The Counterfeit Spy*. New York: Harper & Row, 1971.

D'Este, Carlo. *Decision in Normandy*. New York: Harper Perennial, 1994.

Farago, Ladislas. *The Game of the Foxes*. New York: Bantam, 1973.

Graham, Helen. *The Spanish Civil War: A Very Short Introduction*. Oxford, UK: Oxford University Press, 2005.

Harris, Tomás. *Garbo: The Spy Who Saved D-Day*. Bath, UK: Bath Press, 2000.

Helm, Sarah. *A Life in Secrets: Vera Atkins and the Missing Agents of WWII.* New York: Anchor, 2007.

Hesketh, Roger. *Fortitude: The D-Day Deception Campaign.* Woodstock, NY: Overlook, 2000.

Holt, Thaddeus. *The Deceivers: Allied Military Deception in the Second World War.* London: Phoenix, 2005.

Howard, Michael Elliot. *British Intelligence in the Second World War: Strategic Deception.* London: Her Majesty's Stationery Office, 1990.

Irving, David. *Hitler's War.* New York: Avon, 1990.

Johnson, David Alan. *Righteous Deception: German Officers Against Hitler.* Westport, CT: Praeger, 2001.

Juárez, Javier. *Juan Pujol, el espía que derrotó a Hitler.* Madrid: Ediciones Temas de Hoy, 2004.

Kahn, David. *Hitler's Spies.* New York: Macmillan, 1978.

Levine, Joshua. *Operation Fortitude: The Story of the Spies and Spy Operation That Saved D-Day.* Kindle e-book. London: HarperCollins, 2011.

Liddell, Guy. *Diaries. Volume II: 1942–45.* London: Routledge, 2005.

Lochery, Neill. *Lisbon: War in the Shadows of the City of Light, 1939–1945.* New York: Public Affairs, 2011.

Macdonald, Scott. *Propaganda and Information Warfare in the Twenty-first Century: Altered Images and Deception Operations.* Oxford, UK: Taylor & Francis, 2007.

Macintyre, Ben. *Operation Mincemeat: How a Dead Man and a Bizarre Plan Fooled the Nazis and Assured an Allied Victory.* London: Bloomsbury, 2010.

Masterman, J. C. *The Double-Cross System in the War of 1939 to 1945.* New Haven: Yale University Press, 1972.

McManus, John P. *The Americans at D-Day: The American Experience at the Normandy Invasion.* New York: Macmillan, 2005.

Miller, Russell. *Codename Tricycle.* Kindle e-book. London: Vintage Digital, 2010.

Orwell, George. *Homage to Catalonia.* London: Secker & Warburg, 1938.

Patton, George S., and Martin Blumenson. *The Patton Papers.* New York: Da Capo, 1996.

Perrault, Gilles. *The Secret of D-Day: Where and Why?* Boston: Little, Brown, 1964.

Philby, Kim. *My Silent War.* London: Grafton, 1989.

Phillips, Gene D. *Some Like It Wilder: The Life and Controversial Films of Billy Wilder.* Lexington: University of Kentucky Press, 2010.

Pujol, Juan, with Nigel West. *Operation Garbo.* New York: Pocket Books, 1985.

Ruby, Marcel. *F Section SOE.* London: Grafton, 1988.

Sebag-Montefiore, Hugh. *Dunkirk: Fight to the Last Man.* Cambridge: Harvard University Press, 2008.

Speer, Albert. *Inside the Third Reich.* New York: Avon, 1970.

Thomas, Hugh. *The Spanish Civil War.* New York: Random House Digital, 2001.

Waller, John H. *The Unseen War in Europe: Espionage and Conspiracy in the Second World War.* New York: Random House, 1996.

Weber, Ronald. *The Lisbon Route: Entry and Escape in Nazi Europe.* Lanham, MD: Ivan R. Dee, 2011.

Wheatley, Dennis. *The Deception Planners.* London: Hutchinson, 1980.

Young, Martin, and Robbie Stamp. *Trojan Horses: Deception Operations in the Second World War.* London: The Bodley Head, 1989.

ACKNOWLEDGMENTS

I'd like to thank the Pujol and Kreisler families for their generosity in allowing me full access to Juan Pujol's letters and speaking to me so openly about his life. Tamara Kreisler was especially gracious in welcoming me into her home and sharing her family memories. I wouldn't have been able to write the book without her help.

Tessa Estévez was my tireless interpreter and researcher in Madrid, and contributed enormously to the project. Her husband, Richard, gamely read over the translations and the final manuscript. I'm grateful to them both for their hard work and friendship.

José Antonio Buces, nephew of Tommy Harris, graciously allowed me access to his archives and enlarged my understanding of that remarkable man.

Thaddeus Holt gave me indispensable advice on the deception operations and was always willing to field the next question. Nigel West was kind enough to talk about his search for Pujol, as well as offer his insights into the period and the intelligence agencies.

Jaysa and Mariano Faz, our upstairs neighbors on Calle Velázquez, welcomed us warmly to Madrid. Many thanks.

My editor, Bruce Nichols, strengthened the book with his clear eye. And my agent, Scott Waxman, saw the potential from the beginning.

Once again, my love to Marie, Asher and Delphine for sharing the adventure.

INDEX

Abwehr: agents defect to Allies, 226
   attempts to infiltrate MI6, 59
   Canaris as head of, 99, 100, 101–2
   confidence in Pujol, ix–x, 45–46,
      51, 58–59, 84, 94–95, 103–4,
      112–13, 118–19, 148–49, 161,
      183, 184–85, 189, 206, 218,
      230
   Franco and, 31
   German companies work with, 98
   high attrition rate, 103
   interest in chemical warfare, 88
   Jebsen as agent for, 198
   Jodl and, 103, 107
   known as "Santa Clauses," 99
   MI5 analyzes thinking of, 86–87,
      88, 118–19
   and Operation Fortitude, 159, 176,
      182–83, 190–91, 212–13
   operations in England, ix, 44, 59,
      102–3, 107
   operations in France, 102–3
   operations in Lisbon, 36
   operations in Madrid, 30–31,
      104–5, 171–72, 184, 187–88,
      191–92, 199, 207, 223–24,
      228, 239
   Pérez as agent for, 182
   permits Pujol to use wireless radio,
      96–97
   Popov recruited by, 198
   and preparations for Normandy in-
      vasion, 159, 189–90
   Pujol as intelligence analyst for,
      149–50, 187–88, 192, 216
   Pujol begins spying for, 43–46
   Pujol feeds fake intelligence to,
      47–50, 58–60, 67, 83–84,
      92–95, 107, 128, 143, 144,
      149–50, 158–59, 170, 171–72,
      177, 187–88, 191–93, 194, 201,
      215–16, 224–25
   recruitment in, 100–101
   researches gas masks, 88
   rivalry with SD, 161
   rushes agents to England, 103
   scope and methods of, 98–99
   shortcomings in deception opera-
      tions, 105
   Strangeways feeds fake intelligence
      to, 164
   and supposed Nazi sympathizers in
      England, 189
   and V-1 attacks, 223–24
Agent J (fake agent), 86, 187, 188–89,
      192
Agent No. 1 (fake agent), 127–28, 129
Agent No. 2 (fake agent). See Gerbers,
      William
Agent No. 3 (fake agent), 86,
      92–93, 110, 113, 127, 209, 211,
      223, 226

WITHDRAWN

28.00   7/6/12.